W9-ADO-989

My Way Was North

Other Books by Frank Dufresne

Animals and Fishes of Alaska
The Great Outdoors
Lure of the Open
No Room for Bears

¶ My Way Was North

by Frank Dufresne

An Alaskan Autobiography

Introduction by Corey Ford

Drawings by Rachel S. Horne

Holt, Rinehart and Winston · New York Chicago San Francisco

Published simultaneously in Canada by Holt, Rinehart
and Winston of Canada, Limited.
Library of Congress Catalog Card Number: 66–21630

Published, August, 1966
Third Printing, August, 1967

Designer: Ernst Reichl
8599755
Printed in the United States of America

Dedicated to daughter Ginny and son Frank
whose early years were spent
in tents and cabins in the wilderness,
and who saw more wild beasts before they
were of school age than most children
would see in all their lives.

¶ By Way of Introduction

by Corey Ford

Frank Dufresne says in this book that we first met in the Alaska Game Commission office in Juneau sometime in the early thirties. Maybe he's right, but it seems to me I've known him all my life. I can't remember how often I've gone back to Alaska to be with him, how many miles we've traveled together up trout streams and down bear trails, how many hours I've sat beside a campfire at night and listened to him talk.

Frank worked a kind of magic when he talked. He might be in a roomful of people, with twenty conversations going at once; gradually, almost imperceptibly, the other conversations would die away and presently everyone would be silent, held spellbound by his descriptions of primitive Eskimos, of dog-sledding over the Bering ice, of sourdoughs he knew along the Yukon, of caribou and mountain goats and bears, of the old Alaska which will never be again.

Over and over I urged him, all his friends urged him, to set down his life-story. Certainly no man had a better first-hand knowledge of Alaska's birds and fishes and animals, we argued, no one else had visited so many remote spots in the Arctic or savored more deeply the lure of the north. Like the famous naturalist Steller, first white man to set foot on Alaskan soil, Frank Dufresne had a fantastic memory, a keen eye that missed no detail of the wilderness around him, a boundless excitement over each new discovery. If he could convey that excitement in words, if he could capture the magic of a talk around a campfire, his book would be an enduring American classic.

Well, he did, and it is. *My Way Was North* is an unforgettable picture of early days in Nome and Fairbanks, a tale of breath-taking adventure in the white cold, but it is more than that. It is the story of a career devoted to the conservation of Alaska's natural resources. "Most of my life," he writes in his preface, "has been spent watching, and watching over, wild animals." He was always their devoted champion. "They were on earth long before we were," he told me once, "they have the prior right, and now that we're on top after millions of years they deserve our respect and help." Among his many accomplishments, Frank was proudest of the fact that he helped to write the original Alaska Game Laws which protected and preserved the territory's wildlife for two decades, until statehood allowed the commercial interests to take over.

My Way Was North concludes with his departure from Alaska to take up government duties in Washington; but his career as a conservationist went on to new heights. Director of Information for the United States Fish and Wildlife Service ("I began to perceive that management of wildlife must also include management of people," he explains, "and that it was not much use to know merely what the fish and game needed unless the people approved and supported the necessary laws."); associate editor of *Field & Stream;* outstanding authority on Alaskan natural history; author of innumerable books and outdoor articles, perhaps our finest nature writer since Rachel Carson. In recent years, he and his wonderful wife Klondy—one of the truly great women I've ever known—lived in a comfortable home in Paradise, California, where they played host to a freeloading army of raccoons and other wild creatures who invaded their back porch nightly for handouts.

But Frank's heart was still in Alaska, and his crusading zeal never faltered. His recent and enormously successful book, *No Room for Bears,* is a plea to save the matchless rain-forests of Admiralty Island before they are timbered off and the historic range of the brown bear ruined forever. Those who value Alaska's wildlife as a national heritage should be grateful that Frank Dufresne, in his books as in his life, remains its champion, that his way will always be north.

ɋ Foreword

My oldest sister Eva, who bore the brunt of watching over me when I was a toddler back in the White Mountains of New Hampshire where I was born, said she could always shush my howling by pointing somewhere and saying, "Look at the pretty bird!"

She was right, except it didn't have to be pretty, nor even be a bird. Any kind of woodsy thing would do—a chipmunk, a deliciously-slimy pollywog, a "devil's darning needle" swishing over the reeds, a chain pickerel warily curling amber fins in the shadow of a lily pad, ready to scoot.

Now, there is nothing unusual about a small boy's fascination with nature. Given a chance to live on a farm, as I was, most boys and girls will become friends with all kinds of wild creatures, even uglies like warty hop-toads and squirmy worms. The difference is that, as they grow up, children tend to lose interest in these underfoot creatures. I never did. Most of my life has been spent in watching, and watching over, wild animals. These interests have taken me into faraway places; by dogteams, boats, airplanes, calked shoes, and rubber boots.

I find it difficult to credit myself with any special traits for my chosen job. My schooling was normal and I was an average student. An old taxidermist, behind drawn blinds, taught me the then black art of "upholstering" small dead things and deer heads when I was in my high school years, and it served me well. With my earnings I bought a gun, a camera, a fish-pole and all the books on natural history I could afford. In 1917 I enlisted in New England's own 26th Yankee Division and spent two thoroughly useless years in the trenches of France, from which country a paternal ancestor had migrated two centuries earlier. I was not a very good soldier and won only the medals they handed out to rank and file. I remember I kept watching the red-legged partridges and lapwing plovers running around among the barbed-wire entanglements, and wondering how in the world they would ever survive the next barrage of enemy shrapnel.

My sister Eva, now in her spry eighties, recently reminded me about one other oddity of character. When I was a lad, fishing a New Hampshire brook, and wanted to get at what I thought was a better hole on the other side, I devised a crossing method that never failed. I hurled my fish-pole over to the other shore. Though I frequently got soaking wet, and sometimes half drowned, no power on Earth could prevent me from retrieving that fish-pole!

My wife, Klondy, who thinks she is pretty good at analyzing me, says I never outgrew the habit. She says I have been hurling my fish-poles across rivers ever since. Retrieving these fish-poles has taken me into every state, and into regions far south of our borders.

But mostly, my way was north.

Contents

My Way Was North

¶1 From the Whale's Mouth

In the summer of 1920 when I was still trying to find myself after two lost years in the muddy shell-holes of France, I traveled by slow stages across Canada to Seattle, and with no real purpose in mind bought a round-trip ticket and boarded the aging Steamer *Victoria* bound for Nome. A week later the old coal-burner moored briefly at a lonely whaling station in the Aleutians to discharge cargo. There I had my first look at the land which was to dominate the rest of my life. It was at once the foulest and most excitingly beautiful place I had ever seen.

The ship lay berthed alongside a rendering plant huffing and puffing nauseous mushrooms into the mist. So blood-soaked was the dock from epic scale butchering, so penetrating the odors, that most of the passengers remained in their staterooms with portholes screwed tight. But beyond the fuming factory the island of Akutan rose steeply out of the squalor, greener than any land I had ever visited, and I knew I had to see more of it. When I followed a foot-trail up its slope I found myself brushing through soft, damp grasses and patches of giant buttercups, and bright blue lupines the size of cultivated delphiniums. There was not a tree in sight; nothing larger than a willow bush. As the mist cleared, I saw above me a fairyland of brilliant wildflowers shining in the sun, and heard strange calls from unseen creatures unfamiliar to my New England ears.

I heard something else, too, and it cut short my first exploration in Alaska. There was a blast of black smoke from the whaling station below, a hoarse, echoing sound followed by tooting of whistles and the clanking of heavy chains across the dock. I thought it might be a boarding call, but when I reached the pier I found it signaled a far more interesting development.

Dressed in gurry-spattered slickers and rubber boots, a gang of workers came spewing out of the steam-filled rendering plant and scurried to the waterfront. There were warning shouts, the sound of chains drawing up tight and straining, then more whistle toots and steam puffs. Slowly out of the bay rose an enormous black monster, bigger by far than I thought any of Earth's creatures could ever grow. Tail first, it came sliding up a greasy chute and shuddered to a stop. I could hear it sighing and groaning with escaping gasses as it collapsed belly-down on the planks.

Someone placed a stepladder alongside a head as big as a school bus. Without conscious direction my feet carried me up the risers to where I could peer through fringes of hairy whalebone into the domed cavern of its mouth. It looked big enough in there to hold a New England town meeting. Toward the throat the vaulted chamber tapered away into dark mystery. Though I had a vagrant thought about the huge jaws suddenly clapping shut behind me, I knew I would have to go inside and do further inspecting. Never again would I be in better position to find out what really happened to Jonah. I had no fish-pole to toss, but my hat served the same purpose.

In retrieving it, I was in the act of stooping over to wedge my body between giant louvers hanging pendant from the whale's upper jaws when I felt something nudge me in the seat of my pants. I nearly jumped down the whale's throat, then spun around to face a bearded man wearing horn-rimmed glasses and carrying a tin bucket and notebook. He said he was Dr. Gill and he was the station's biologist. I told him I was nobody at all, and if there was one place in the world I had no business tossing my hat, I guessed this was it.

Dr. Gill grinned. "Step in," he invited. "Plenty of room in there."

Balancing on a rubbery tongue the size of a prostrate elephant, I managed to touch finger tips to the whale's palate. Dr. Gill moved up and down the edge of the tongue gathering small objects trapped in the frayed ends of the baleen and placing them carefully in his bucket for microscopic scanning in the station's laboratory. I tagged behind, peering over his shoulder at what looked like undersized shrimp, miniscule greenish flecks no bigger than pinheads, and odd-shaped wigglers of which there seemed to be no two alike. The spectacled man of science said he always tried to pick up samples of whale feed before they'd gotten crushed in the whale's stomach.

The origin of these primitive organisms, explained Dr. Gill, seemed to be a spontaneous creation taking place in the colder currents of the ocean near both poles, forcing the whales to migrate from one end of the world to the other. They formed a beginning link in a food chain, being fed upon by small fishes which were in turn preyed upon by bigger fishes and so on up to the top. He called this plankton substance the mother of life. The doctor, a man of imagination talking to a young fellow he knew was all ears, had a sudden thought. He could explain it all better, he said, if we could be standing right here in the mouth of the whale when it was feeding.

"Hang on," he called out to me. "Let's take this whale back to sea!"

Under Dr. Gill's make-believe guidance the great blue monster seemed to slide down the slick chute in the bay and start cruising for its dinner. I could almost feel the giant tail flukes, wide enough to shade the village square, beating up and down in ponderous cadence as the blunt nose broke the wave tops. At a speed of 10 knots, the whale would slant down to 300 feet, then rise after a few minutes until the nostrils on the top of its head came to the surface. At that instant the monster would breathe, an explosive changing of air audible for a mile. A column of hot, vapor-filled discharge from lungs weighing a ton would mix with spray from overlapping wave tops to whistle high into the air; a fresh supply of cold air would be sucked in, and once more the whale would sink into the depths as it searched for the plankton growth known as krill.

As we stood in the mouth of the giant, Dr. Gill explained that it was guided, by a sense we have later come to know as sonar, to an immense patch of krill. Other plankton feeders were there, too. Billions of herring flipped at the surface, skittering into the air, pursued by salmon. Other kinds of baleen whales plowed open-mouthed through banks of densely packed vegetable plankton and tiny crustaceans. Sea birds from the mist-shrouded cliffs of Akutan swarmed like bees over the tide rips; auklets, clucking fulmars, gulls, and long-winged albatross—all finding their favorite food on a surging dining table 50 miles long. Outnumbering all other species in the winging hordes were brownish, cigar-shaped, narrow-winged birds which had come a long way to be with the whales. They'd reversed the usual order of migration by flying north across the equator from nesting grounds around South Australia, and now they covered the sea in fluttering multitudes. In the bird guides I'd fetched from New Hampshire I had known them as Slender Shearwaters, but the doctor used the sea-farer's name, "whale-birds."

Into this mass the behemoth would shove its gaping jaws, opening wide as a barn door. A torrent of saltwater would come gushing in and go screening out through the baleen fringes, leaving the tiny morsels of krill the size of ants and grasshoppers entangled in the whale's whiskery strainers. When the whale had a fair mouthful—something like a few barrels said the doctor—it would shut off the ocean intake and press a rubbery tongue up against the roof of its mouth to expel surplus water. The crushed mass remaining then went sluicing down its amazingly small throat.

I stumbled along behind Dr. Gill to the rear of the mouth as he began probing in the semi-darkness until he located the passage leading to the whale's stomach. Although I shoved with all my strength I could not force my fist into the throat opening. After a while, I said I guessed the story about the whale swallowing Jonah must be all fiction.

The doctor smiled indulgently. The Jonah story, he said, might be *half* true because some of the toothed whales like the giant Sperm and the Orca could easily swallow a man—and leach the life out of him in seconds. But none of the whalebone types could do it, not even the biggest species in the world, like the blue whale we were studying. Its mouth had become specialized through millions of years. In the beginning, Dr. Gill said the whale—like all other life on the planet—had originated in the sea. Rudimentary legs buried deep in its flesh indicated it had tried, perhaps through millions of years, to adapt itself to living in the Silurian swamps, but had returned to the sea to chase oceanic bugs, and develop into a modern hundred-ton monster!

Dr. Gill, who had been wallowing in whale gore and lore for several years, supplied some other astonishing data. This blue whale was 87 feet long. Its heart weighed more than 500 pounds, and pumped approximately 8 tons of blood through more miles of arteries than anybody would ever get around to measuring. Its liver was the size of a grand piano and tipped the scales at close to a ton. When the flensers got at it with their long-handled knives they'd strip off 25 tons of blubber, and butcher out a hundred thousand pounds of red meat. When the last chunk of blubber was dissolved in the rendering pots, they'd pour out 150 barrels of oil. The stuff was in great demand, he said, especially in foreign countries like Japan, Russia, Scandinavia, and England. They'd make it into margarine, glycerin, soap, candles, varnish, paint, and a hundred other items like solvents for tempering steel and cutting screws.

The odors in the whale's mouth were beginning to make me gag. Dr. Gill had worked up an immunity against the smells but I could have used the gas mask the army had issued me in Belleau Woods. I clawed my way out through the baleen whiskers into the fresh air and stumbled down the stepladder. I'd seen and sniffed enough whale to do me for a long time, but the doctor wasn't through yet.

"Everything about a whale is big," he said. "They're even born big."

The blue whale calf came into the world fully a third as long as its mother, and it grew faster than anything else on land or sea. It suckled 400 gallons of rich, yellow milk a day from gargantuan nipples pushed out from folds in the smooth hide and exposed at the waterline when the cow rolled on her side; and gained a ton every 8 days. In 7 months its length doubled from 25 to 50 feet. In 36 months it was sexually mature, and 12 months after titanic, romantic carryings on, produced its own calf. It would make annual round trips between the Arctic and the Antarctic, and during its lifetime the blue whale would daily consume enough proteins to nourish a town of twenty-five hundred humans. In 20 years it would succumb to old age.

That seemed to wrap up the blue whale's biology, and not a bit too soon because the *Victoria's* steam whistle sounded a hoarse summons: "All Passengers Aboard!" The good Dr. Gill had a parting gift for me. It was a thick, dark-red whale steak from his private refrigerator where he kept his krill specimens. He told me he considered it tastier than the finest range beef, and he bribed the ship's steward to cook it for me that first night at sea.

I never did get a chance to tell Dr. Gill what I thought about whale porterhouse, and it is just as well. The truth is that it tasted exactly the way a whale smelled. So did everything on the bill of fare. The indelicate effluvia of the gory carcasses and the melting pots of the rendering station had penetrated every cranny of the old *Victoria* so that everything coming out of its galley reeked with defunct whale. With the rolling motion of the *Victoria* wallowing in the trough of the waves, women passengers were holding handkerchiefs to their pursed mouths, pushing back from the tables and making hasty exits. Even strong men quailed and fled to the rails.

By opening wide every porthole, vent and passageway to the cool breezes of Bering Sea, the *Victoria* was fairly well purged of its whale odors in a couple of days. There was only one spot of contamination left on the ship. I was it.

The session with Dr. Gill in the whale's maw had thoroughly saturated my clothes and the reek of it sunk into my pores. Running the gauntlet of uplifted noses, I hurried to my cabin for a change of wardrobe, but succeeded only in fouling everything else in the stateroom. Though I scrubbed and shaved and donned new clothes from socks to hat, I still stunk like a glue factory.

The little schoolteacher from Kansas who sat at my table, let herself be coaxed by a new swain to another table. She even smiled when the fellow made what I thought was a very unfunny remark about somebody having a bad case of "whalitosis." It was a thoroughly frustrating situation. There I was, bursting with important statistics on the life history of a whale, and nobody wishing to have their knowledge enriched. For the rest of the voyage to Nome aboard the *Victoria* I was shunned like a carrier of bubonic plague.

2 Uncle Charley

Nome in 1920 was a fading gold camp. From a noisy tent city strung helter-skelter along the beach sands where thousands of stampeders had washed out quick fortunes, it had shrunk to a few hundred diehards. False-fronted saloons, once staffed with gamblers and painted ladies tolling newly-rich prospectors in off the street, now stood empty and forlorn. Battered by twenty winters of shrieking blizzards off Bering Sea, the jerry-built structures sagged badly out of plumb, propped up with two by fours like tired old men leaning on their canes. Boardwalks resting on the soggy tundra, squirted water up through cracks and broken boards at my every step. On my way through town a pack of loose sled dogs bounding down the narrow road spattered dirty water on my Sunday pants.

During the few days the *Victoria* would be anchored off Nome Beach "lightering" freight through the shallow breakers, we round-trippers were free to meander through the famous old gold camp. I had a special mission. I'd promised to make inquiries about a lost uncle who in 1897 had up and quit his steady job as a Boston shoe clerk to join the Klondike Stampede. There'd been reports that Uncle Charles had later left Dawson to float down the Yukon River for the big strike at Nome, and then there was no more word. Nobody had heard from him in several years, and the members of the family weren't sure he was alive. Other passengers were likewise ferreting around for vanished kinfolks, but I hit paydirt first.

A stubble-faced Goliath in Stetson hat and rubber boots bellied out through the sagging doors of a place called the Board of Trade and came clumping down the sidewalk. He looked like one of those shaggy characters from "The Shooting of Dan McGrew"; one who had tramped across many a far place. When we met head on, I asked him if in all his travels he'd ever run into a man named Charles Rice. The tipsy giant rolled back on his heels as if I'd kicked him in the shins, and roared loud enough to halt all foot traffic in Nome.

"CHARLEY RICE!" He started to shove me off the boardwalk, then stopped to peer suspiciously. "Ya' tryin' t' get smart with me, sonny?" Lumbering off down the spurting sidewalk, he bellowed a final remark over his shoulder. "HELL, CHARLEY'S MAYOR OF THE TOWN!"

So, I quickly found the lost uncle, and that night I stayed ashore to bunk on his spare cot. He told me he'd several times struck enough gold to return home and buy his own bootery, as he'd planned, but in the process he'd lost all interest in selling shoes, or ever seeing Boston again. "This is the land, boy," he said. "Right here around Nome. Gold all over. Only the cream has been skimmed. You'll make your stake in no time, young fellow."

I told him I'd have to make it pretty quick, because I was due to sail south again as soon as the steamer finished unloading. Uncle Charley was speechless for a moment, staring at me as though he suspected all the weak-minded blood in the family had settled in this one nephew. In his probing blue eyes, his bulging muscles, his out-thrust black-bearded chin, I saw a man who would never again be content to bow and scrape and polish his hands before lady shoe customers. Something very drastic had happened to him. He'd changed to fit the new country, and I liked what I saw.

He took me for a stroll down Front Street which ran within a few feet of the thundering surf, past all the half-collapsed wooden buildings. They'd looked dismal when I first saw them. Now, under Uncle Charley's reminiscing, the ramshackle places seemed to straighten up on their old foundations and come alive with history.

On our left, the lettering "Northern" still could be made out through the flaking paint. Here, said Uncle Charley, his friend Tex Rickard used to run a square gambling hall and pour whiskey fit for a man to drink. "We served on Nome's first city council together," remembered Uncle Charley. "Good man for the country. Maybe he'll come back some day after he gets through promoting all those prize fights down in the States."

A great barn of a place, heaved out of shape by the frost, held special memories for Uncle Charley. It marked Nome's once famous Eagle Hall where musicians and actors from as far away as New York came to entertain with concerts and stage shows. It was also the center of local talent performances. "Before he wrote that book about the Spoilers, a young fellow named Rex Beach used to put on blackface skits in there," said Uncle Charley. "I like to died laughing at him. The town lost its best end man in the minstrel shows when Rex took up writing for a living."

I could hear pool balls clicking when we passed the swinging doors of a place called the Nevada. Tourists stood watching a couple of halfbreed Eskimo boys idly knocking the balls around. To Uncle Charley it was nothing now. But take it a few years back . . . "Bartender in there was a man who used to be marshal somewhere in the southwest, name of Wyatt Earp. Guess he was the only real gun man in camp. You'd see him walking along the beach flinging empty whiskey bottles in the air and smashing them with his six-shooters. Didn't stay in Nome but a short time; went back to Nevada or California or somewhere."

Uncle Charley had seen an endless parade of important people pass through Nome. He'd met Jack London, already a famous author when he boated down the Yukon to catch a steamer to San Francisco. There'd been Frank Gotch, the wrestling champion, meeting all comers and pinning their shoulders to the mat with the greatest of ease. Prize-fighter Jack Twin Sullivan, fighting under assumed names, had barnstormed the gold camps, knocking local hopefuls stiff. Roald Amundsen, Norwegian South Pole discoverer, was a familiar figure around Nome with his big eagle-beak nose, his Homburg hat and tight-fitting gray suit, and courtly manners. Through the years, Uncle Charley had greeted big name globetrotters; dukes and counts, potentates and grand poobahs from all over the world coming to look at a real gold camp.

Go back to the smug obscurity of a New England bootery? Not Uncle Charley! Not while Nome needed him (though he didn't get a penny for serving as mayor); not while there was gold hiding right under the grassroots waiting to be found! Why, all you had to do was strap a pick and gold pan on a packboard, go out there on the tundra, and look for it!

That's what he had me doing next day, and in style. In the days of the Spoilers a narrow-gage railroad led for miles across the flat tundra to the foothills and up through the bare mountains. Like Nome itself, the flimsy affair had fallen to ruin, its light-weight rails warped into fantastic curves. Snowslides had carried away entire sections, while across the swaybacked trestles the rails dangled perilously.

To negotiate this roller-coaster horror, Uncle Charley had contrived a railroad buggy of sorts from the wheels and axles of abandoned equipment, and used it to exercise his sled dogs during the short Arctic summer. After we'd loaded a prospecting outfit aboard, and with the mayor's guiding hand on the brake, the dogs took us on a wild ride to the hills, careening, twisting, jumping the rails, splashing through bogholes in clouds of spray. Uncle Charley kept pointing with his free hand at old gravel piles overgrown with weeds where some early day prospector had hit it rich. Right over there Joe Brown made his fortune in a single summer. On the other side of the tracks a character named Snakehead Dooley had taken out a cool million and headed back to Ireland with it to kiss the Blarney rock again. Nobody had missed; they'd all hit it big.

But I had a hard time paying proper attention to all these success stories. What took my eye were the chattering "sic-sic" spotted squirrels scooting tails-up ahead of the racing dogs and scuttling into their burrows just in time. Little birds called longspurs, fluttered aloft like skylarks, singing their heads off as they slowly parachuted back to earth. Flocks of sandpipers, hook-billed curlews and robin-breasted dowitchers whipped around our heads, whistling their shrill alarms. Between knee-high tussocks grew carpets of salmonberry vines loaded with luscious soft berries that looked like clusters of salmon eggs. Brilliantly colored wildflowers were everywhere; patches of cotton-tipped sedges and masses of bright blue forget-me-nots. Never had I seen the likes of the wild mushrooms—acres of scarlet capped russulas, boletas, and giant puffballs! Every pool had its pair or two of ducks with broods of half-grown young flapping into the weeds.

At the base of Anvil Mountain we passed an active mining operation; streams of water from giant hydraulic nozzles cutting away a hundred feet of overlying frozen muck to lay bare an ancient shore of Bering Sea. Uncle Charley said that gangs of "shovel-stiffs" had in earlier years heaved enough pay dirt into old-style sluice boxes to make a dozen millionaires. Now, mining syndicates were getting ready to ship some big dredges up from California to rework this same third beach line. They'd take out more and more millions, he admitted, but it wouldn't be like finding new gold. That was the real challenge! Prospectors like him were still looking for the source of all this wealth; some place back in the mountains from which the nuggets had been flushed by floods in ages past; some place richer than anything yet uncovered in the Nome country; a mother lode just waiting for the lucky man to find it!

Uncle Charley was thinking of this hidden pot of gold, not the scenery, when he halted the pupmobile on a high dome, staked the sled dogs in a patch of scrub willows alongside an alpine rill, and tossed them each their daily ration of one dried salmon. "They'll be all right until tomorrow night," he said, as he busied himself stowing paraphernalia into a couple of packsacks.

I turned to look back over the way we had come, and the sight was enough to make a man's breath catch in his throat. An immense, colorful panorama of tundra stretched for more miles than I could see across a treeless expanse, dotted with hundreds—no, thousands of potholes winking in the afternoon sun. Creeks and rivers looped in endless convolutions across the boggy muskeg to the turbid sea, and Bering Sea itself curved away past the coast of Siberia, lurking in the haze, and on into infinity across the top of the world. In this grandeur of unpeopled space, Nome was but a dot of coal-smoke smudging out on its once golden sands, fading away in the past. From our far distance, all the rest—the deserted, wind-torn miners' shacks and puny gravel heaps—looked to be all but reclaimed by the wilderness, so that it looked like it was in the beginning. It was profoundly moving. Before I weighed my words, I blurted out to Uncle Charley, "No wonder you never came home from the Gold Rush!"

Uncle Charley didn't seem to hear me. His mind was on the present. "Hold still a minute," he ordered. I stood like a horse while he flung a loaded packsack across my withers, cinched up on the surcingle, and made motions like putting a bit between my teeth. He finished draping the load with assorted items like picks, shovels, gold pans, skillet and gun, then gave me a final slap on the rump. "Giddup, Dobbin!" he said. "We got a few miles to go before making camp."

He shouldered a somewhat bigger pack and led the way around the mountain to where a sizable flow of water came thundering down a rocky chute to plunge into a deep pool before leveling off across the tundra. Melting summer snow and every rainstorm sluiced fresh deposits of sand and gravel out of the high country. Uncle Charley said that some day he hoped to find this river hole loaded with "color." That would be the day to trace the upstream source, testing with samples of dirt in his gold pan until he found where it came out of the ground.

We shucked our packs, and I watched the pioneer prospector kneel at the water's edge, expertly dipping and twirling until the lighter material was carried away over the lip of the shallow pan. I leaned close to see what remained. A couple of pin-point yellowish flecks glinted in the bottom. Uncle Charley tilted the gold pan into the current and let them wash away. "We'll try it again," he said.

It wasn't any use—not this time, anyway. Colors, yes, but definitely not the big find. He sampled several other places along the shoreline with similar results. There would be no baring of the adenoids and shouts of "Eureka!" on this trip. Uncle Charley was only mildly let down. He'd panned thousands of creeks without finding a sign of gold. It was all part of being a prospector. This one was, temporarily, just another blank.

But not to me! Never had I seen a better fishing hole. A run of bright blue salmon had moved in from Bering Sea until they were blocked from further upstream migration by the falls, and now the air was full of them trying to leap the obstruction. Among the milling salmon were schools of red-spotted trout, and a fish called a grayling with fan-shaped dorsal fins, color-speckled like miniature peacock tails. There wasn't the slightest sign of a fisherman's boot heel, and the thought of it nearly drove me out of my mind, because in all our back-packed gear there wasn't a scrap of angling material.

Uncle Charley took care of that in his own way. He waded out into the shallow end of the pool, and when a salmon swam past he swung a shovel and bashed it on the head.

I helped him pitch the begrimed, spark-holed tent he'd carried on many a stampede, then spread sleeping bags on a natural mattress of gray reindeer moss inside. We rigged the sheet-iron stove and Uncle Charley crumbled dry willow twigs, and lit the fire with an old-fashioned sulphur match torn off a thin, wooden comb. While he was mixing a batch of biscuits from his sourdough starter, he had me gathering a bowl of sugar-sweet blueberries to stir in the batter. By the time they were browned, the coffee pot was boiling over, and the red slabs of salmon were smoking in the skillet with a tantalizing aroma.

Afterward, we lay in our sleeping bags looking out the open tent flap while the sun dipped down like a great blob of molten copper into the pale green Bering Sea. In its dying rays of magenta and deep purple, we watched an enormous migration of sandhill cranes float down from the sky like five thousand open umbrellas and settle with noisy clamor on the hills around us. I told Uncle Charley that this was the feature of his Alaska that stirred me deepest; not the gold, but the primitive land itself with its exciting plenitude of wild things; that if I stayed, this was what would hold me.

3 A Switch in Plans

When we came pupmobiling back to Nome and looked out across the booming surf of Bering Sea, I could scarcely believe my eyes. Except for a school of small beluga whales arching their white backs out of the turbid water, the sea stretched empty to the skyline. The Steamer *Victoria* was gone.

Uncle Charley explained. Nothing to fret about. He'd fixed it with the Purser for me to stay over in Nome until a later sailing. A reservation had been made for me on the old coal-burner when she returned on her next and final voyage of the season. My steamer trunk had been fetched ashore and placed in Uncle Charley's spare room. While he stood by, I opened it to reveal my meager possessions: a .22 Savage Hi-Power rifle highly touted in those years as an all-around weapon for everything from a prairie dog to a charging rhinoceros; a camera; a few articles of raiment definitely not fabricated for Alaska's frigid winters; some bird and animal guide books, and a second-hand typewriter I'd hammered on since school days. If Uncle Charley hoped to see the tools by which a man might earn his keep, he had to be disappointed. The look in his eyes told me he would have traded the whole kit and kaboodle for a short-handled pick and a No. 2 shovel.

He left me fondling over these cherished possessions while he called at his cubbyhole office in the Nome Volunteer Fire Department Hall where the town business, when any, was carried on. He hadn't come right out and said so—he didn't have to—but I guess he was beginning to realize I didn't have the makings of a prospector. Nor did I try to deceive him. In truth, his ringing whoops, "The ground hasn't been scratched yet" had fallen on my empty ears. If I had to do it, the ground was already scratched as deep as it would ever be. To me, the stuff might just as well stay where it was under Alaska's grassroots as gathering tarnish under Kentucky's Fort Knox.

What then could I find of interest up here at the cold tail-end of the Continent? The answers were not all negative. Already, I'd seen for myself that the tundra was far from being the frappe waste described in my natural history books. Beyond the tundra, dozens of snow-dusted mountains sawtoothed against the blue, begged for exploration. And the icy-cold sea, bending out of sight across the largest uninhabited space in the northern hemisphere, really stirred my imagination. There was apparently an endless assortment of wild life.

The more I thought about it, the more I was convinced that for me the real gold in Alaska had wings and fins and hair on it. Before leaving the farm in New Hampshire, I had pecked out a few manuscripts and managed to place enough of them to stay ahead on postage stamps. Now, I felt the writer's itch again, and this time I figured to try a really big subject. I'd start with whales.

Looking back on it now after nearly fifty years, I'm bound to admit that it wasn't a good article. It deserved to be thumbed down with a printed rejection slip and it was; but long before I knew the bleak results, events in Nome took an odd turn.

Uncle Charley made a last try to inoculate me with the virus of the gold bug that flowed in his own veins. Walking along the beach past strange, rusty contraptions half buried in the dunes, he explained that miners of the early days had merely worked the ruby sands above tidewater; that beyond the pounding breakers the bottom of Bering Sea was practically lined with gold. It had been waiting twenty years for some inventive miner to make himself richer than Midas. Charley gave me a fast rundown on man's futile battle against the forces of nature.

What looked like a head-on collision between a couple of bulldozers had actually been a device for scraping the bottom of the sea and hauling the rich sands ashore to put through a sluice-box. A heap of eroded cogwheels and buckets had once been a sea-going suction dredge. Nearby was the dream child of his friend Rex Beach where the husky young novelist had romped in the surf with a go-devil rig until he'd "turned blue as a tuna and started snapping at bait." A huge, iron cylinder rolling in the wash of the waves represented an attempt to sink a caïsson and dig gold dry-shod within its walls. Somebody with real Buck Roger ideas had spent his last dime constructing a giant straddle-bug to stalk the shallow waters, lowering clam-shell buckets to haul up the pay sand. Every one had met the same fate. Bering Sea had waited with benign calmness until the right moment, then risen up in its cold fury to hurl man's offerings back into his face.

The sorry sight of these rusty derelicts in no way discouraged Uncle Charley. He picked up a piece of driftwood and began scratching in the sand his own design of an apparatus which couldn't miss. Before he had it finished, a big breaker came hissing across the wet beach to wash it all out. This seemed rather symbolic to me, but Uncle Charley in his optimism saw something else.

"Look!" Where the backwash had obliterated his stickmarks, a mote of yellow shone in dampness. By the happiest calculation it couldn't have been worth a penny, but it was all Uncle Charley needed to prove to his complete satisfaction that pots of the stuff lay waiting out there on the floor of Bering Sea.

But what I liked best along the cold ocean were the living things. Though it still lacked a few days until the end of August, freezing nights had already put a skim of ice on tundra potholes to the north. Broods of waterfowl had begun to move out to the coast to assemble for the southern migration. All manners of web-footed birds bobbed on the waves beyond the surf, and the cloud-puffed sky was laced with skeins of ducks, geese, and myriads of shorebirds sweeping down out of the Arctic nesting grounds. Flocks of black brant were strung for miles across the whitecaps, their calls oddly like the sound of beagle hounds on the hot trail of a rabbit. The clangorous cries of the beautiful blue Emperor geese joined with the organ-like pealing of old squaw ducks, the mewing of glaucous-winged gulls, and the piccolo trills of curlews and plovers, all swelling into a great symphony, then dying away as the flocks drifted south.

In their passing was a note of urgency, of shortening days, of a warning to all summering visitors to be gone. Already, there was a nippy feel in the air; a notice to prepare for the abrupt ending of a too short summer. "There are only two seasons up here," said Uncle Charley somewhat soberly, "Fourth of July and winter."

Nome veterans were already beginning to cache food supplies. Busiest of all were the Eskimos who lived along a sandspit across Snake River. A hundred or more of these genial natives were tending their gill-nets in the breakers and tossing out salmon and silvery char which the women split deftly with their round oola knives and hung across wooden racks to cure in the ocean wind. Others among them were pulling a community seine through the surf, sagging with tons of 10-inch tomcods to be strung through the eyes and thrown across the fish-racks. The wondrous abundance of fish had attracted whales and seals, and the crack of rifle shots and spat of bullets ricocheting off the wave tops came echoing in from the fruitful sea.

In the rapidly darkening days of fall the white people were also storing food. Those who planned to "winter in" were making their deals with Nome's trading posts for wholesale case lots of canned goods, crates of eggs and vegetables, sacks of flour and sugar, all to be held in warm dry storage at gradually rising costs until called for during the winter. When the last steamer left for the south in early November, Bering Sea would freeze over shortly afterward and there would not be another shipment until the breakup in June. "Wintering in" had all the ominous implications of bears crawling into dens to hibernate. I began to feel a kinship, instead, with the wild geese who lived in perpetual summer merely by shifting locations with the seasons. It was a comfort to know that my return fare to

Seattle had been set up by Uncle Charley for that last sailing of the venerable *Victoria*.

There was a national election that fall. Although Alaska's territorials could not vote for President, nor even for their own Governor, they were, nevertheless, intensely aroused. As a result of the election, several juicy political plums were due for the plucking at Nome. All of this meant less than nothing to me until fate thrust me into the role of catalyst. It started when the town's elderly barber, known to clients as Shaky Sol, saw a chance to improve his lot by applying for appointment as local game warden at a salary of $2,000 per annum, which was a princely figure, indeed, in that there was nothing to do and he could keep right on cutting hair. Uncle Charley had spread the news about his boy with the hottest typewriter on the beach, so Shaky Sol asked me to compose a letter from him to Democratic inner circles in Washington, D.C. With tongue in cheek, I suggested, "Why don't you write one to the Republicans, too. That way, you double your chances."

Soon I was applying for jobs as Deputy Marshals, Jailers, Janitors, and Officer for the Suppression of Liquor Traffic Among the Natives. The list of hopefuls for these modest appointments grew to astonishing numbers. I gave each applicant my all, endowing every man with sterling qualities they'd never suspected, though none hesitated to sign on the dotted line. I offered my services to Uncle Charley, but he looked at me curiously and said he had other plans.

As increasingly cold weather in the mountains froze off the water supply needed to wash paydirt through the sluice-boxes, miners began rubber-booting into Nome with their gold pokes. Most of them would catch the *Victoria* south to the "Great Outside." Others planned to "winter in" and among this group were more candidates for appointment. I had by this time exhausted my superlatives and had to take a short refresher course with Thesaurus before launching the new group. Business rose to a final peak in the fading light of October when Nome's boardwalked streets clattered and thumped with miner's bootheels for twenty-four hours of the day, and I thought nothing of being aroused at two-thirty in the morning to turn out another wheedling letter.

I was beating the drums for one last deserving office-seeker when bedlam erupted outside my window. Miners began yelling, and suddenly there was a hoarse hooting of a steamer whistle, joined by mournful ululations from every sled dog in the community. I hurried out to see the *Victoria* slow to a stop in the open roadstead and let go anchor. Lighters were being launched through the smashing icy breakers to bring in the six weeks' accumulation of mail in the Seattle postoffice, and the last freight Nomeites would see until next summer. News had spread that a big storm was brewing in the Arctic and that the steamer would lay off Nome Beach only long enough to rush offloading and take on passengers.

Before packing my steamer trunk I had to finish another letter, this one in behalf of a son of Sweden who wanted a "yanitor yob" at the Court House. The typewriter keys were singing their swan song when I became aware of two men pushing through the door to look over my shoulders. I swung around quickly to say I'd closed up shop. One of the newcomers was an important looking big fellow whom I'd never met. The other was Uncle Charley. I wasn't sure I liked the look on their faces. The big fellow spoke first and came right to the point. He'd just got the word that he was going to be the new United States Marshal for the

Second Division of Alaska, and he needed a young deputy who could wrangle a typewriter. He'd heard about me playing John Alden for just about everybody in Nome; how about taking some of my own medicine? I said I couldn't do it because I had a ticket in my coat pocket good for one first-class passage back to Seattle.

Then it was Uncle Charley's turn, and now I knew what he'd meant when he said he "had other plans for the winter." He'd been up here in the cold and snow for twenty years, he said, and if I'd stay in and watch out for his interests he'd like to go "outside" and thaw his bones in California. He'd catch the first boat back in the spring. I looked at him long and hard, then silently handed him my ticket.

Bering Sea had become an ocean of slush rolling ponderously up on the sands, crashing and splattering an icy enamel on everything it touched. The temperature had turned bitter cold, and a razor-edge gale came ripping out of the Arctic. It seemed to me that half the people of Nome had managed to stow aboard the old steamer, and I had the feeling of being deserted on an ice floe. The wind brought the clanking of anchor chain to those of us who lined the shore, and there was a loud *Chunk!* as the steam winch drew it taut. The whistle hooted its harsh good-bye, there was the sad keening of the malemutes, and soon the *Victoria* was a wind-whipped plume of coal-smoke flattening out on the gray skyline. The memory of it is still sharp in my mind. It was the worst day I ever spent in Alaska.

4 The Deputy

I didn't last long enough on the job to learn all my duties as Deputy United States Marshal, Second Division, Territory of Alaska. There were four of us loafing around in the Nome headquarters with almost nothing to do; free to pursue our various hobbies. A white-maned patriarch named Addy, who looked like a deacon, spent most of his time trying to peddle a worthless mining claim. Another fellow sentenced himself to hard labor during every weekend sinking a 40-foot prospect hole through frozen ground to bedrock on the Second Beach Line. The artist among us secreted himself behind hung blankets in the toilet where he spent hours developing photographs of Eskimo babies in fur parkas.

I was the nature boy of the outfit. I was drawn as if by a magnet to newly frozen Bering Sea where a field of ice now stretched all the way to Siberia, veined with open leads where seal heads bobbed to the surface to be picked off by

Eskimo hunters. Nearer shore, in holes chopped through the ice, fur-bundled native women jigged out heaps of watery tomcods which flopped briefly before freezing hard as icicles, and tasted about the same. But red spider crabs hauled out through the same holes were a gourmet's delight, and I learned how to eat them like the Eskimos, feeding the legs into one corner of my mouth, spitting out shells on the other.

The temperature fell to 15 degrees below zero, then to 20 and finally to 30 before Christmas, and the wind howled like an invasion of banshees as it heaped up drifts higher than the houses. Yet, it was not uncomfortable outdoors when one dressed in reindeer parka, sealskin boots, and wolf-skin mitts tested by the Eskimos for centuries. I spent hours snowshoeing across the tundra where now every pothole was under a blanket of white, every willow thicket buried so that only the brittle tips showed above the surface. White though it was in every direction as far as one could see, buffeted by gales which swept the snow in shrieking ground-storms, the tundra still remained a place of teeming life. There was a solid network of lacy patterns made by the scurrying feet of lemmings, field mice, and sharp-nosed shrews. Weasels poked their glistening black eyes out of snow tunnels and stared boldly. Ptarmigan, now turned from brown to white, gathered in huge flocks invisible against the snowscape until they thundered away into the storm on loudly clapping wings. They were the very epitome of Arctic hardihood, an example of a grouse which had learned to live in the midst of apparent desolation. Ever since the first snowfall the ptarmigan had been on their winter diet of willow buds, and their dark flesh had become bitter to the taste. Only a hungry man would kill one now, though I was told that the open season would continue until the cocks started crowing in the spring, and the hens started hiding their eggs among the tussocks. Miners thought nothing of potting a duck or a goose in the spring but the ptarmigan was a homesteader like themselves, and every miner admired it and gave it a fair chance to nest.

One reason there wasn't much work for the deputies in early winter was the annual love affair Nome had with itself. Right after the last steamer departed in November, leaving a disconsolate band of "stay-ins" to fight off frozen noses and the blues, the townspeople drew together and vowed they'd be kind to one another. There'd be no nasty feuding as in the past; this winter they'd all be one happy family.

It was quite a family! A rough count of those who had "missed the boat" showed a population of 900, of which about 750 were men. Mostly, they were crabbed old gaffers whose true names were not always known, but who answered—if they felt like it—to such monickers as Goofy Gus, Bloodpoison Bill, Kobuk Red, Scarface Louie, Scurvy Kid, and the King of Denmark. The remaining 150 were all known as "girls" be they white-haired grandmas, the minister's and the judge's proper spouses, or newly arrived schoolmarms. "Girls" also designated the twenty-five or so rouged ladies who lived in a red-lighted compound behind a boardwall enclosure, among whom—waiting to answer the doorbell—might be such lovelies as Dawson Kitty, Halibut-face Mary, Deepwater Dorah, Toodles, Betsy the Bitch, and the Oregon Mare.

Nome's main amusement during the long winter, nevertheless, was attending Billie Code's Theatre, a hall as run down as its old movies of the pre-1920 days, featuring

Mary Pickford, Fatty Arbuckle, and the Keystone Cops. Several times during each performance there would be long intervals for rewinding of films, re-threading to cure flutter, splicing breaks. Once in a while an arc light would flame out and send a cloud of smoke out over the audience, then plunge the hall into darkness for as long as an hour. Usually, the hand operator would have to crank like mad at the end to make up lost time, and the film characters would dart like flies all over the screen.

Because the "odor of their mukluks resembled not the rose," Eskimo patrons were politely asked to sit together in the balcony where they watched with wonder as the white people on the flickering screen belabored one another with billy-clubs and tossed custard pies in each other's faces. All kindness and gentleness among themselves, at the end of each show the Eskimos would wend their way back to their igloos on the Sandspit, tongues clacking, heads shaking sadly at the white man's perfidious ways.

Many veteran Nomeites whiled away the long, dark hours of winter with their feet on a hot stove and their noses in a book. They were amazingly well-informed on the most obsolete subjects, and after boning up on some obscure point in past history would slyly inveigle a newcomer into an argument. After taking my lumps from a few of these boreal bookworms, I became very bait-shy and learned never to rise to a lure hooked into a subject of the other fellow's choosing. This was right after I'd been shellacked by a quiet little man who just happened to mention Gibbon's *Rise and Fall of the Roman Empire.* It turned out he'd been reading the thing two or three times a winter for twenty years. When the next sourdough tried to badger me into a debate I ran like a coward, fearing the subject might be something like "Strange Customs Among the Headhunters of Interior Borneo."

There was almost no court work to mar the serenity of the winter until the beginning of "feuding time" in February. It happened every year, they told me, ushering in the annual period when the 900 brothers and sisters in Nome's one happy family began spreading snide rumors and snapping bites out of one another's rear ends. It was probably a mere coincidence that at this time the town's supply of cold storage eggs, now six months away from the hens, started turning green in the shells and smelling like asafoetida. While it is possible that the poisonous intake of Chinese-style eggs might be cankering the minds of the Nomeites, the real reason was probably the constant association at social gatherings like whist parties, lodges, and box suppers. There was no way to escape seeing the same old faces everywhere and hearing the same old jokes staler than the eggs. Gradually the town folks organized into cliques, each one set on character assassination of the other. It was a kind of epidemic "cabin fever," and no amount of pre-planning could hold down the virus beyond February's dark days.

A diversion was desperately needed to uplift the ice-locked community into nobler feelings toward his fellow man, and this winter the job fell to a squat, toad-faced character known as Sleepy Pete. Pete did it by getting nabbed by an itinerant squad of prohibition officers who caught him asleep amid the fumes of a moonshine plant. When Pete faced judge, jury, and a courtroom jammed with old customers, the floor was covered with evidence, to wit: copper still, barrels of yeasty sourmash, sugar, cornmeal, and a dozen wicker-bound jugs filled to the corks with reputedly the best hooch brewed in the entire Nome precinct.

Sleepy Pete wasted nobody's time on alibis. He said he just happened to be passing by the place when he smelled good liquor and came in to bum a drink. Nobody was there, so he helped himself and was sleeping off the lovely effects when the Bone Dry agents pounced on him. The judge, into whose home Sleepy Pete had several times been observed making clandestine deliveries, sent the jury out to deliberate. Shortly, they filed back into the jury box and announced they had reached a unanimous verdict. "We find the defendant," declared the foreman, "Not Guilty!"

Nobody had expected any other decision on so flimsy a case. "All they had was evidence," said the defense attorney. But now he tossed in a surprise. "By reason of the fact that my client has been found innocent," he moved unctuously, "we pray for the return of all such evidence."

His Honor, an old hand at dispensing frontier justice, peered mildly down at Sleepy Pete over his steel-rimmed spectacles, and remarked dryly, "The Court will take this motion under advisement."

We deputies waited in vain for Shaky Sol, the new game warden, to christen his badge by bringing a culprit into court for shooting a ptarmigan, or something, out of season. But he fooled us by remaining discreetly in his barber shop all winter. Then, at breakup time along Bering Sea, Sol made his move. When the first goose—closed to shooting by international treaty—came flying over the melting ice in front of his window, Shaky Sol headed for the hills, leaving a sign in his window that he wouldn't be back until after the migration. This was the glad cue all the good citizens of Nome had been waiting to hear. Oiling up their shotguns, they went out to fetch in the first fresh meat the town had seen in more than six months. On the night of Sol's return, the grateful folks showed their esteem by hanging a brace of fat brant on his doorknob; plucked. dressed, and oven-ready.

Meanwhile, the tundra behind Nome stirred under the impetus of spring sunshine. The ptarmigan, which had been snow-white all winter, seemed to change color overnight. The hens became speckled with brown to match the willow patches emerging through the shrinking drifts. The pugnacious cock birds, now sporting bright russet necks and fiery red combs above each eye, jousted like game roosters for possession of the high tussocks. All day and most of the night their guttural challenges, "Come Here! Come Here! Go Back! Go Back!" sounded all over the tundra, followed by raucous cacklings and bold strutting. The only time they slacked off was when a snowy owl came winging low and silently across the broken snowfields.

Such is nature's way that coincident with rising hordes of rodents on the tundra, and the rising populations of ptarmigan, came extraordinary numbers of their predators. The fierce Arctic snowy owls had taken over all the highest hummocks for nesting sites, in each of which there were from five to seven round, white eggs laid on alternate days. Because the nights were still sharp enough to chill the embryos, the adults started brooding as soon as the first egg was deposited, with the result that the first woolly white owlet to hatch was almost half grown before the last egg was pipped. All eyeballs and snapping beaks, they fed voraciously on every dead creature the parents brought in. The mounds looked like butcher shops with carcasses of lemmings, field mice, ground squirrels, and ptarmigan ringed around within reach of the gluttonous owlets.

From a single lookout point, I counted upwards of twenty such nest mounds spaced across the tundra. Their toll of lesser wildlife about them must have been enormous, yet the rodents and ptarmigan showed neither scarcity nor signs of fear. I spotted a ptarmigan hen hovering quietly over a dozen freckled eggs of her own within a dozen feet of an owl nest, and the hummocks occupied by owls continued to be swarming with rodents.

Back in the Marshal's office sitting in front of an idle typewriter day after day, I finally succumbed to an urge to write something about this strange "balance of nature" at work on the Alaska tundra. I mailed the manuscript to a small eastern magazine, and this time it paid off double. The first payment was a check for $18.75. The second was a letter that made me gasp. It was from the Chief of the United States Bureau of Biological Survey, Department of Agriculture, in Washington, D.C.

It developed that the eminent scientist, Dr. E. W. Nelson, had spent several years of his early career in Alaska as a field agent, and in the 1880's had himself made notes on the occurrence and habits of snowy owls in the Yukon River Delta. He had penned extensive journals on the life histories of other wildlife of such detailed correctness that they had led him into the highest office of its kind in the land. My inexperienced reporting on the same subject matter had stirred poignant memories in the great man. He was eager to learn more, not only on snowy owls, but on all the other Alaska fauna, most of which he hadn't seen for nearly forty years. His letters, typed by a secretary, then interlined and expanded on the back of the page with his bold handwriting, conveyed his nostalgia. They kept pressing me for more information, and wanting to know my background, my plans.

There had been several such lettered exchanges between this famous biologist and the greenest wildlife amateur in the country, when Dr. Nelson took the short-cut of a wireless message. I have saved it all these years: WILL YOU ACCEPT APPOINTMENT FIELD AGENT MAKE WILDLIFE RECONNAISSANCE NORTHWESTERN ALASKA PURPOSE PROMULGATING FIRST COMPREHENSIVE GAME CODE? LETTER FOLLOWS.

Dr. Nelson had opened the door and pointed the trail. What happened on the way, where the trail might lead, was up to me. I wired back immediate acceptance, then went over to the Marshal's office and turned in my star.

5 Voyage to Reindeer Land

In that year the Bureau of Biological Survey had transferred one of its top field men to Nome to help develop what was then believed to be a budding industry to replace Alaska's petering out gold mines. Small shipments of domesticated reindeer from Lapland and Siberia in 1892 to provide a means of living for the Eskimos, had in thirty years multiplied to half a million. Santa Claus' steeds had far outgrown local appetites and now there were rosy schemes for supplying butcher shops all across America with the meat called "rennon."

My first assignment called for sharing Nome quarters with the experienced L. J. Palmer, and sailing with him aboard a native-built schooner to inspect reindeer herds scattered along the Arctic shorelines. Neither of us knew jib from boom and we couldn't have started the decrepit make-and-break distillate-burning auxiliary engine if our lives depended on it—which they later did. Fortunately, the *Hazel* came to us manned by an Eskimo who had grown up with the old trading ship, besides which he could find his way through the densest fog with the instinct of a homing walrus. Napook was a barrel-chested, bandy-legged little fellow, with arms like a blacksmith which he'd acquired in a lifetime of kayak paddling. A perpetual grin split his high-cheeked, copper-toned face. His nose was flat, and his big teeth white as bleached clamshells. Napook could understand and speak English, except in an emergency when he could do neither. He'd been living aboard the *Hazel* several weeks, fitting her for sea duty, and when we knocked the chocks out from under her skids on the banks of Snake River, she coasted down into the muddy water and floated like a loon.

Provisioned for weeks of summer travel, we chugged out through the breakers into Bering Sea, shut off the engine to conserve fuel of which the *Hazel* carried only a hundred-hour supply, and sailed north. In four hours we were abeam of Sledge Island, which meant we were making about 6 knots, and late in the afternoon we scudded under a village on King Island where a hundred Eskimos dwelt in hide-covered hovels propped up against slanting rock walls with driftwood poles. The natives lined the cliffs waving their arms like the flapping wings of the sea birds around them as they beckoned us in for a visit. But there was no time to stop. We were overdue for a series of reindeer roundups in Kotzebue Sound. Also, Napook said we would soon be delayed by ice. How did he know? "Me smellum!"

It was exactly midnight when the sun, a huge garnet disk, dipped its lower half into a peasoup-colored sea. Today became yesterday and tomorrow was today, as the blazing orb rose almost immediately to start another 24-hour journey around the sky. Passing through narrow Bering Straits into the Arctic Ocean, our sails seemed to be aflame in its low rays. Alaska's Cape Prince of Wales was floodlighted until each lowly igloo shone like a palace, and the deserted heap of rocks marking Russian Diomede glinted with life. I had the exhilarating feeling of sailing on and forever into the luring brilliance of the red polar sun. Then, suddenly, like somebody slamming a door in our faces, we were cut off by an impenetrable bank of fog.

The air chilled many degrees, and now we could all "smell" ice. Napook slowed the *Hazel* to avoid colliding against an enormous mass of upthrust ice slabs and jumbled bergs that loomed in the gray opaqueness. Then, he put his shoulder to the helm and swung the schooner to skirt the edge. After several hours, in the distance, we could hear the faint far away howling of malemutes. Napook said we were passing Shismaref, a sandspit projecting into the sea. Invisible in the mist, the sound of the village sled dogs was still audible when Napook found what he was looking for; a churning river of shattered ice particles. While Palmer and I wielded pike-poles to fend off the larger bergs, he probed cautiously into this grinding chaos for several hours.

As quickly as it had come, the mist vanished. The *Hazel's* bow cut through the fog blanket into dazzling sunshine and we were immediately blinded by reflections and mirage effects. Clouds of gulls and eider ducks spattered off tiny open spots among the floes to wheel overhead.

Arctic foxes, airy as powder puffs, scampered alongside. In the distance a polar bear tossed its snaky head high in the air as it scented our engine exhaust and shuffled swiftly away until it disappeared right through the wall of the sky.

Just when I was hoping this spectacular show would never end, the *Hazel* came a cropper. Without warning, the river of swirling ice cubes pinched down to a crack. There was no time to stop the forward progress of the schooner; all Napook could do was steer her into the narrowing slot. Heeling on her side, amid crashing of ship's crockery and tableware, and accented by Eskimo yells, the *Hazel* climbed onto the floe and collapsed on her scuppers.

There was a moment of dumbfounded silence before Napook let go the tiller and slid down on the ice where Palmer and I were untangling ourselves. I looked up at his mouthful of big white teeth and I thought he'd gone crazy. He was grinning like a chimpanzee. "*Adegah!*" he called out assuringly. "Everything dam' good!"

Palmer and I picked ourselves up off the ice and waited for the Eskimo to tell us how dam' good. I guess he did, but it was all in Innuit jargon and we didn't know what he was talking about. It seemed to be a thoroughly desperate situation—the *Hazel* lying on her side, high and dry, helpless as a foundered whale—and worse yet, the fog choosing this moment to come rolling in again. With visibility, and our spirits, at nil, we clambered aboard the schooner to escape the sudden dank cold. Napook managed to brew a pot of coffee on a primus stove, and we gnawed on sea biscuits and waited in murk thick enough to slice with a knife.

After what seemed an eternity we heard dull roars out in

the fog, gradually becoming louder, spreading and echoing in the gray void until it was impossible to locate the source. In our predicament, the unearthly din was well calculated to breed morbid thoughts. I shuddered and glanced at Palmer, and he was doing the same. We both looked hopefully up at Napook, perched on a slanting top bunk. He was grinning again, as he cocked one ear and then the other. With one ear he was hearing a great herd of walrus deployed on the ice field; with the other he was listening for something more important. It was the wind.

Soon, the bergs around us began rubbing together and creaking like rafters in an old barn, lifting and falling, tumbling and crashing, gradually pulling apart. The *Hazel* came alive, groaning from stem to stern as she struggled to right herself. When the ice under her side finally separated, she rolled up on her keel and settled back into the opened channel with a splash. Napook went below to squirt priming ether into the cylinder petcocks. We heard him clanking the Johnson bar against the heavy flywheel to heave it over, and suddenly the old engine began pop-popping. At slow bell, the schooner started creeping through the mist. I stole a look at the compass. The *Hazel* seemed to be headed for the North Pole. I was about to call Napook's attention to this glaring error in navigation when I realized that at our present Arctic latitude, the compass needle would not be pointing to the True North, but to the Magnetic Pole in Baffin Land, due east of our position.

The neighing and baying and bellowing of the walrus faded away while we pushed through the gray curtain. Many hours later as the floating ice thinned and the water became calm ahead, Napook called on his native wild instincts again, swinging his head like a polar bear, questing the air. After another spell of time he seemed to have picked up a message, and his almond eyes blinked.

"You ketchum?" he asked me.

I didn't "ketchum," not at all; not even after I'd heaved the lead line to find bottom at 3 fathoms, and tossed the stock anchor over the bow. I didn't know what Napook had in mind until after he went down to shut off the engine, came back rubbing his hands with satisfaction, and announced, "Reindeer Camp!"

We turned in then for some badly needed sleep, and when we awoke every last vestige of fog had burned away. Brilliant sunshine bathed the tundra that ringed the *Hazel* as she swung at anchor in a small bay. Floating silently alongside the schooner was a flotilla of kayaks, the occupants politely waiting for somebody on ship to wake up. At Napook's bidding they pulled themselves aboard and he brewed them a pot of tea which they preferred to coffee.

There was no need to ask them about their co-operatively owned reindeer. We could see for ourselves. A great rippling gray and brown carpet, polka-dotted with white animals, covered the tundra. The near edge mingled among tents pitched along the shoreline, and in the far distance there were more reindeer streaming down out of the mountain draws. Palmer estimated there were ten thousand in sight. Nasharluk, the chief herder, quietly revised the figure. "We think maybe many more."

There was a way to find out and that was one reason we were here. It was the first time in a year that the Choris Peninsula herd had been assembled. For weeks not a man had crossed their paths; they had been free to roam the nearby hinterlands like their close American relatives, the caribou. For several days prior to our arrival from Nome, Eskimo and experienced reindeer herders brought over from Lapland, had been combing the hills, routing out small bands, taking advantage of the reindeer's natural tendency to drift down to the sea in summer to lick at salt-encrusted objects on the beach. A narrow neck of land leading out to the bottle-shaped peninsula formed a perfect lead-in to a trap. Cunningly concealed over the brow of a low hill was a corral through which all the reindeer would then have to pass before they could get off the peninsula again and back into the mountains.

Here was where the action was about to take place; where the reindeer would be counted and ear-marked to show ownership among half a hundred Eskimos; where the young bulls would become steers; and where I would take my lumps at the connivance of fun-loving Napook.

The first reindeer to come through the squeeze-gate was a mouse-colored fawn. "Ukalasuk, one female," the chief herder sung out. Three half-circular notches were cut in one ear, a triangular slash in the other, and Ukalasuk's female fawn went dashing into the scrub willows, not likely to be touched again in her lifetime. Three adult females ear-notched in previous summers, were checked off by the counters and passed unheeded through the gate.

There was a wild commotion. A 200-pound bull with spreading antlers in the velvet, came dashing down the chute to the gate, snorting and grunting its anger. Napook was there to meet it. Grasping the left antler, he gave the Eskimo words for, "Let him out!" Into the open bounded the bull with Napook hanging on. I had a blurred vision of flying hoofs, sharp as razors, flailing the air around Napook's head. There was a flurry of dust, and when it cleared the bull was on its side breathing heavily. Sitting astride its shoulder, Napook calmly unsnapped his pocket knife, leaned over, and performed the operation.

News of the roundup had spread with incredible speed from mouth to ear—Mukluk Wireless, they called it—from one fish camp and village to the next all along the shores of Kotzebue Sound. In skin boats the Eskimos came, bringing their wives, children, and sled dogs to set up a temporary village. Reindeer were being slaughtered to provide hides for garments, sinews for fraying into thread, and flesh for the feasting and dancing that went on at all hours of the night and day. With tons of fresh meat to store, it looked to me like an ideal place for some enterprising salesman to achieve the ultimate triumph of his calling by selling a refrigerator to an Eskimo. But I was wrong. They already had one.

The tundra for miles around was one vast, underlying strata of frozen silt, into which the Eskimos had dug a labyrinth of tunnels. Thermometer in hand I descended the pole ladder into a shaft. Surface temperature stood at a warm 70 degrees that day, and I stopped to pluck a handful of wild berries from a matting of dwarf bushes before going down. Three feet below ground level, the thermometer reading dropped to 50 degrees, and at the bottom of the shaft, twenty feet down, it stood at 24 degrees—8 below freezing! The Eskimos had rigged sliding racks to hold hundreds of reindeer carcasses in permanent cold storage.

The purpose of it all was not merely to preserve their own food, but to cold-store shiploads for transfer to the States. But somehow it didn't work out. Exorbitant freight charges, aggravated by the fact that it was almost impossible to get the meat to market without it being thawed, re-frozen, and re-thawed was too great a burden to overcome. After an early boom, the reindeer export business slacked off, and the herds settled back to their original purpose of supplying local needs.

Down at the corral there was a thundering stampede as the herders brought in another big band of reindeer, and ran them into the funnel leading to the trap. Clouds of dust billowed up. Along the edges I saw terrified fawns bleating as they hunted for lost mothers in the blinding turmoil. Reindeer were being rushed through the squeeze gate at the rate of two to the minute, and the young Eskimo bucks whose job it was to wrestle the bulls to earth for altering were beginning to show signs of battle. Napook took his turn, then came panting over to where I stood on the sidelines.

"Maybe you like try 'um?"

All the young Eskimo bucks were watching. I shed my jacket and tossed it out of the way—that hurled fish-pole trick again—and went forward to meet what must have been the biggest and maddest reindeer bull in all the churning thousands. I seized his left antler confidently, and I remember how soft the coating of summer velvet was in my hands. There wasn't much else to remember. For a moment I stood eyeball to eyeball with this bulging-orbed demon, then he flung me over his shoulder, flailed me around in the air, and sent me flying into the corral fence. I managed to sit up in time to wave good-bye as he fled across the tundra to his freedom. I didn't blame him a bit. I hoped he would live to sire a thousand sons.

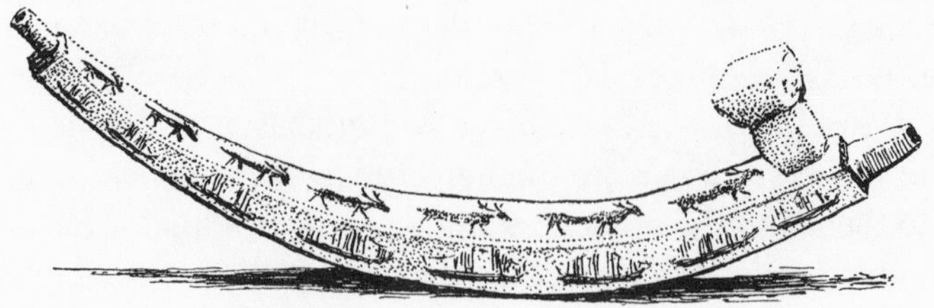

¶6 Old Bones

On the chart the place was called Elephant Point, which seemed an odd name for an Arctic landmark until a reindeer herder explained what it meant. The Eskimos had an unpronounceable name which Napook translated roughly as "Old Bones," because along its base were found many skeletons of long dead creatures. It was directly across the bay from the reindeer corral, and I noticed it first because its front was a wall of solid ice. The aged native recalled that when he was a boy, "Old Bones" had projected much farther into the sea. Now, the thudding waves and summer sun had eroded it back until it looked like the broken-off end of a bridge. A bridge which once might have extended clear across the Arctic Ocean to Asia!

They told me that the icy façade was studded at times with bony remains of beasts from another age, and as the exposed front melted away and crumbled, many strange objects toppled into the surf below. For years the natives had been visiting the place to gather fossil ivory for carving into tools and artifacts, and of late years for making into strings of beads and bracelets to peddle among the white people. That same day, Napook and I moved over there in the *Hazel* and rowed ashore in the dory. Standing at the bottom of the most remarkable glacier I was ever to see in all my Alaska ramblings, I took a look around at this scene out of the past, and imagined a world that hadn't existed for thousands of years.

Out on the surface of the sea, bits of floating ice sparkled like gems. Bright-plumaged eider drakes flew by in bachelor groups. Pigmy white whales rose and fell beneath the ripples like blobs of snow dissolving. In the swirl of the surf, Napook picked up a mammoth molar as big as a cobblestone. I pried loose a massive bison skull half buried in the wet sand, then began struggling with a thighbone off the ancestor of Paul Bunyan's Blue Ox. There were bones sticking up all around, and I was hurrying from one to another when Napook pointed upward and yelled. "No more diggum! Here comes whole one!"

It looked just like that at first. It looked like an emaciated elephant in the very act of breaking through the walls of its icy crypt where it had been in deep-freeze for hundreds of centuries. Two enormous tusks of stove-pipe diameter, curling back against themselves like fish-hooks, hung suspended in the air. Part of an incredibly huge skull was exposed, with ice water trickling from its open jaws. A poised foreleg the size of a tree trunk gave the impression of probing cautiously for a foothold which wasn't there any more because it had melted away. Napook pursed his breath at the sight of a beast, a hundred times bigger than a reindeer, slowly emerging out of the frozen darkness into the sunlight. He said such a beast lived in the legends of his forefathers.

There wasn't anything we could do to hurry the miracle. In its own good time the gigantic skeleton would project farther out, finally to break out of its icy prison and plunge into the sea. We waded into the chilly breakers under the awesome spectacle, gathering handfuls of dark hair long as those on a horse's tail, and we picked up bones with fragments of hide still attached. There had been reports of mammoth finds on the Siberian steppes so perfectly preserved and of such recent entombment that undigested forage was pulled out of their stomachs, and the flesh was sufficiently preserved to cause fighting among the native, sled dogs. When I told this to Napook, he sunk his white teeth into a grisly joint, quickly spat it out, and grunted "plenty old."

Observations made at many points around the world indicated that the mammoths and other now extinct animals had not all been killed in one cataclysmic upheaval of nature. Some had been buried for millions of years; others had roamed the northern tundra in enormous herds possibly within the past twelve thousand years and had probably been neighbor to primitive man in the Arctic. Some had escaped one glacial advance down over America and Eurasia almost to the tropics only to fall victim to the next. Some had died of peaceful old age; more had been caught up in fierce floods and roaring avalanches of ice and snow, killed and frozen within hours.

At least three, possibly four or more times in intervals of ten thousands of years, the polar ice cap had spread down to cover the present sites of New York, Ohio, and California, driving the wildlife ahead of it, or trapping it in pockets to perish. None of this implied a catastrophic change in climate. An average drop of only 15 degrees in temperature was enough—*and would again be enough*—to send icy tentacles several thousand miles into the southlands; a corresponding lift would melt off the tentacles and restore the land to lushness. At one extreme, mammoths and superbisons trumpeted and bellowed where Los Angeles now stands, and at the other extreme strawberries grew on the shores of the Arctic Ocean. But the change did not occur in one lifetime, nor in a hundred. Nothing hurried a glacier. It counted time in multi-centuries.

During the implacable advance and back-up of the polar ice, lakes and rivers had been gouged out, filled in, and gouged out anew. Mountain tops were sheared off like anthills, and the original face of America had been at times puckered out of shape like that of a man sucking lemons. Wildlife trying to adjust to such drastic variations had to alter its way of living, move out if it could, or die. I was convinced that Elephant Point—"Old Bones"—was disgorging some important clues as to what had happened. Definitely, it appeared to be one end of the land bridge which in a past age had united the new world with the old. Over it had trooped all manners of strange beasts, and it had been two-way traffic.

From the Asian side came most of the species we regard as native fauna today: deer, elk, moose, mountain sheep and goats, caribou, grizzly bears, wolves, and a long list of smaller animals. On their way across the land span, they met face to face with herds of primitive horses which had originated in America millions of years earlier as spaniel-dog-sized creatures with five toes, but migrated to the old world before they became saddle mounts and plow nags. We didn't see them again until the Spaniards brought them back in the sixteenth century.

Intermingled with all our existing forms were some of the most grotesque and fearsome monsters that ever cavorted through a drunkard's dream: high-domed mammoths taller than elephants with hair sweeping the earth; giant buffalos with horns to match; ground sloths fifty times bigger than any living today; beavers the size of black bears; long-limbed, short-faced bears to make our present Kodiak brownies look like yearling cubs; camels with necks that seemed to be grafted off giraffes. There were heavy-headed wolves that looked something like giant hyenas, great cats to outmatch African lions, and saber-tooth tigers with killer fangs long enough to stab an elephant to death.

Miners on Seward Peninsula did not always appreciate all this prehistoric big game. They'd been complaining about old bones ever since the gold rush. It was trouble enough to cut down through a hundred feet of frozen muck in order to reach the gold-bearing gravels at bedrock. Streams of snow water gathered in ditches dug around the mountain slopes were led down onto the tundra through flexible canvas hose, and shot through tapering nozzles to shred and thaw away the overlying debris. But when the sluice-boxes were in place and the long-awaited "cleanup" at hand, more troubles appeared.

Long strands of hair and rust-colored wool sometimes clogged the riffles and sluice-boxes. Skulls bigger than the camp stove, too bulky to be carted off in wheelbarrows, had to be rolled out of the way. Ivory tusks up to 15 feet long required the strength of two men to carry them from the pits, and occasionally the water streams would loose nauseous odors and have everybody holding their noses. The busiest creatures at some of the mine pits were the camp dogs trying to re-bury the old bones.

For all these long gone beasts who crossed the land bridge between Alaska and Siberia, the icy abutment at Elephant Point might well have been one of the clover-leaf approaches. The bridge had at times widened to a broad, fertile plain. Then, ever so slowly, the waters had risen to flood it over, allowing the fishes, whales, and seals their turn at migrating. Thousands of years had passed before the oceans gradually receded to block off the fishes, and the highway opened to land animals again. This off-again on-again topographical switch might have started a million years ago, and the last land bridge might have existed within the last twelve thousand years. Before it sunk for the last time, there is much evidence that our "original" people, the Eskimos and Indians, came across, swinging their clubs among the swarming game herds.

If, as the old reindeer herder had told me, Elephant Point had visibly shrunken within his own memory, it meant that it would likely be gone entirely within another generation or two. What was left would be a part of the mainland, and its old bones hidden under a matting of moss and crowberry. The prehistoric remains already washed into the sea would probably be buried forever. With thoughts like this goading me on, I wallowed in the surf like a sea lion and dug into the foam-flecked sands like a terrier. Once in a while Napook extended a helping hand on a gargantuan knuckle, but most of the time he was busily stuffing his seal-skin poke with fossilized molars and fangs for carving into beads, bracelets, and cribbage boards.

When the *Hazel* headed back to Nome her forward lockers were crammed with king-size skeletons, and a tangle of mammoth tusks and super-bison horns were lashed down on the open deck. There wasn't enough room in the Bureau of Biological Survey quarters to store them, so I piled them along the boardwalk in front of the door where they attracted a crowd of tourists when the *Victoria* anchored offshore again. They also attracted a very cagey little merchant, and his name was Napook.

As he stood on the steps of the office, dressed in full Eskimo regalia of fur parka and fancy seal-skin mukluks, Napook would display his ivory trinkets while putting on a show of not being very bright. Grinning amiably, pretending not to understand English, he would point to the bone display stretching up and down the street, and quickly sell out at fancy prices. Getting into the spirit of the game one day—and remembering how Napook had inveigled me into wrestling the bull reindeer—I said to the assembled tourists, "Beware this Eskimo. He is slyer than a fox, and he'll cheat you blind."

Napook stood by, understanding every word, bowing and grinning as though he were being paid the highest compliment. His reply fractured me. "Prank, him punny pellow," said Napook, who had trouble pronouncing his f's. "Inside good. Outside kickumass."

The crowd roared, and that day Napook sold out quicker and for more outrageous prices than ever before.

This schill game might have gone on all summer except that I ran out of old bones. I'd wired Washington, D.C. to ask if the Bureau would pay shipping charges on some prehistoric specimens I'd collected at Elephant Point, and when they said they would, I filled up three huge wooden crates and got them aboard the *Victoria*. The consignment must have been transferred at Seattle to a tramp steamer by way of Cape Horn, because weeks passed before it reached Washington.

But there was nothing slow about the Bureau's acknowledgement, and I reeled with the blow. "SEND NO MORE BONES," the wireless message shouted. "FREIGHT TOLLS ARE ENORMOUS. LETTER FOLLOWS."

The message came too late. The last crate of old bones was already aboard the *Victoria* on its way south. I was still cringing when the letter arrived. It had been written by a Professor of Science attached to the Smithsonian Institute, and it explained that what they wanted, and had expected, were not big bones but small ones. The Professor said they had already classified the larger beasts of the Ice Age, but there was an important and fertile opportunity for discovery among the lesser creatures.. He mentioned a long list of rodents and shrews. Look for tiny slivers of bones, he urged, the kinds which went largely unobserved by amateurs.

The letter closed by giving me a chance to redeem myself. "Send me all the fossil teeth you have on hand," the Professor wrote.

But I had none. Napook had carved them all into trinkets and sold them to the tourists.

7 Island Hopping

I received another rebuke during my early efforts to please Dr. Nelson and on this one, too, I had an assist from Napook. It began as a summer of rare adventure, of island hopping in the Arctic Ocean as we sailed the *Hazel* through broken ice fields from one lonely Eskimo village and bird rookery to another. Our first scheduled stop was at the 40-shack community of Ukivok on the steep slopes of King Island.

The hovels looked as if a gust of wind would send them all tumbling down into the sea, and in some places the slightest mis-step would result in a plunge to death. There wasn't as much as a bush growing out of the all but perpendicular walls. With all the vast, unoccupied space in northwest Alaska, I wondered why any people would choose to live on this wind-scourged brink of eternity.

I didn't find out, not this time. The entire village from suckling mikinninnies to aged folks with faces like puckered russet apples had all been loaded in open walrus-hide oomiaks, each almost as long as the *Hazel.* With crude sails hoisted aloft, paddles flying, singing like children on their way to a picnic, the King Islanders grinned and waved at us as they rode a spanking breeze to Nome. There they would set up camp on the beach and spend the summer trading carved ivory and exquisitely sewed fur slippers for some of the white man's staples they'd learned to like; flour, sugar, tea, condensed sweet milk, woollen red underwear, calico, chewing gum, and bottles of strawberry soda pop.

Favorable winds and tides had separated the ice pack, opening many channels to the north. Napook thought we'd better push right on past Fairway Rock and the Diomede Islands to a flyspeck on the mariner's chart named Chamisso Island. Two days later, in the far distance we sighted its two pinnacle rocks. A mirage effect produced by the midnight sun dipping into the Arctic Ocean had cut them off at the base, and they appeared to be floating in the air. I was staring wide-eyed at the wonder of it, when suddenly the rocks disintegrated as if an explosion had blasted them to smithereens. The red sky filled with gray and whitish flakes. Then, like confetti in a ticker-tape parade, the cloud drifted back into place and the stone spires were reformed. As we drew nearer and focused binoculars on the phenomenon, Chamisso Island let us in on the secret. Its vertical slopes were plastered with uncountable thousands of nesting sea birds. Periodically, they filled the air with a mighty crescendo of wings, slowly floating back to the island to settle down on their eggs and young on the narrow shelves.

The performance went on and on until the anchor chain of the *Hazel* went clattering over the side, and then came the grandest show of all. A living waterfall of birds poured down the sides of the rock, and just when it seemed they were all about to crash headlong into the sea, they leveled off along the wave tops, and shot upward, higher and higher, in an atomic mushroom of flailing wings.

Strangely enough, the murres—which looked like small penguins, but with stubby wings enabling flight—soon became accustomed to our presence as we scaled the cliffs among them. Murre eggs enough to supply omelets for the city of New York were spread along the bare ledges, row upon row, from the ocean's spray to the topmost pinnacle. Among zillions of eggs I saw no two of like color or shape. They were blotched, daubed, and streaked with every hue in the rainbow, presumably to help the returning murres locate their own single egg. And to prevent them from rolling off into the pounding surf, nature had pointed each hard-shelled egg so that if disturbed, it spun around in a tight circle. Squatting among the unhatched eggs were murre chicks in all stages of growth, and gorging on both eggs and chicks were fierce, gluttonous gulls. Yet, so great was the reproduction among these sea fowl that the predation of the gulls—like that of the snowy owls I had observed on the Nome tundra—appeared to have no effect. As happens so often in wildlife colonies undisturbed by man, the prey species were multiplying as fast as natural enemies could destroy them.

While Napook took advantage of a clause in the Federal laws permitting natives to gather sea fowl eggs for food, I watched at close range while the swarming inhabitants of the Chamisso Island bird-city settled into their daily routine. Outgoing murres headed for the feeding areas, tipped off the cliffs, took wing, and flew high and fast until they faded in the distance. Beneath them in a separate layer, the incoming birds, loaded with spoils, barely skimmed the surface until at the last split-second they zoomed upward, spread their tail-brakes, and landed precisely in front of the gaping bills of their own chicks. It was a traffic control and delivery system worked out through eons of time.

As we boarded the *Hazel* ready for the next island wonder in the Arctic, the murres demonstrated still another skill—how to fly underwater! Leaning over the rail I watched them dart through the emerald translucence, back and forth under the schooner's keel in a wild game of tag. Unlike ducks who paddle with webbed feet, the murres let their legs trail astern as rudders and use their cupped wings for oars. Their speed was fantastic, like tiny jet-planes racing ahead of phosphorescent contrails. Flurrying small fishes were slow-pokes in comparison. As we hoisted anchor, every murre shot to the surface and took off in full flight.

While the *Hazel* was sailing southwest from Chamisso toward Bering Straits, it was difficult to separate the passage of time into its proper days. The sun kept circling around the horizon, low in the true north at midnight, high in the south at noon, while the course of the schooner took it back and forth across the international date line where it might be Monday on one side and Tuesday on the other, or vice versa. Which was one and which was the other, I never could be sure and soon it didn't make any difference. From the Asian shore, which had been clearly visible less than 40 miles away, a fogbank came rolling out across the sea to envelop the *Hazel*. Napook said this meant ice lurking beneath, so we lowered the sails and began a drift that lasted for hours in the eerie, opaque silence.

We were below, heating a pot of coffee, and Napook was boiling some of his precious murre eggs for breakfast when something nudged the schooner's hull. I rushed up on deck to witness one of the most exciting wildlife reviews I have ever seen in the Arctic.

A great mass of bergs had crept around the *Hazel* to grip it tight. And now that the fog screen had played its insidious role, it thinned to let the sun glisten across alternate stretches of white ice and green water. A chocolate drop island seemed to push up out of the sea dead ahead. There was no sign of human habitation on this Fairway Rock. We were alone among the Arctic floes.

Polar explorers have often remarked how some ice packs appear to be biological deserts devoid of life, and how others swarm with abundance. This one was loaded, and I thought I could see why. The water was tinted pink with billions of tiny shrimp, and flashing with the silver of small fishes. The whole area was an incredibly rich food bank which in turn had drawn larger forms of life. Every species of hair seal known to inhabit the western Arctic lay sprawled on the floes, loafing in the summer sun; little spotted *kasageuks* and the handsome ribbon seals, cream-colored ringed seals, and the larger bearded *oogruks*. Dwarfing the lesser seals with their massive hulks weighing up to 3,000 pounds each were the walrus. Most of them were sleeping in brown blubbery heaps, raising their tusked heads off the ice now and then to stare stupidly in our direction through myopic eyes the size of hockey pucks, then flopping heavily on their sides again to snore like fat men with clogged sinuses.

Not far away a bowhead whale pushed up through the loose bergs like a surfacing submarine, and shot a thin column of mist into the air. The next time it blew, the behemoth had narrowed the distance between us to half, and on its third expulsion of breath it was so close to the

Hazel that the warm, wet air from the dilated blowholes on the top of its head drifted across the open deck into our faces. Abruptly, for no reason then apparent to us, it turned flukes up—high as the schooner's mast—and I counted the barnacles on its black hide as it slid straight down under the ice never to show again. Something had frightened it, and what it took to frighten a 50-ton whale I wanted to see.

The napping seals and walrus were alerted too. They had lifted their heads and were sniffing the air. Pods of swimming walrus bobbed up alongside the ice floes, hooked two-feet long tusks over the edges, and heaved themselves out onto the pans. Napook, who knew what to look for, and whose black eyes were sharp as a raven's, spied the invading enemy and pointed. I saw a dozen sabers flashing in the sun, slicing the surface in perfect formation, almost as if directed by a single brain. Short bursts of spray blossomed above the water, and as the blunt heads came bludgeoning through the sea I caught glimpses of ivory-colored markings under the chins and bold eyes oddly positioned near the corners of the wide mouths. There was something so ominous about these carnivorous killer whales that Napook's copper-colored features turned ashen. He kept muttering, "*Akhluk! Akhluk! Akhluk!*"

The carnivorous monsters swung toward a small berg on which several small *kasageuk* seals were hauled out. Their impact turned the ice cake over, and the next thing we saw were terrified seals leaping wildly high out of water. With exact timing, a pair of jaws armed with pointed white teeth opened beneath one of the flying seals and it vanished in a single gulp. The bloodthirsty pack swept on past the *Hazel,* led by a bull about 30 feet long, and trailed by smaller cows and calves. We watched the razor-fanged butchers skirting the ice pack, deliberately rocking the bergs to dump more seals into the water. Napook sighed with relief as they disappeared in the distance. Shortly afterward the sea lanes opened up again and allowed us to sail the *Hazel* to the last island on our summer schedule—Little Diomede, only three miles from Russian soil!

Actually there were two Diomede Islands, and they belonged to two different countries. The smaller one, a conical pile of rocks with only the crudest forms of dwarf vegetation on it, was the westernmost possession of the United States in the Arctic. Just across the swirling saltwater gut through which ran the international date line was Big Diomede, nearly always lurking behind a fog screen, and at that time uninhabited. Little Diomede, on the other hand, housed on its bleak slopes a small tribe of the happiest, most hospitable Eskimos in all of Alaska. When Napook and I scaled the cliffs to the tiny shacks shored up by stilts over shuddery drop-offs, we were invited into the chief's home for tea and birds.

The birds were fish-flavored greaseballs and there was a neverending supply of them nesting among the rocky crevices. As they came waddling out of their burrows and tipped off in space to gain take-off speed, the Eskimo youngsters showed me how they grabbed them off in midair. I got into the line-up with the giggling boys and girls to pick off enough "fowl-balls" to identify crested, paroquet and least auklets, white of eye and quail-sized. For the last "out" of the game I caught a "hot" liner by snatching an angry *katukpuk* sea parrot out of the air, and it nearly tore my fingers off with its stout, orange-colored bill. Everybody screamed: the Eskimo tads with delight—me with pain. Afterward, we held a picnic with hardtack and chewing gum off the *Hazel,* following which the happy little imps shyly gifted me with bits of crudely carved ivory which I have saved to this day.

The little Diomede Eskimos lived well on seals and walrus and the occasional bowhead whale to vary their diet of auklets, eider ducks, and huge ivory-billed loons of which they were especially fond. Once in a while one of the native hunters would steal across to Siberian Big Diomede in his kayak. But they always kept a watchful eye out for the Russian ice-breaker *Red October* and if they saw its black smoke anywhere on the horizon they hustled back to their own island. There had been no sign of the dreaded gunboat for several days, and when moody Big Diomede Island cast off its fog-mask to stand revealed with rare brilliance in the morning sun, I couldn't resist the temptation. Napook waited to be assured that I, not he, would be the one to set foot on the alien shore, then cranked the *Hazel's* distillate engine and we moved across to anchor in a bight.

Napook rowed me to an exposed shoreline where ocean swells flailed the rocks with foaming breakers. There seemed to be no way of setting foot on this alien land until, suddenly, I again remembered that old fish-pole trick of my youth. As I stood in the stern of the dory, Napook eased it in as close as he dared, and I took off my jacket and hurled it onto the rocks. On the next back-up of the dory, I timed a leap onto a boulder, got soused to the waist, but scrambled to safety and retrieved the jacket. I was clawing my way up a rock chimney when I happened to glance toward the Russian coast. A black pennant of coal smoke was trailing across the water! My heart sank. I couldn't have picked a worse moment for a sneak visit, because it was most certainly the *Red October* on boundary patrol.

I shouted for Napook. He didn't seem to hear me, nor see me, either. He had also spotted the dreaded Russian "smoke-boat," and had only one thought in mind; to reach the American shore. This left nothing for me to do except to try to find a hole in the rocks and crawl in with the sea parrots. But there was no place to hide until I had climbed to the very top of the island.

At any other time I would have considered the scenery spectacularly beautiful. From the mesa-like crown of Big Diomede Island, the Siberian mainland, no more than 30 miles west, was revealed with startling clarity. Beyond patches of floating ice lay the tiny Chukchi village of Naukan. Above the coastal outpost, stacked tier upon tier into the blue infinity, rose the wild peaks of Chukotsk Peninsula where only a year or so before the American sportsman John B. Burnham—though he had gone to great pains to secure a permit to enter the country for a sheep-hunting expedition—told me he had been seized by the Russians and grilled mercilessly before being deported back to Nome. The charged crime—if it was a crime—was that Burnham's companion, Andy Taylor, couldn't resist panning for gold when he was washing the camp skillet in a mountain creek. Somewhere near, unseen eyes had been spying, and the informer had told the Russian police.

I had the same feeling of being under surveillance, if not by suspicious eyes close at hand, then through binoculars from the bridge of the *Red October*. The ice-breaker's curling bow wave was like a bone in a dog's bared teeth as she steamed straight to the spot where I had come ashore, reversed engines, and floated with sinister stillness in the water.

From a half mile up I peered over the top of an up-ended rock almost straight down on the gunboat. Several officers and crew members were standing on the deck, and I caught the glint of field glasses scanning the shore. After a while, the *Red October* got underway again. Not until she had pushed her steel-shod nose far into the ice floes did I dare get started on the project that had brought me ashore: to collect a series of small birds and rodents on this highly important transitional zone between the new and the old world; to take wildlife samples from an island which at various periods in prehistory had been a mountain squarely in the center of the land span once connecting the two continents. With "dust" pellets fired from special .32 caliber cartridges fitted into a double-barreled shotgun, I soon had a sackful of small "game" for skinning and making into scientific specimens aboard the *Hazel*.

I kept looking hopefully across the three-mile gut to Little Diomede so that I could come sliding down the rocks when Napook brought the schooner over to snatch me out of my predicament. But the canny Eskimo made no move, and soon I learned the reason why. The *Red October* had turned about in the ice fields. She was cruising back to the island! While there was still time, I hustled across the flat, boulder-strewn, treeless top to get as far away as possible from where the *Hazel* had deserted me. And there I found a perfect hideaway.

It was a grave, an ancient tomb containing a very large and moss-grown human skull, together with fragments of rodent-gnawed bones. I squeezed under a shelving rock, slid the lid back to block off the opening, and decided to spend the night with the giant chieftain in the bed where he had been sleeping, for all I knew, since the year of the mammoth.

Sometime during the rosy glow of the midnight hours, the *Red October* sent a scouting party ashore. I heard their alien shouts—they reminded me of bloodhounds baying in the distance—though none came close. Next morning when I cautiously pushed aside the rock-slab, I was relieved to see a black smoke trail on the sea, pointing for what was evidently the gunboat's base in St. Lawrence Bay beyond Cape Nunyagmo. From his hidden bight on the other shore, Napook had likewise taken note. The *Hazel* came chugging across the channel, and when Napook backed the dory into the wave-pounded rocks, I first tossed my bag of specimens over the surging swell, then followed with a wild do-or-die leap.

At Nome I wrapped each precious bird and mouse in a roll of cotton-batting with tender loving care, and mailed the collection to Dr. Nelson, together with identification tags and a detailed report as to locality taken. Forty years earlier when he was a young man of about my age, the great Doctor had cruised these Arctic waters aboard the old coast guard cutter *Corwin*. He had passed close to the Russian Diomede Island and had surely yearned to set foot on this key spot on the crossroads of migrating birds. What would be his reaction, after all these years, to seeing this rare lot of specimens?

His response came by return mail—which was approximately six weeks elapsed time. I read the terse, typewritten message with a shock: "Never again, so long as you are an employee of this Bureau, will you place a government vessel in jeopardy of being seized by a foreign power, nor will you risk our further embarrassment by trespassing on alien soil."

I sat stunned as the bottom of the world fell away. I felt like crawling back in the grave with the old Diomede chief. Then, as I started to fold the letter and put it back in the envelope, I noticed a penned message on the back of the sheet. It was unsigned, but unmistakably in Dr. Nelson's bold, slightly shaky, handwriting: "You have given me a most enjoyable evening . . . trust you will continue to display personal initiative beyond your regular duties . . . report fully to me . . ."

I let out a whoop that fetched Napook running from the back room. He said he thought something had happened to me, and it had. I had just elevated Dr. Nelson to the status of a god.

8 A Novice and His Dogteam

Early in the winter of that year I suffered a misadventure which was never "fully reported" to Dr. Nelson, nor to anybody else. The incident occurred on my first solo dog-team trip into the wild Aghiapuk Valley. A veteran of dogsled travel along the lower Yukon River forty years earlier, and aware of the dangers of traveling alone, Dr. Nelson had instructed me to engage the services of an experienced musher for my winter surveys. But I had wanted to do it on my own, and this ambition was due in no small part to one of my Nome neighbors at that time, a Norwegian by the name of Roald Amundsen.

The Captain, as he was called around Nome, had covered thousands of miles by sledge, and had already become famous for his dash across the Antarctic to discover the South Pole. Now, by driving a team of sled dogs to the end of land at Point Barrow, then taking off across the Arctic Ocean, in a single-engined airplane, he hoped also to be first over the North Pole. During my practice sessions on the Nome tundra, I would often meet the distinguished, hawk-nosed viking out hardening his muscles for the perilous journey ahead. Sometimes he would be poling along on his skis as graceful as a swooping bird. At other times he would be driving a string of especially selected, high-spirited Siberian Huskies. As they overtook and swept past my malemutes, Amundsen would raise a mitted hand in courteous salute. In his spotted reindeer parka with its white wolf ruff and his sealskin snowboots, the arrow-straight Captain—always handling his own team—cut a heroic figure. In that early winter, life held no higher ambition for me than to emulate this great man's skill on the snow.

"If Captain Amundsen can do it, so can I," I said grimly to myself, and soon came the day when with sled loaded for travel, I set out from Nome to prove it.

The winter mail trail through the Sawtooth Mountains led along the "pupmobile" railroad, now buried under the drifts. As the dogs scratched their way up the hard-packed slopes around Anvil Mountain I looked down on the frozen river pool where Uncle Charley had tried to teach me how to pan for "colors," and where he had bashed a salmon on the nose with the flat of his shovel. High up in a snow-drifted gulch a streamer of blue smoke rose thinly out of the whiteness, and I knew that in a shack deep out of sight an old sourdough was hibernating like a bear in its den.

The weather was clear, calm and comfortably cold at 30 degrees below zero. Once over the first rise of mountains, the dogs trotted easily, heads in the air as they routed out occasional white Arctic hares and foxes, unseen against the snow until they went racing away. When we stopped at a government shelter cabin that night I was brimming with confidence at my ability to handle a dogteam, and when I cooked my first "trail" meal and then crawled into my warm sleeping bag, I felt as superior to ordinary mortals as Roald Amundsen looked. This dog-handling was a cinch!

The next day was even better. The trail to the Eskimo village of Mary's Igloo led down into a quiet river valley and through a forest of sheltering, tall willows. Hordes of ptarmigan from the surrounding, snow-heaped wastelands had assembled here for the winter. They hung like popcorn balls from every willow, the branches sagging with their combined weight as they nipped off the frozen tips on which they would be subsisting until next summer's sun again uncovered the bountiful tundra.

The vast valley was of peculiar interest to Dr. Nelson as one of the most important ptarmigan wintering areas on Seward Peninsula, and he had asked me to give him a rough count. The white grouse were subject, like the snowshoe hares, to drastic rise and fall in populations, reaching unbelievable numbers only to die off with dramatic suddenness. For a year or two scarcely a bird could be seen, then slowly over the next eight or ten years they would mount into the millions again.

This was one of their peaks of cyclic abundance. As they clung to the bushes almost within touching distance, their challenging cackles were almost deafening. In their enormous numbers they had lost much of their normal awareness of man. Only once or twice did a flock, directly in the trail, roar into the air with thunderous clapping of wings. Trying to count them was like trying to count snowflakes falling. My estimate of those within near distances rose to ten thousand, then the job got entirely out of hand before I reached Mary's Igloo. I had no idea what kind of a guess to submit to Dr. Nelson, and the village Eskimos weren't much help. They said that whatever number I decided on, I'd better multiply it by all my fingers and toes to take in that part of the valley bottom I hadn't seen from the dog trail.

Mary's Igloo consumed hundreds of ptarmigan during such mountains of plenty. Mostly, they gathered the birds without firing a shot, by the aid of snares strung in the willows. Though they were sharing the harvest with extraordinary numbers of foxes, weasels, hawks, and owls, the toll of all predators could not keep pace with the booming populations when the native grouse were on the upswing of their cycle. It took something more drastic in the way of Nature's control to prevent the ptarmigan from devouring their willow-bud food supply. Every nine or ten years a deadly epizootic disease scythed down the millions until scarcely a grouse could be found on the tundra, and then they would have to start another build-up. The Mary's Igloo Eskimos told me they feared such a big die-off would occur this very winter.

In a sing-songy mixture of Innuit and English they also told me of danger on the uninhabited stretch between their village and the trading post at Teller on Bering Sea: something about tides and winds on Imuruk Basin, a saltwater estuary at the mouth of the Aghiapuk River. I was so eager to tackle new adventures, I didn't wait to hear more details. The dogteam trail led out onto the frozen river, slick with windswept ice, and I had to keep pressing down on the foot brake to prevent the sled over-running the loping dogs. I was fifteen miles downriver when the sled runners under my feet suddenly broke through the ice and water started spurting up. Instantly, I gee'd the lead dog toward the nearest shore and stepped off the sled to investigate this puzzling phenomena of thin ice at 30 degrees below zero.

It wasn't as bad as I feared—at least, I thought it wasn't. There was less than an inch of water below the top sheet of ice, and beneath the slight overflow was another layer which appeared to be several feet thick. I swung a camp axe to test its strength. "Heavy enough to bear a horse," I concluded, as I swung my dogteam back onto the river and went racing merrily downstream with twin roostertails squirting into the air behind me.

I was thoroughly enjoying the ride when calamity struck. The top skim of ice began undulating ahead of the dogs, the sled runners began settling, and water rose up around my mukluks as I stood on the runners at the rear of the sled, hanging onto the handlebars. There was a sloping bank some distance ahead and I swung the team toward it, cracking a blacksnake whip in the air to urge the dogs into a full speed race for dry land. We didn't make it. Suddenly, the thinning ice collapsed under the entire team. I rode the sled runners down to the second layer of ice, strangling for breath in water up to my armpits. The dogs, burdened by their harnesses and the heavy load behind them, were paddling madly to hold their noses above the icy caldron, and it seemed to me they would all perish within seconds. My own chances looked no better. The water was paralyzingly cold, and I had been told that no human could stand more than ten minutes' exposure to it and live. Even if I could reach shore, my sodden fur garments would become an icy straitjacket.

I have learned that in such sudden peril there is no awareness of reasoning; only a blind instinct to stay alive as long as possible. This is what saved me now; this and a higher power. I floundered to the lead dog, grasped him by the collar and towed the struggling huskies to a low place on the shoreline where they could scramble out of the churning ice-water. I could not get them to pull the waterlogged sled clear, but with an inherent sense of what to do for themselves, they rolled in the snow to blot the water out of their thick fur. Soon, they were all on their feet, shaking off the frozen clods, apparently none the worse for their frigid ducking. While I was still able to move, I wanted to help them more by unsnapping the towline to the sled. My hands were too stiff; my fingers already turning white and without feeling. I had to desert them. When the situation became desperate enough, they could always chew themselves free from the rawhide harnesses. They had a chance, which seemed to be more than I had.

Realizing that whatever action I took would have to be fast, I started to climb a sort of path, or game trail, leading from the river bank up into a copse of willows from which I could get a view of the surrounding wilderness. As I left them behind, the sled dogs lunged wildly into their collars. Their yowling uproars filled the air, and suddenly, unbelievably, there came an answering howl!

There was no way of knowing whether it came from a wild timber wolf, a tame sled dog, or was but an echo of my imagination. It meant only that there might still be a slim chance to live. If I could reach the bank-top and look into the willows! My mukluk soles, frozen hard as glass, skidded out from under me on the steep incline. I fell with a bone-jarring thump and for a moment lay half conscious while my furs froze fast to the snow. I was aware of no pain, no discomfort, only a creeping weariness. Was this what it was like to freeze to death?

The leaden feeling passed, followed by a panic of energy. Suddenly, I was struggling with every ounce of strength, ripping myself free of the snow. On hands and knees I clawed my way up to top the river bank, and there I came face to face with the most beautiful sled dog I have ever seen. It was a battle-scarred malemute, and it appeared to be blind with age. Its ragged coat was rimed with frost, and as it sensed my presence its curled bushy tail wagged a greeting; its gray muzzle pointed straight up into the sky as it poured out another long, tremulous howl.

The old dog was chained to a stake alongside a low, sod-covered igloo from the top of which curled a thin wisp of smoke. With a surge of hope, I finished crawling to the entrance to this underground hovel, and tumbled down through a skin-hung doorway onto a twig-covered floor to look up into a face that appeared to be all red whiskers and bugged-out blue eyes. For a long moment, the shock of what he had seen was too much for the surprised occupant to grasp. He hadn't seen another human for months. Now here was a total stranger dropped at his feet. Eyes fastened on me in utter disbelief, he continued to fry a skillet-full of flapjacks, turning them with care. Then as the full meaning of my unannounced visit slowly became clear to him, Redbeard flipped the flapjacks onto a tin plate and shoved them toward the back of the sheet-iron camp stove. Not until then did he speak. His voice was oddly falsetto, I remember, loud like that of man with defective hearing.

"Where's ya' dogs?"

I croaked a reply. The trapper didn't hear me and had to cup an ear close while I shouted at the top of my lungs. Stone deaf, I thought, but Redbeard had heard enough to send him charging up out of the underground hovel. When he had gone, I struggled to my feet and stoked the sheet-iron camp stove with dry willows until it glowed cherry-red, then stripped down to my bare hide. Teeth chattering uncontrollably, I picked up the sodden clothes and hung them on pegs around the low wall of the igloo, wherever there was room between the cased peltries of foxes and mink and ermine. As the heat of the stove warmed me and started the blood circulating again, I began to experience the torture of frost-bitten toes and fingers, ears, nose, and cheeks coming to life. I knew then that another few minutes of exposure in the 30-degree below zero winds would have maimed me for life; that in an hour I would have been frozen stiff as a board—all for a mistake that only a dumb cheechako would make!

How the lone trapper accomplished it, I'll never know, but after a while there was a clamor of sled dogs outside the igloo. When Redbeard came pushing down into the dark hole he was carrying a canvas sack over his shoulder. Not only had he managed to drag the sled out of the river; he had also credited me with enough sense to have a change of clothing in a waterproof duffle bag. Without a word, he went outside again to unharness the dogs and stake them out among the willows with a dried salmon ration to chew on, after which they would dig into the snow and curl themselves up to sleep. My reindeer sleeping bag, soaked and frozen into a block of ice, was dragged in and stretched behind the stove. Then, Redbeard handed me a tin plate and calmly resumed his flapjack cooking.

His name, he yelled, was Dunc MacBain. He was the only man on the river, and who the hell was I to be pulling such a fool stunt? I told him humbly, and slowly we began shouting ourselves into a friendship which was to endure through all my years in Alaska. Trapper MacBain insisted that I share his igloo until every item of clothing and equipment was thoroughly dried out, and while we hunkered shoulder to shoulder in the confines of his "beaver house" home, he explained why I had broken through the ice. There had been a gale from Bering Sea, washing saltwater across the anchored ice and pushing a wind-tide far up the Aghiapuk River. When I came along, the first spurts of water around my sled runners should have been enough to warn me that the ice would become weaker, the overflow deeper, as I traveled downstream to meet the sea.

Redbearded Dunc didn't let me make the same mistake twice. When he figured it was safe for me to travel again, he snowshoed a trail through the willows upstream to a narrow place, led the way over to the other side by swinging his axe to test the new ice, and put me on the overland dogteam trail to Teller on the coast. From this trading post the winter mail route led 85 miles south to Nome, and there shouldn't have been any further trouble or delays. But when I came to the government shelter cabin at Cape Douglas I ran into what I thought was a sort of polar cyclone, a seething wall of horizontally driven snow which seemed to rip the breath from my lungs, and into which I could not see the length of the dogsled. Frostbitten and unsure of myself, I retreated to the empty shelter cabin to wait for better weather.

I was still there the next evening when two dogteams from Nome bucked through howling gale, and a pair of fur-clad figures stomped the snow off their fur mukluks and pushed into the cabin. One was Ralph Lomen, a prominent merchant and reindeer owner in Nome. The other was his good friend Roald Amundsen. They were on their way to Teller—where several years later Captain Amundsen was to land down in the dirigible *Norge* after flying non-stop across the North Pole from Spitzenberg, Norway, with the Italian Commander Nobile.

Just before sacktime, the Captain stood beside his sleeping bag doing his daily calisthenics; stripped down to his flaming red long johns, acquiline nose ruddy of hue, resplendent as a scarlet ibis flapping wings at the edge of its nest. After he had finished his gymnastics, I asked him about the blinding gale through which he and Lomen had come that day. He peered at me curiously. It was nothing, he replied after a while, just a narrow snow belt blowing down out of Tishou Pass, as it did practically every day all winter. Only half a mile wide, and beyond it clear as a bell all the way into Nome.

The great explorer added that what a dogmusher really had to watch out for along the coast were the overflowed river mouths. His wise blue eyes had been studying my face, all purpled and bruised like an over-ripe plum from freezing, and now I saw a twinkle of crows' feet forming at their corners. Plainly, he wanted to know what had happened to me. But I wasn't about to do any explaining, neither to Captain Amundsen nor to Dr. Nelson.

9 The Deep, Deep Cold

I had the odd experience of following my next report more than halfway, in elapsed time, to the Bureau of Biological Survey in Washington, D.C. The manila envelope left Nome on a long sled drawn by twenty-six big huskies, and I tagged along with a dozen malemutes. Though mail-carrier Pete Curran quickly outdistanced me on that first day, his trail was easy to follow. He chewed tobacco incessantly, and every few yards there would be a brown pancake splattered on the snow. I was sorry to lose these markers when at the end of three days' travel down the coast, the outgoing letters were transferred to a relay team and Pete turned back to Nome with the incoming mail from the States. From here on, I would be picking up a new dogmushing carrier about twice each week. The system was like the pony express of the old west, only done with dogs instead of horses.

I had two reasons for following closely on the sled tracks of the mail-carriers. At that time the lawmakers in Congress had decided to provide the Territory of Alaska with its own set of game regulations, and Dr. Nelson wanted me to interview outlying residents to get their ideas on seasons, bag limits, and other special features like allowing residents to kill game any time they needed it for food. By arriving with the mailmen at the scattered trading posts along the trail, I would have an opportunity to take notes from trappers coming in to pick up letters. In those days before radio, Pete Curran and all the other dogteam postmen were more than bearers of the U.S. mail. They performed countless errands between communities and families, and faithfully repeated all the gossip. Sometimes they delivered native brides from one village to waiting grooms in the next, and months later brought medicine and instruction from a doctor many miles away on what to do when childbirth came. They knew all the shortcuts along the trail, were all experts in care and handling of dogs, and could judge when the weather was too severe to travel. By riding tail on one dogmushing carrier after another, not only did I pick up pages of notes to be considered in the new Alaska Game Law, I also learned how to survive in the blizzards; how to keep from freezing on the trail when the mercury fell to the bottom of the thermometer.

The mail route led south along the Bering Sea shoreline 200 miles to Unalakleet, then cut across a hundred miles of uninhabited scrub willow and dwarf spruce portage to Kaltag on the banks of the Yukon River. The coastal-dwelling Eskimos gave way to river Indians, and I had to learn a new set of names for the wild creatures. Ptarmigan, for instance, were no longer *a-kuzh-gik*. Now they were *da-goo*. The term for beaver changed from Eskimo *pa-lok-tuk* to Indian *t'see;* caribou from *tun-tu* to *vad-zaih*. I was glad to start using the Athabascan Indian name of *zi-chooh* for the sharp-shinned hawk, because the little blue darters were always out of sight before I could get the Eskimo word out of my mouth. It was *chu-kub-vi-ug-shu-guk*.

The mile-wide Yukon River water level fell steadily, and the collapsing ice crashed and boomed like field artillery. The thermometer dropped lower and lower, and a sinister wind whispered its warning. A detachment of soldiers at old Fort Gibbon had their strict orders never to venture away from the barracks when the mercury registered 40 degrees below zero, but the dogmushing mailmen continued to drive their huskies thirty or forty miles daily between places of shelter, and I had no choice but to follow along as best I could. In the short days of December it was dark when we left one log-cabin postoffice in the morning, there would be a pink streak along the southern horizon at midday, and it would be dark again long before we pulled into the next settlement.

I have never met a hardier lot of men than these winter mail-carriers of the early days. Toughest of them all, was veteran Ben Derrick of Whiskey Creek. He had never been known to miss a day on the trail because of bad weather. He drove a team of giant timber wolves, so malevolent in disposition that only old Ben dared go near them. Even Ben, who must have been a lion-tamer at heart, knew better than to try any Clyde Beatty whipcracking around his sullen lobos lest they panic and turn on him. When he had to single out a wolf for punishment, he would set the brakes at the rear of the sled, walk quietly forward to the malingerer, talk to it in low tones so as not to arouse its savage teammates, then give its ear a slight twist.

As I sat around the big heating stoves at the roadhouses with the mail-carriers after their daily runs, the talk often turned to Ben Derrick as the great daddy of all dogmushers, though to me all the postmen were gutful heroes. Some of them had frozen to death at the handlebars of their mail sleds, sacrificing their lives in getting the mail through on time. Whatever they were paid, they were worth more, because what they gave no one could really buy.

At the confluence of the Yukon and Tanana River my letter to the Bureau went one way, and I another. I had convoyed it for three weeks during which I had trotted 550 miles behind my dogteam. It would continue for another five days to Nenana where the winter trail from Nome intersected a narrow-gauge railroad, then it would travel south two more days to be placed aboard a steamer at the open port of Seward. When it finally reached Dr. Nelson's desk in Washington, D.C., my report would be six weeks old, and on that very day I would be fighting for my life north of the Arctic Circle during a cold spell so intense that trees cracked open like over-boiled frankfurters.

The mail-carriers along the Yukon had warned me that it was going to be a rugged experience, so this time I took Dr. Nelson's advice. I engaged the services of two strong young Indians from Alatna who had mushed into old Fort Gibbon (now Tanana) to sell their furs and who would be returning to their home village along the route of my journey's beginning. The way lay directly north for 200 miles to the Indian mission at Alatna on the upper Koyukuk

River over a seldom-used trail. Then the course veered northwest through the mountainous headwaters of Kobuk River *over no trail at all.*

Every step of the totally uninhabited high country would have to be snowshoed ahead of the dogs to break a path. Finding the right route would depend on use of the compass, tied in with the Indian trappers' recognition of landmarks as handed down to them by their fathers, because neither of them had ever made the trip. We would have to pitch tents at least a dozen nights in deep snow. The amount of food we could haul on the sleds for ourselves and our dogs would be strictly limited. We would have to ration it carefully to make it last to the next point of supply. A mistake in navigation, taking us down a wrong valley, could lead to fatal consequences. The darkest days of winter were upon us, and the ghostly white wilderness ahead was known to be one of the coldest regions of North America. But it was important that it be visited and reported on, because it represented a transitional zone, a key boundary, in the forthcoming Alaska Game Act.

No expedition could have gotten off to a more dismal start. On our second day of snowshoeing up a narrowing canyon-walled tributary of the Alatna River we ran into a snowstorm so overwhelming that it blotted out our snowshoe trails as fast as we could make them, so blinding we could not see the lengths of our dogsleds. We had no choice except to stop in the first clump of trees and make camp, first pitching an eight by ten tent with sewed-in floor cloth, and over it a larger, bottomless tent measuring ten by twelve to provide an airspace. With a sheet-iron camp stove set up on a base of green billets inside, rumbling at its fare of dry spruce, we were not uncomfortable. That wasn't the problem. We had food enough for the trip only if we kept moving.

Moses and Aaron, the two young Indians with biblical names bestowed on them by the Alatna mission fathers, solved this problem in their own way. They started living on rabbits. From their dogsled they produced a coil of light picture-cord wire which they fashioned into snares and hung at snow level among the willows. Next morning they dragged in a heap of frozen snowshoe hares, and reset the snares a foot high to stay even with the rising snow. They dressed out enough rabbits to fill our biggest kettle, and flung the rest to the sled dogs. On the third day our tent was almost buried in the white fluff, and though Moses and Aaron continued to eat rabbit mulligan with gusto, I could barely choke down the stuff.

As it so often does in the Arctic, the temperature rose to well above zero during the smothering snowfall. Strapping on my snowshoes, I made endless circle around the tent, always being guarded by Moses or Aaron who thought I might get lost. Though we were immobilized by the mass of snowflakes, the wild creatures about us seemed to be at their busiest. Trails of snowshoe hares led everywhere and among them were the big pad-marks of the Canada lynx who helped themselves to our snared victims. Ptarmigan, feathered to the toe-tips and with additional long, flat nails extending farther out at this season to furnish them with their own snowshoes, cackled all about the tent. A lone wolf howled its spine-chilling ululations close by, though unseen behind the descending curtain of snow. Flocks of chicadees twittered chipperly over our heads. Moses pointed to a bird and said, "He slap his face on the wood." It was a rare Arctic three-toed woodpecker.

The Indian boys said there were flocks of white mountain sheep not far away on the windswept ridges. One morning our huskies, who had been quietly curled nose to tail under their deep snow blankets, began howling and lunging at their chains. A band of caribou had come churning through camp. Before the boys could bring rifles to bear, the caribou vanished in the downfall, and we continued to eat snowshoe hare mulligan until the snow stopped falling.

The first hour of the next morning told me how exasperatingly tedious the long portage would be from the Alatna drainage over the mountains into the Kobuk headwaters. Our moccasin-clad feet, insulated against the cold with four pairs of wool socks, sank almost to ground level in snow higher than our heads. The dogs could no longer haul the loaded sleds over a single snowshoe track. Now it had to be double. This meant that Moses and Aaron and I had to take shifts plowing a hundred yards ahead, turning about to press down a parallel track back to the sleds, then catching a ride as far as the undisturbed snow and repeating the operation again and again during the day. In late afternoon we had covered no more than ten miles. By the time we had set up camp, staked out, and fed the dogs their dried salmon and whale blubber, and closed the tent-flaps behind us, the moon had risen round and silver-clear over the peaks, and it was deathly cold.

The temperature had dropped alarmingly. In less than 24 hours it had fallen from 15 above zero to 50 below—a decline of 65 degrees. But when I came in from reading the thermometer hanging on a guyline of the tent and announced the news to Moses and Aaron, they showed no surprise. They said, "We think it get much colder."

For the first time I began to wonder if I had the right to

ask Moses and Aaron to share such a risky trip. When I put it to them, the boys shrugged, conversed at length in Indian tongue, and finally gave me their answer. "If we turn back to Alatna, better do it now," they said. "Two more days on trail, we closer to Kobuk side. You speak."

I didn't "speak" that night. I didn't know what to say. Stripped down to a heavy woollen union suit while my outer garments hung over the stove to air out, I had donned a pair of hip-length boots made from untanned mountain sheep with the dense white hair inside, and crawled into my reindeer-sleeping bag. But sleep would not come. I watched Moses and Aaron pull on their own night boots and roll up in their marvelously warm robes made from woven strips of snowshoe hare pelts. Soon, they were breathing evenly, curls of vapor marking the position of their faces in the fur cocoons. But I was not only wide awake with foreboding; I was shivering, and I stoked the fire several times during the night as I pondered the situation into which I had drawn these young Indians. A hundred more miles of excruciatingly cold weather; ten more nights of pitching tent in the Arctic wilds; the grave danger of taking the wrong turn in the labyrinth of ridges and valleys; the peril of another storm: I was still undecided what to do when the morning came, and we wolfed down our limp fried bacon, poured the drippings over thick bannocks sluiced with warmed syrup, and downed mugs of hot coffee. The Indian boys were watching me for a sign, but said nothing, as I toed into my slim, six-feet long "pickerel" snowshoes to begin the day's travel.

Even then I wasn't sure which way the webs would take me, until without conscious direction I found myself bucking into the unbroken stretch that lay before us. I looked over my shoulder at Moses and Aaron. They were waving mitted hands and grinning. I knew now they also would rather look ahead than behind. They had been non-commital only to find out whether or not I had any yellow feathers.

They had pulled knitted masks over their heads, and I was wearing the long silk and wool muffler given me by mail-carrier Ben Derrick. "Never, never suck in a deep breath of air when its colder than 50 degrees below," he had warned. "It could frost your lungs. Keep this muffler wrapped around your face, try to filter the air through a couple of layers. It could save your life."

Another tip old Ben had given me was never to over-exert at extreme low temperatures. "When you ease off," he explained, "your sweat-soaked underwear will turn to ice, and you'll be worse than miserable; you'll be in the process of freezing to death."

We made another ten miles or so that day, and pitched camp west of the remote Hogatza River on the shore of Norutak Lake. The cold had reached a frightening intensity. When I looked at the thermometer outside the tent, the red spirits had fallen into the bulb at the bottom of the glass—72 degrees below zero!

On this night occurred the most awesome display of northern lights that I have ever witnessed. Toward the north pole a pinkish glow suffused the horizon, building up like an atomic mushroom until the night was bright as day, then fading away to leave the cold heavens glittering with billions of icy stars. Suddenly, ten thousand searchlight rays stabbed the zenith—red, blue, green, and violet—so brilliant as to penetrate the two layers of canvas over our heads and illuminate the interior of the tent like sunlight coming through the stained glass windows of a church. There was a definite electrical swishing sound, an ominous hissing and crackling, and for the only time on the trip Moses and Aaron did not try to hide their fears. They said it was a bad sign; that somebody up there was angry with us. *Down here, too,* I thought, because beneath its overlay of snow the ice on Norutak Lake resounded with ringing explosions. Around our tent the stunted spruces, frozen to the core, popped like rifle shots.

All day we had seen only two living wild creatures. I had all but snowshoed onto a bull moose, yarded up to its long ears in a small patch of willows. It was noontime and the crimson rays of light from a sun still below the rim of the northern mountains shone on its frost-spangled coat until it glistened like an overlay of jewels. Shoulder hackles on end, nostrils spurting steam, the desperate beast charged fiercely to the edge of its self-made prison, and I beat a hasty retreat. There was not a sign of the snowshoe hares, nor of the ptarmigan and fool hens presumed to live in the area. They had all taken refuge from the deathly cold air by plunging deep into the feather-light snow. The only other life we saw that day was a gray Alaska jay, known as the whiskeyjack, or camprobber. On silent wings it followed us into camp, and that evening it snatched bacon scraps from our extended hands.

Two days later as our caravan topped a rise and started down a frozen river, the sled dogs began barking and surging against their collars. Moses, who was snowshoeing ahead, held up a mitted hand and let us come abreast of him with the teams. What he said was to me, after eleven days in the midwinter Arctic wilderness, as memorable as the meeting of Stanley and Livingston in darkest Africa.

"I smell smoke!"

It was an Eskimo family on Pah River, and downstream

a few miles was the furtrading post of Shunknak. Our ordeal was over. Later in the week, when I bid good-bye to Moses and Aaron, the temperature had practically soared up to 45 degrees below zero. Their sled was loaded with trade goods as they started back to their home in Alatna before more snow buried our hard-won trail. Then, I looked ahead to the end of my own dogteam journey. The way would be easy, now. A mail trail led down the middle of the Kobuk River, cutting across the bends. It would be well traveled, and there would be Eskimo villages and trading posts for shelter every night all the way down the coast around Seward Peninsula. When I waved good-bye to trader Harry Brown at Shungnak, I still had 600 more miles to go, but it seemed no distance at all. I was almost home! If I hadn't accomplished anything else on this expedition for the Bureau of Biological Survey, I had become its best—its only—dogmusher.

¶10 Funeral for A Painted Lady

As soon as I got back to Nome from the long dogsled trip, I plotted to get rid of five belligerent malemutes. The snarling brutes had started furious free-for-alls almost daily, and every dog in the team carried scars from their slashing fangs. Shortly, in the weekly tabloid the Nome *Nugget* appeared the following advertisement: FOR SALE. 5 SLED DOGS. SPIRITED BUT GENTLE.

Only one reader responded. It was the prettiest and most talented girl in camp; a slim, blonde daughter of the gold rush who had gone "Outside" to win a name for herself as a concert violinist, and who had come back to spend another winter with her relatives. I had observed Klondy Nelson with considerably more than casual attention, as had every other male in town, and she was certainly the last person I wanted to flim-flam on a dogteam deal. Nonetheless, the situation did seem to have certain advantages, such as getting to meet the proud beauty, so I decided to explore the subject. Before showing off the battling demons, I took them for a hard drive out on the tundra, sparing not the lash. At the first hint of a growl, I sent the blacksnake whip curling around their ears, and not until they had cooled down and were on their best behavior did I bring them around to the fair damsel's home for a demonstration. Just as I had planned it, the slant-eyed rascals stood at attention like a group of trained tigers while the unsuspecting Miss Nelson counted the money into my guilty hands. Though I shuddered to think what would happen when the innocent maid attempted to harness the savage team all by herself, it was on this very point that my plot hinged—a scheme to make a villain twirl his mustache.

Everything was proceeding according to script when I strolled toward the new owner's home next morning. Suddenly, horrified neighbor women were standing in their doorways, wringing their hands at the goriest dogfight to occur in Nome for many a day. Roaring like wolves closing in for the kill, enjoying every bloodcurdling moment of it, all five malemutes were locked in a fury of flying fur. The helpless young lady seemed about to be swallowed up in the fray.

This was my cue to come dashing to the rescue. But suddenly, the plot backfired. The blue-eyed slip of a girl was not pleading with palms together; was not beseeching the hero to save her. Instead, she had waded into the center of the melee and was flinging malemutes right and left. Her blacksnake whip, whirling with cool precision, popped off like pistol shots among the brawlers. When I reached the blood-flecked arena, the malemutes' snarls had changed to startled howls. Without a look in my direction, the dainty Miss Nelson yanked each cringing canine to the tow-line of the sled, snapped it in place, and took her stance at the handlebars. I made one last try to save the day, to establish myself as a needed friend. I offered to help handle the dogs on their first trips under new management; maybe go out with her a few times until the malemutes got to know her better.... That was as far as I got.

"I don't need you, or anybody else, to teach me how to drive a dogteam," snapped the flashing-eyed Miss Nelson. Her whip whistled through the air and cracked like a bunch of firecrackers. The dogs went tearing off across the tundra like a bevy of frightened jackrabbits, and I slunk back to the Biological Survey office gnashing my teeth.

When it was too late, I learned that the Swedish miss had grown up with sled dogs in the mining camps of Council and Nome, and had been mushing her own team since she was a little schoolgirl. Her father had, in fact, helped originate the greatest dogsled races the world ever knew! The All Alaska Sweepstakes had been a grueling, go-as-you-please, round trip contest between Nome and Candle over frozen Bering Sea, across the blizzard-swept tundra and through the mountains, covering a distance of 408 miles! The winners' stakes had mounted into huge sums, and the dogs had been the fastest and toughest selected from thousands tested in Alaska, Canada, and Siberia. Klondy Nelson had known all the champion mushers—Scotty Allan, Iron Man Johnson, Fay Delezene, and the incredible Finn, Leonhard Seppala. She had even driven some of the superdogs in short races, and probably knew more about handling malemutes than I would ever find out during all my years in the north country.

Though the dog derby spectaculars of Nome's gold-spangled years were gone with the wind, the sled dog population still exceeded that of its humans. For a while each winter, most of the social life revolved around their doings. Every week there would be a *ka-moo-gan* race, and between times the trails radiating out of Nome resounded with whoops of the mushers training their dogs. Recently, something new had been added; a Ladies' Race with special prizes and a victory dinner hosted by explorer Roald Amundsen. I found myself involved when one of the new schoolmarms in Nome borrowed my remaining dogs for the affair. The cheechako teacher finished near the tail-enders. Among the winners—mushing the "discards" I'd sold her a short time before—was the pretty Klondy Nelson.

But exciting as were the dog races, they could not quell the annual winter feuding among the inhabitants. As usual, the howling blizzards and spoiling eggs of February coincided with a sharp division of local folks into cliques and enemy camps, and no man was big enough to avoid becoming embroiled in guerilla warfare. Sooner or later, he would hear some monstrous bit of gossip about himself or his wife or girl friend, and then he'd be out there on the firing line shooting back at the snipers. It was going to take something bigger than a dogsled race to halt the slanderous rumors, and this winter it came from a source nobody suspected. The heroine who effected an armistice, healed the wounds and brought unity to the town—though she had to depart this mortal world to do so—was a shady lady from behind the boardwall.

The incident became known around Nome as the "Funeral For a Painted Lady," and before the chief character was laid away practically everybody in camp became involved. The town was ready to rally around the first good cause that came along, and the demise of the Painted Lady became the most important affair of the Nome winter.

It seemed that beneath her scanty attire and pink feather boa, the Painted Lady (nobody seemed to know her real name) had possessed a heart of gold. She had plied her art in the finest traditions of the ancient calling, and had left behind scores of admiring old timers who muttered in their beards that the camp would never be the same without her. They said she had never been known to roll a drunk, but instead had stashed his gold poke away until he could sober up and resume spending it where he'd left off. She had grubstaked many a prospector down on his luck with a "see me later when you strike it rich." She was ever ready with the voice of experience gained in camps from Dawson and down the Yukon to Nome Beach to advise a client down on his luck, and no lonely man had ever been turned away from her door as long as the Painted Lady was alive.

With such tales running rampant, a rush of warm fellowship soon spread through the camp. Donations started pouring in to make the Painted Lady's funeral one of the most colorful ever held in Nome. There wasn't a fresh flower to be had at any price, but the ingenious women of Nome knew what to do. They bought rolls of colored crepe paper at the trading post, fashioning them into sprays and wreaths, and when the services were held at the little snow-covered church there wasn't an empty pew in the house.

For the first and only time in the history of Nome, the good people of the town had an opportunity to gratify their curiosity about the "girls" who lived their dark lives behind the mysterious board fence and who seldom ventured out on the streets except to get some fresh air in the wee hours of the morning. Now, they emerged as a solid platoon in the full glare of daylight, trudging through the snow to pay final tribute to one of their departed members. Alaska Lizzie, Bighearted Bess, Toodles, Dawson Kitty, Deepwater Dorah, Halibut-faced Mary, Pile-driver Kate, the Oregon Mare, Betsy the Bitch and all the other veteran camp followers, filed into church and took their seats in the front row.

Married women of the town stared with envy as the "girls" threw back their mink coats which were rewards of the trade in the days of the gold rush. The soft-coal heater warmed the long unused church, and the air became heady with perfume. Blue-bottle flies hibernating in the cracks of the ceiling, now restored to life, started spinning and falling to the floor. Old time prospector friends of the deceased filled every pew to overflowing. Among them appeared to be a total stranger in the community. It was only after I had carefully studied the giant with his oddly pale face all nicked with razor cuts that I finally recognized him as Big Hans who had been in Nome for twenty years. He had shaved off his whiskers for the occasion.

Center of all eyes was the plain wooden coffin made of tongue-and-groove hemlock flooring by Dutch Schmalz, the local carpenter. Heaped around the sides were masses of the crepe-paper flowers, and inside, resting on a padded lining of white muslin reclined the Painted Lady. Embalming had been neither possible nor necessary. The body had been allowed to freeze hard as a piece of marble statuary, and the "girls" themselves had dusted flesh-colored powder on the face, applied a bright spot of rouge on each frozen cheek and painted the frigid lips a vivid red.

Four local talent performers who had once sung in Nome's early day Minstrel shows with Rex Beach, shuffled forward in their seal-skin mukluks to stand behind the coffin. Another took his place at the organ to run off a few chords, and then the old barber shop quartette rendered "Rock of Ages," not once but several times before organist and vocalists could all get together on the ending. As the last note of the organ droned away many a bearded miner surrendered to his emotion, and I stared with helpless fascination as Big Hans tried to stanch his tears with a wad of toilet paper such as all dogmushers carried on the trail. There was a slight murmur of voices when the perforated tissue slipped from Big Hans' trembling fingers and unrolled across the floor, but proper decorum was quickly restored when the vestry door opened to reveal the beautiful Klondy Nelson with her violin. Taking her place alongside the organ, Nome's own home-reared artist rendered Schuman's "Traumerai" with such purity of tone and finished technique that a long spell of silence fell upon the mourners.

Afterward, a deacon of the church delivered a short eulogy on all "fallen women," and on the deceased in particular. Carried away by his own oratory, at its conclusion, he brandished an angry fist in the air and thundered a challenge: "Let who will among you cast the first stone!" Of course, nobody did. Instead, all the mourners came forward for a final look at the Painted Lady; at the henna-dyed hair, gray at the roots; at the pink ostrich-feather boa draped around the wrinkled neck; at the frozen face daubed with rouge, and at the bright red lips pursed in a mysterious icy smile as if the Painted Lady carried many a secret to her grave.

This marked the end of the rites. As the mourners filed up the aisles, Dutch Schmalz, the carpenter, was already fitting the lid on the coffin and nailing it shut for cold storage in an unheated warehouse until the tundra thawed in the summer. Then, with no further ceremony, the remains of the Painted Lady and others who had died during the winter would be carted out on the tundra and lowered in graves dug down to the permafrost where they would be preserved in frozen condition forever.

There was a brief scene outside the church door before the mink-coated "girls" paraded back to their cribs behind the boardwall. Overcome with gratitude at the words of praise and the town's turnout for one of their kind, big Deepwater Dorah, with a façade like the super-structure of a battleship, addressed herself to the miners and prospectors gathered around. In a deep, gravelly voice, choked with emotion, she invited, "Come down and see us, boys. Everything's on the house for the rest of the day."

Another group of citizens had surrounded the talented Klondy Nelson to compliment her on her rendition of "Traumerai," and when I could get close enough, I added an invitation. Now that the dog races were over, I asked, how would she like to combine our teams for a ride out on the tundra? To my pleasure, she was willing, and as we took turn about at the handlebars of the speeding sled, I confessed my earlier scheme to become acquainted with her. Later in the week we made another trip, and this time I went a step further. I hinted how nice it would be if we could keep the team together all the time.

The blonde Miss Nelson smiled. "I was about to suggest the same thing," she replied. "It would be nice to leave my dogs in good hands. You see, I'm taking the first steamer south in the spring."

11 The Wild Yukon Delta

On mail-carrier Pete Curran's next trip into Nome with a sledload of letters from the "Outside" he brought me a five-page message from Dr. Nelson's desk in Washington, D.C. It was the most exciting assignment he had ever given me. A party of Biological Survey scientists was leaving the eastern states for the "end of steel" at Nenana in central Alaska, and from there they would journey by dogteam caravan several hundred miles into the windswept wilderness of the Yukon-Kuskokwim Delta. They would spend the spring, summer, and fall exploring the greatest waterfowl nesting grounds in all the Territory. How, asked Dr. Nelson, would I like to drive down from Nome to intersect this party? How would I like to guide these noted ornithologists and act as liaison man between them and the primitive Eskimos of the little known region? How would I like to help them photograph the teeming bird life, and collect scientific specimens for the Smithsonian Institute?

How, indeed? The wise old doctor knew I would turn handsprings at the opportunity, because at the end of the typewritten pages of formal instructions there followed his customary private note in the bold, slightly shaky, India-inked handwriting. I would be heading into an area where he had spent four years of his own early manhood in the period from 1877 to 1881, and he said it had been the most adventurous, the happiest part of his life. I could sense the nostalgia in his postscript, and was touched by the desire of this fine old gentleman to live it all over again through me: "This expedition is very close to my heart, as you know. Please write me directly and fully on all phases. Send progress reports whenever possible through the summer. E.W.N."

From Nome the way was south along the blizzard-scourged shoreline of Bering Sea, mostly across the jumbled ice to the port of St. Michael, some 300 miles away, where Dr. Nelson had made his headquarters four decades past, at a time when few white men had ever visited the bleak region. Twenty years after the Coast Guard Cutter *Corwin* came to bear him and his bales of specimens and sketches away from the tiny outpost, St. Michael had been hit with a gold rush. Suddenly, it had found itself acting as a gateway to the Klondike stampede of 1897. While thousands of prospectors toiled up over the Chilkoot Pass out of Skagway far to the south, many others had traveled by steamer from Seattle to St. Michael and crowded the decks of newly commissioned paddlewheel steamers for the 2,000-mile battle up the muddy Yukon to the diggings around Dawson. A tent city had sprung up along the shores of St. Michael Bay. It had filled with painted harpies, and with saloon keepers pouring whiskey from barrels upended on the beach. Gamblers had fleeced hundreds of miners long before they could sink a shovel into pay dirt. The government had had to send in a company of soldiers to quell riots.

Everything had gone wrong for the stampeders at St. Michael. No sooner had the last batch of prospectors finally cleared the port and headed upriver for the promised land when word was flashed that the Klondike was petering out, and that the new strike was on Nome Beach behind them. Abruptly, the Yukon River traffic was reversed. Steamers spun about in midriver and churned back to St. Michael, headed the other way in a race to reach the golden sands of Nome. With them came hundreds of small, whip-sawed boats and barges from the Dawson country, drifting down the muddy whirlpools to saltwater, and in the rush and the bedlam St. Michael had been one of the wildest and wickedest camps in all the north.

Now, it was all over. A small gas launch handled all freight, mail, and passenger business from St. Michael into the Yukon River mouth a hundred miles away. The colorful old sternwheelers had been towed to a bight known as the "graveyard" and hauled up on skids to wait for another stampede that had never come. Their gingerbread trimmings hung forlornly in the wind, the gilded names all but scoured away by pelting sand and sleet storms. The barracks where blue-clad soldiers had "lived by the bugle" were silent now, their weathered shiplap walls flattened by the gales. A herd of domestic reindeer, driven in to feed the miners during the gold rush, had trampled into extinction the colony of rare, black-beaked Aleutian terns discovered by Dr. Nelson on adjacent Stuart Island. Otherwise, St.

Michael had reverted to the little native village it had been in the doctor's time.

It has always been a puzzle to me how various species of wildlife are able to breed themselves to staggering plenitude in the rigorous far north. As I drove my dogteam along the frozen rim of Bering Sea and into the mouth of the Yukon, the countryside appeared unsuited for any kind of wild creature. Mostly, it was a frigid, blank whiteness stretching far away into the low skyline, and as my team struggled across the jumbled ice-slabs on the sea and the mountainous drifts piled along the lower river we were lashed by one punishing blizzard after another. It appeared that only the sparsest distribution of living things could sustain themselves in such harsh habitat. Yet, the very opposite soon became apparent. Nowhere in any part of the milder lower States had I ever encountered such staggering abundance of wildlife.

When I searched for the key to this amazing plenty, I didn't have far to look. The magic ingredient filled every ravine and lined every bank. Willows! Its scraggly tips were supporting endless flocks of ptarmigan through months of the snow-heaped winter, powering the snow-white birds with vigor to thunder into flight ahead of the dogteam. Beavers built their dams and houses from these same willows, and the big rodents impaled cut willow sticks in the muddy bottoms of their frozen-over ponds to gnaw on from November to May. In the leafy litter among the willow roots scurried voles and lemmings, shrews, and many kinds of wild mice. Owls, hawks, weasels, and other carnivorous mammals hunted the willow thickets and grew fat. And by some strange alchemy of Nature, the snowshoe hare, favorite food for most of the predators, bred themselves into such towering numbers on a diet of willow bark, that no combination of natural enemies could hold them in check.

I noted the first evidence of their runaway populations near Kotlik in the North Yukon Mouth. What I saw first was not live rabbits, but their amputated legs left by foxes, lynx, horned, and snowy owls. In a single day's travel I counted thousands of the furry "snowshoe" feet scattered along the dogteam trail. When I stopped for the night at an Eskimo village, every igloo was heaped with dead rabbits. They hung in huge, frozen clusters from the high-pole caches. Inside one of the sodwalled hovels where I hoped to find space on the floor to unroll my sleeping bag, the native women folks were holding a quilting bee, cutting the green pelts into strips and weaving them into rabbit-skin robes. Naked babies crawled about among the debris in the fetid air, sucking "lollipops" of half-cooked rabbit flesh. A big iron "trade" pot simmered with boiled rabbit carcasses to which the bulging-eyed heads were still attached, and I was politely invited to join in the feast.

"Better try some," urged chief Johnny. "Next winter maybe no rabbit. All gone. Today, me see *ma-ga-gu-uk* jump little ways; fall dead."

At this extraordinary prediction, my ears grew longer than those on a rabbit, and before I crawled into my sleeping bag amidst the squalor and odors and the clacking tongues of the blanket-weavers working late in the flickering light of the oil lamps, I made a deal with chief Johnny to see for myself this significant spectacle of a snowshoe hare being stricken with death midway in its leap. I had a hunch what it meant.

Next morning at daybreak Johnny and I recruited all

the youngsters in the village and tramped across the river ice to a thousand-feet long island so choked with willows that one could scarcely push into them. Where the lower end of the brush island tapered to a point, I dug a trench in the snow to conceal myself. Johnny and his army of beaters formed a tight cordon at the upper end, then began whooping and beating the bushes to start the drive.

At first the rabbits were reluctant to show themselves in open daylight, and kept hopping back into the brush, trying to sneak through the beaters. But, finally, when the shouting youngsters were no more than a hundred yards away, I peeked up over my trench wall. The snow between us was carpeted with them! I waved a go-ahead sign to chief Johnny; there was a pandemonium of yells and jumping rabbits, and suddenly the whole mass of them stampeded right over my head. One knocked my fur cap off, and my face was pelted with snow kicked up by their clawed feet. When the last rabbit cleared the hurdle and they were all bounding wildly across the exposed river ice to the next cover, I jumped up and tried to make a count.

There had been at least a thousand in that 20-acre patch of willows, and though I watched carefully, not one among them exhibited the slightest tendency to keel over dead. I was about to tell chief Johnny I'd never seen a healthier bunch of bunnies when I saw a lifeless rabbit swinging from his hand.

We took it to his igloo and I performed a crude autopsy with a pocketknife. There wasn't a mark on the animal; it was in plump condition, and its paunch was well-filled with chewed willow bark. I couldn't find anything wrong until I laid bare its insides. There I spotted something! There were grayish lumps on its liver, and bloody pinpoints on the lungs. I swung around then to tell the chief that I guessed he was right, after all; that this was the beginning of the end for practically every rabbit along the Yukon.

In a cycle of roughly ten years they had bred themselves into a population explosion such as I had never heard of among any wild animal in the States. No amount of predation by their carnivorous enemies, no amount of usage by the native Eskimos and Indians, had been able to stem their phenomenal increase, and now Nature was stepping in to wield the scythe among them, and by so doing, prevent these dizzily multiplying bunnies from totally destroying their food supply. The controlling agent had not alone been tularemia fever, the well known tick-borne killer communicable to man. This was something different, and far more devastating to the rabbits. This was the deadly epizootic later to be termed "shock disease," a breakdown of the vital organs through lack of sugar in the diet. There was nothing in all northern wildlife comparable to this death-dealing malady that blots out the snowshoe hares about once in every decade. To judge from past records maintained for more than a century by the Hudson's Bay trading posts across sub-Arctic Canada, population densities running from three to four thousand to the square mile were on the verge of being wiped out so completely that a man might snowshoe all day without flushing a single rabbit. Chief Johnny had lived through several such debacles. The moment he picked up the first dead *ma-gu-gu-uk,* he figured what was about to happen, and now I had to agree with him.

But why had the willows, principal winter food of the snowshoe hares, failed in this one year to supply enough sugar for their livers? Why did such dire calamity occur only about once in every decade? One of the theories had to do with flares and spots on the sun. Every ten years—

note the coincidental timing—solar spots reached a point of abundance, *followed by sudden, sharp decrease*. Study of northern willows and other browse indicated that they somehow failed to produce certain essential vitamins in this period. Research on this odd phenomena was, of course, by no means conclusive.

No one will ever know how many millions upon millions of varying hares—so named because they turn from brown to white in winter—keeled over lifeless in the Yukon Valley in that year of 1924 when chief Johnny and I observed the fatal epidemic at its onset. There was no way for us to estimate the number of predators who likewise perished when their meat supply vanished. But we reasoned that Nature would never kill off her last rabbit, nor those who preyed upon it. Even where the pestilence hit hardest there would still be a few widely scattered animals—perhaps two or three out of a hundred—and these survivors would start building again to another colossal ten-year climax.

Meanwhile, during the lean years of the rabbit cycle, other resources would be tapped by the energetic Eskimos of the lower Yukon. As I mushed my dogteam up the frozen river, I saw the first evidence of an unbelievably strange migration that had taken place *under the ice*. In the distance was what appeared to be a sizable pile of willow sticks cut for fire-wood, and I wondered what it would be doing out in the center of the river rather than along the bank. Unaccountably, the sled dogs tossed their heads into the air and surged against their collars full speed toward the obstruction, and the mystery was heightened as a pair of red foxes went scampering away from it across the river ice. But it was not until tht malemutes reached the heap and began snapping at the frozen mass that I identified the "wood-pile." Because what I saw, though it looked like a wagon-load of dead snakes, was actually uncountable thousands of lamprey eels!

The things were somewhat less than a yard long, round like a water adder, colored sulphur-yellowish, with seven gill pores extending down each side from a beady eye. The mouth was a hideous tool, shaped for rasping a hole in the flanks of a worthier fish like a salmon or a trout, and for hanging on like a leech while it proceeded to suck the life fluids out of its helpless victim. The lampreys possessed no true bones; only cartilagenous skeletons. They were classed among the lowest order of fishes, and an uglier tangle of creatures than those on the ice I never hope to see. They were stacked higher than my head, each one so reeking in its own oils that not even the subzero winter weather had been cold enough to freeze them stiff.

Within sight of the first dark heap another loomed upriver; beyond it still another, and at this one an old grey-headed Eskimo was loading a hand sled with the greasy spoils. Kwavuk, (meaning crow) told me the Russian name for the lampreys. "*Me-no-ga,*" he said, had filled the Yukon channels every winter as far back as he or his forefathers could remember. "We like, he added, "but not very much."

As soon in early winter as the Yukon ice was strong enough to bear their weights, old Kwavuk's people had been out on the great river cutting test holes and watching for the first lampreys to show up. Without fail, the first of the snaky fish had appeared in early December, the topmost layer finning just under the ice in a solid mass extending from surface to bottom and all across the main channel in numbers utterly beyond any computation I knew how to make. At the first heavy showing, the Eskimos then cut a trench crossways of the current, and arming themselves with forked sticks began flipping lampreys—several at a time—out on the ice. In the three weeks it took for the school to pass a given point, the pile of squirming lampreys grew bigger than an igloo. If the villagers wanted still more, all they had to do was move upstream a few miles and do it all over again, because the progress of the migration averaged scarcely more than a half-mile an hour.

Not in the slightest affected by the toll, the main body of lampreys which was strung approximately 250 miles along the river, would continue its slow progress under the Yukon ice. Having attained full growth on victims at sea, they would now live entirely off the oil in their bodies as they traveled fully six months to their spawning beds in the Yukon headwaters more than a thousand miles from saltwater. I knew of no greater massed migration of fishes anywhere else in the world. The total lamprey numbers in this one school must have mounted into the billions. Every one of them would die immediately after depositing its eggs in the river gravels, to be replaced in a short interval by multiplied billions of larva-like creatures. In spite of their staggering numbers the parasitic young lampreys would seldom be seen as they drifted down the muddy Yukon and into Bering Sea where each of the baby vampire fish would have to find a host on which to latch its rasping mouth in order to attain maturity.

Gray-thatched Kwavuk finished loading his hand sled with the frozen "snakes" and started back to the village. He invited me to help myself off the remaining pile, because in another month when the ice along the Yukon melted, the lamprey heaps would be washed out to sea. In this big year of the rabbits, Kwavuk and his people had made little use of the lampreys. But next winter when the rabbits had disappeared, the repulsive creatures would be fulfilling the old Innuit legend that as long as *me-no-ga* came out of the sea to fill the Yukon, there would never be famine among these Eskimos.

Though lampreys were once considered a great delicacy in Europe and were, in fact, known as the diet of kings, I have yet to meet the white man who could stomach the Yukon variety. Always the experimenter, I gave it a try. I boiled a piece Eskimo-style. It tasted like rancid grease, and I could not possibly induce my epiglottis to freight it down to my innards. It kept coming back, threatening to bring up the rest of my dinner with it. I made another attack by frying a skinned lamprey and it turned into a skillet-full of hot oil. The only solid matter I could dredge out with a fork was its gristly body shrunken to the size of a pencil. It tasted like nothing I had ever eaten, or would ever try again; a doubtful alternative to death by famine.

12 Strictly For the Birds

The dogmushing scientists arrived at our designated rendezvous a week late. Their dog teams, stretched for more than a mile along the trail, had been the biggest winter caravan to leave the railroad terminus at Nenana since the gold rush, and it had started rumors that a mysterious new strike was about to be made somewhere in the wilds of the lower Yukon. No one would believe the expedition leader's story that they were interested solely in ornithological field studies, and every night as members of the party sat around the big wood heaters in the trailside roadhouses, they were surrounded by eavesdroppers cupping their ears for one small hint that might touch off another stampede.

At the old ghost mining camp of Fortuna Ledge where I joined the group, a deputy marshal—himself an old prospector whom I had known in Nome—led me off into a corner. "If there's gonna be some more claim-staking around here, I gotta right to be in on it," he whispered. "The camp's dead right now, and needs another strike."

I wished I could have helped him, because Fortuna Ledge was, indeed, in sad shape. We'd quartered our dogs in the old movie house, and had the empty town hall in which to spread our sleeping bags. Vacant store fronts lined the streets, most of them with broken windows through which snow had blown in to fill the buildings. Once a community of several thousand, it was now down to less than fifty aimless individuals, most of them with no visible means of support.

"Where is it?" pressed the deputy, "Is it gold or platinum?"

"Neither," I had to reply. "This one is strictly for the birds." The old deputy gave me a withering glance, and without saying a word, called me a liar.

What happened next morning aroused his suspicions still more. As we trudged through the snow on our way to the camp's only remaining restaurant for breakfast, the ornithologists suddenly froze in their tracks. A tiny chicadee had landed on a bush and was hanging upside down twittering at us. "Good heavens!" exclaimed our party leader. "Can that be a *Parus cinctus lathami?*"

"Let's not take snap judgment," counseled the assistant party leader cautiously. "The crown is a shade too brownish for *Parus cinctus lathami.* I think I shall list it as *Parus hudsonicus hudsonicus.*"

We lesser minions were polled for our opinions. There were two votes for *Parus cinctus,* two for *Parus hudsoni-*

cus, and one abstention. To me it was just another chicadee, and it didn't seem of any earth-shaking consequence whether it was the Alaska gray-headed chicadee or the Hudsonian boreal subspecies. But binoculars were brought to bear on the subject, and the argument waged on and on. The bird experts were still debating torridly on how to list the tiny puff of soot-colored feathers in their field notes when the old deputy appeared at my elbow.

"Don't tell me a bunch of growed-up men came all the way up here from the States and drove the length of the Yukon just to look at a dam' chicadee," he muttered darkly. "Don't try to pull the wool over my eyes. You fellers are up to something big."

When we left the petered-out gold camp with our dogs strung out along the white bosom of the Yukon, the deputy marshal was down for a final try to smoke out the truth. And when I looked back a couple of hours later I saw the lawman and his dog team tracking us to our next destination.

A few days earlier, on my way upriver to meet the ornithologists, I had made arrangements for the party to occupy an empty schoolhouse in our jumping-off place at Mountain Village. And that night, on the brink of our departure from the mail trails of the Yukon into the untracked wilderness of the treeless delta, we held a council. Before us stretched a hundred miles with no shelter except isolated Eskimo family groups, if we could find them. If they could be persuaded to let us move into one of their igloos overnight, the accomodations would be cramped and filthy beyond anything the bird men had ever seen. We would have to carry our own food from Mountain Village, not merely for the four days' travel across the tearing winds of the delta, *but enough to last us through the entire summer.* When we left Mountain Village during this last week in April we would not see another trading post until we came out of the delta during the following September. It would take some careful planning to feed all hands, and before I threw in my lot with these bird-loving zealots, I wanted to have a peek at the grub list.

On this score I needn't have worried. The provision department couldn't have been in better hands. Herbert W. Brandt, private collaborator from Cleveland, Ohio, who was paying most of the expedition's expenses, had made his ample fortune in the food-handling business. He ate well, and wanted the rest of us to do the same. His problem was the simple logistic factor that a sled dog could haul no more than its own weight. In his generosity, if our malemutes had been the size of elephants I think leader Brandt would have provided the grub to overload them.

I watched him cleaning out the shelves at that last store in Mountain Village, working with the efficiency of a vacuum cleaner, and stacking foodstuffs on the floor: sacks of flour, cornmeal to be used in bird-skinning operations, salt, sugar, dry beans, and rice; cases of dried fruits, canned coffee, and evaporated milk; whole hams and slabs of bacon; cartons of crackers and cookies; tins of butter and jam; cheese, dehydrated vegetables, and powdered eggs; bales of dried salmon for the dogs. Though the assortment already outweighed the combined capacity of our dogs to haul away from the trading post, it still lacked the special items on which the success of the expedition hinged—trade goods for the primitive Eskimos.

We would need the natives' help as packers, guides, and woodcutters. We would have to buy their skin boats and rent their igloos. Brandt, whose hobby was collecting eggs of wild birds, would have to hire and train a group of Eskimos in the art of "blowing" the contents of the eggs out through a single pin-hole. None of these expenses could be paid with paper money, which in the year of 1924 meant no more to the aborigines of the Yukon-Kuskokwim Delta than cigarette coupons. So, once more bountiful provider Brandt went sniffing along the almost emptied shelves of the trading post, and soon another pile built up on the floor: 200 pounds of tea which the primitive people loved so passionately they drank themselves "high" whenever they could get it; pounds and pounds of strong, black twist tobacco which both sexes sniffed, smoked, chewed, and spat with gusto; essentials like canisters of black powder, sacks of No. 3 lead shot and primers for reloading their brass shotgun shell cases; luxuries such as cube sugar, glass beads, and bolts of red calico, and finally, a heavy canvas bag jingling with silver dollars which the natives might be induced to accept after our trade goods were exhausted.

When his buying spree was over, Brandt turned to me for approval. "Fine," I said. "Only now you'll need more dogsleds to haul the stuff away." Promptly, the free-spending leader went out and hired the best three dogteams in the village.

Among the trio of new mushers on leader Brandt's payroll when we set out from Mountain Village was an English-speaking native by name of Nick Beans, who solved our navigation problems by saying that he had once made a trip across the storm-beaten tundra to our destination at the coastal village of Napakiagamute. Nick also agreed to act as interpreter on the way, though he was not at all anxious to come face to face with the primitive delta Eskimos.

"Me not like those people," he told me. "Long time ago they make raid Mountain Village. Big fight. Everybody killed."

The delta Eskimos, insisted Nick, were very inferior to the Yukon people and he was quite sure they were descended from dogs. Foul and unkempt far below the usual Eskimo standards, a group of these "dog-people" had captured and bound hand-and-foot a boat-load of women and girls from Mountain Village and were paddling back across the Yukon to hide among a labyrinth of sloughs. Hotly pursued by the Mountain Village men, they had not noticed when one of the captive squaws freed her bonds and began slashing holes in the walrus-hide bottom of the boat. The big oomiak sunk in mid-river and as the raiders floundered in the muddy ice-water, the angry pursuers clubbed them all to death.

"We lose some of our women," admitted Nick Beans sadly, who was speaking not of his own time, but of that of his forefathers. "But we save enough to keep our village going." Otherwise, he intimated, his Mountain Village ancestors would have been forced to try just what the delta barbarians had attempted; raid some other community. He thought all wars—including the recent World War I between the allies and the Germans—were fought over squaws, and considered it a perfectly legitimate way of replenishing women folks when a village didn't have enough to go around.

My field diary shows it was the 27th of April when we left Mountain Village on the north bank of the Yukon, crossed the broken ice, and started on our long journey into the blank white expanse of the tundra. Though the spring breakup would occur within the next half moon, the expedition—now swelled to 7 teams, 8 men, 77 dogs, and 5 tons of freight—was forced to battle against a penetrating cold wind. Nick Beans and Herbert Brandt led the way followed by H. Boardman Conover from the Field Museum in Chicago; Olaus J. Murie, high on the staff of the Bureau of Biological Survey in Washington; an Alaska fur warden named Jack Warwick; and the two hired teams from Mountain Village. I brought up the rear to make sure that none of the party members got into trouble. At first, our guiding beacon, Mount Kuselvak, shone clear and white in the blue sky. But later in the day it was obscured by a blinding snowstorm and we had to fall back on the same kind of "compass" Dr. Nelson had used here forty years ago. It was the "lay" of the grass under the drifts. Fall gales had flattened the stems so that all the tips pointed in the same direction, precisely northeast. Though we were never able to see more than a hundred yards ahead, we all managed to pull to a stop that evening at a designated pin-point in the snow-heaped desolation.

The name of the spot was Chiganamut, and if the ornithologists had turned around here and headed back to their bird-watching clubs in the States I wouldn't have been surprised. Nothing I had encountered among the Eskimos north of Nome and along the Arctic coast had prepared me for the abysmal squalor of the igloo where we had to billet the bird men that night. To begin with, the stench-filled, sod-covered hole in the ground was already crammed with the foulest humans I had ever seen. It was almost as if we'd driven our dogs into a tribe of savages living a thousand years behind the times.

Our problem was to communicate with them; to cajole the evil-smelling chief into moving his family to a neighborhood igloo for the night, and the sly old throwback drove a hard bargain. He finally succumbed to offers of tea and twist tobacco, with a handfull of nails for the clincher, though he took his own time about vacating. The primitive family had been eating their supper when we came crawling down the long snow tunnel into the stinkpot they called home, and we had to stand around while they finished off a mess of boiled fish. I could hear the men of science gasping and gagging as dirt-enscaled brown hands dipped into a pot, snicked fish heads off with their teeth, loudly sucked the flesh loose and tossed the bones on the floor, now and then reaching sticky fingers under their goose-skin tunics to scratch flea bites. But the ornithologists had not spent two months on the road, and traveled 5,000 miles from the midwest to give up now. Instead, as they waited for the Eskimos to leave, they engaged in lively discussion about the identity of the birds that had gone into the making of the filth-plastered garments, and I saw leader Brandt turn to his partner H. Boardman Conover and propound the question, "I say, Connie, isn't that chief's shirt made from the skins of *Philacte canagica?*"

To conserve our dried-salmon dog rations for a possible emergency, Nick Beans and I struck a deal with the chief for a supply of frozen fish to feed the expedition's teams that night. It was the one commodity of which they had an abundance. The sloughs teemed with the tundra blackfish, odd little 5-inch slimy wigglers which the tundra people called *e-mang-uk.* Funnel traps woven from willow shoots and sunk in the channels filled with greenish, reddish-spotted creatures overnight, and they were stored in grass sacks to freeze solidly until needed. And when the icy blocks thawed out a phenomenon occurred.

The bird men were all outside to witness the spectacle. They had tossed each malemute a chunk of iced fish which it promptly gulped down. For a moment the dogs stood around howling for more, then one after another began retching violently as the fish, wiggling with life, came spewing out of their mouths onto the snow. Instantly, the hungry beasts began snapping up the elusive little floppers, crunching them between their jaws, and swallowing them all over again.

Dr. Nelson's own notes on these strange tundra fishes, penned forty years earlier, confirmed what we were finding hard to believe: "*Dallia pectoralis.* Blackfish. The vitality of these fish is astonishing. They will remain in grass-baskets for weeks, and when brought into the house and thawed out they will be as lively as ever. The pieces which are thrown out to the ravenous dogs are eagerly swallowed; the animal heat of the dog's stomach thaws the fish out, whereupon its movements soon cause the dog to vomit it up alive. This I have seen, but have heard even more wonderful stories of this fish."

One of those "wonderful" stories might have been that the blackfish would remain vigorous for months in a bowl filled with tundra water and wet moss; that it would forecast the weather by blowing bubbles at the surface when the skies were about to turn blue, and that it would sink to the bottom and barely stir when a storm was threatening. The Eskimos at Chiganamut were also living proof that its insipid flesh not only carried the essential vitamins to save a starving man's life but to sustain him indefinitely, because they subsisted on boiled *e-mang-uk* and little else all winter.

There were two more such nights for the bird expedition to endure as its long string of dog teams snaked over the interminable whiteness with scarcely a protruding willow tip to relieve the monotony of the drifted snow. Some of the Eskimo children where we stayed had never seen a white person. They clutched their mothers' parka hems, looking at us with fear-stricken eyes, and they thought that *we* were the ones with the offensive odors. In the desolate places where they chose to abide—for no apparent reason except it was the home of their ancestors and that it contained an unfailing supply of *e-mang-uk*—there were few fur animals for them to barter at the trading posts. Consequently, they lived almost independently of the white man's products.

At noon on the fourth day Nick Beans pointed to a jagged spot of color sandwiched between the tundra and a distant fogbank on the margin of Bering Sea. "*Napakiagamute!*" he shouted. It was the end of the long, wearying journey; the center of the greatest concentration of migratory birds in northwestern America; our home for the next four months. It looked like a castle in the sky!

13 The Birds and Belles of Hooper Bay

As we mushed closer to the shores of Hooper Bay our "castle in the sky" took on the shape of reality—or close enough to make us all happy. On a rise of tundra above half a hundred snow-covered igloos stood an edifice toward which I drove my dogs at full speed, and all the other teams came racing behind me. We couldn't wait, because what we had seen looming in the far distance was a new schoolhouse, complete with bell in the belfry. Standing at the open door ready to receive the first white visitors and the first news of the outside world in almost a year were the two teachers, Mr. and Mrs. Ebright.

There were no pupils, they said, and hadn't been any for weeks. The skin-clad aborigine children of the delta had not responded very well to the great white father's call to learn their ABC's. The Ebrights had given up trying, and were impatiently waiting for Bering Sea to clear of ice so that a government vessel could haul them and their belongings far, far away from the smells and ugliness of Napakiagamute. "You can have it!" they told us; meaning the schoolhouse.

Leader Brandt's eyes lighted up at the information. Could our expedition, then, set up shop in the empty classroom? Could the Ebrights be induced to take on our members as star boarders so that our full time could be devoted to the birds? The answers were yes, and soon we were joyfully bedded down on the floor, reveling in the luxury of clean surroundings. All the dogteams, except mine, headed back to Mountain Village in what had suddenly become a race with the melting sloughs of early May. The breakup season had arrived overnight; the dark, cold days were over and soon the pinto-patterned tundra would be shadowed by millions of the wings from the south. The scientists began laying out the tools of their profession; binoculars, cameras, egg-blowing squeeze-bulbs, scalpels, cotton-batting, tags, bird guides, and notebooks.

From the schoolhouse windows we looked across the 3-mile expanse of Hooper Bay to the stranded ice bergs of Point Dall jutting out into Bering Sea. Scouts of the winged hosts to the south, mostly gull and terns, were reconnoitering the honeycombed ice fields watching for open leads which would soon open the way to massed migration into the Arctic nesting grounds. We had managed to time our arrival perfectly. The dramatic spring breakup was almost at hand. Already, the native hunters of Hooper Bay were beginning to collect their first bounties. In late evening we saw their slanting black silhouettes against the red sunset as they leaned into their chest straps, each dragging a hair seal equal to his own weight. Slowly they toiled homeward like a thin, long line of Volga boatmen, and when the first hunter came squishing off the slush ice in front of the mud huts, leader Brandt was there to meet him. We had eaten no fresh meat for several days, and when the Ebrights said there wasn't anything tastier than seal liver, that was all our head man waited to hear. The trouble was that the Eskimos, too, liked this potent ort. After Brandt had shouted pigeon-English for several minutes, pointed at the seal, and cupped his hands in the shape of a liver, the native grinned with understanding and pointed to a slash in the seal's belly. Brandt spread it open and looked. The liver was gone. The native had followed a custom of removing it when he first made the kill out among the ice floes, and had crunched it down on the spot while it was still bloody and twitching with animal heat.

Brandt waylaid a half dozen more incoming hunters before he found an unopened seal. We watched him go into his pantomine, pleading with outstretched arms, and delving into his parka pockets for trade items. When he came slithering and climbing up the icy incline to the schoolhouse he was waving a gory liver triumphantly aloft. But he'd paid a stiff price. It had cost a half-pound of tea, a twist of black leaf tobacco, and three 10-penny nails. The President of Brandt's Food Marts in Cleveland, Ohio said wryly that many's the time he'd bought a truckload of steers with less haggling.

The Ebrights told him he'd made two mistakes. He'd tried to rush the deal. Also, he hadn't known that the Eskimos of Hooper Bay, primitive though they were, were among the slickest traders on Earth. It was a game with them. As they hunkered in their clubhouse, *ka-zhim* all through the dark, blizzard-bound days of winter, one of their chief amusements was swap-talk. They'd spend weeks leading up to a transaction involving a hand-whittled spear-handle and a pair of dog-skin socks, and when they met Herbert Brandt they could scarcely credit their good fortune. For a while I feared they would bilk him out of our entire lot of trade goods in the first month, but in this I had grossly underestimated the merchant prince from Cleveland. He knew he'd been "had" on the liver deal, and took pains to see that it never happened again. What he needed to do, he decided, was to infiltrate the Napakiagamute natives.

"Who's the smartest Eskimo in the village?" he asked the Ebrights over coffee that night.

"Young Tommuk, of course," answered Mrs. Ebright. "Spent a summer traveling with trader Nick Kameroff on a schooner. Speaks some English. Bright as a dollar."

"Tommuk's only seventeen years old," added Mr. Ebright, "but he'll soon be chief of this village."

"That's my boy!" said our leader.

Young Tommuk, henceforth "Tommy," became Brandt's man Friday, acting as go-between, interpreter, and guide. When they started tramping the melting snows of the tundra together, Tommy's quick, black eyes spotted birds long before Brandt could pick them up in his field glasses.

"*A-nee-puk!*" he'd cry out as a big snowy owl came flying silently overhead to stare down at them through its huge, yellow eyes. "*Nyctea scandiaca,*" Brandt would correct. Thus, having established both Eskimo and Latin names, they'd trudge on to more discoveries. "*A-nee-puk-soo-wuk*" Tommy would say as a mop-rag of brown feathers lifted loosely off the tundra and flopped away. "*Asio flammeus flammeus,*" amended Brandt. "Short-eared owl." All went well until one morning as they walked along the sea shore, Brandt spied a tiny V-shaped line of dots far out over the ice fields. Brandt said he thought they were geese, whereupon Tommy stared with wonder, because the phrase used by our leader sounded in the Napakiagamute jargon, like very private business between a man and a woman.

"You like um?" asked Tommy brightly.

Brandt hastened to deny any romantic interest in the village maidens. The flock was duly identified as Cackling Geese—Eskimo, *tu-tan-ga-yit;* Latin, *Branta canadensis minima*—and that evening our leader alerted us all to be very careful never to mention certain words pertaining to geese when in the presence of the Napakiagamute women folks.

They were—in 1924—a sorry lot, decidedly dirtier than the men who lived apart in a sort of stag club called the *ka-zhim* where the women were never allowed except to deliver food to their masters and then waddle back to the family igloos with the other women and the babies. Once in a while the "club" males poured water over hot rocks in the *ka-zhim* and sweated in fetid steam-smoke clouds until perspiration streamed down their backs like rain on window panes. Afterward, they rubbed their copper-toned bodies with oil until they glistened—and smelled—like seals. They lopped their hair off short, but the women allowed theirs to grow rank and wild and densely inhabited by vermin. With no opportunity to bathe all winter, the women were frowsy beyond description, and made themselves weirder looking by tattooing their faces with dye made from wood ashes. They appeared to live only to serve their lords and once each year bear him a child. Most of the babies were born within a few weeks of one another in midwinter, and when we arrived in Napakiagamute we were just in time to witness the general breeding season which followed three months later.

All through the blackness and howling gales of the long winter the Hooper Bay natives had huddled in their crowded sod igloos buried under huge snowdrifts. The nearest supply of fuel was the thinly scattered pieces of driftwood on the open beach three miles away, and days would go by with no fires in the igloos. Hibernating almost like bears in the dens, barely existing on a diet so restricted as to border on famine, their energies fell to a level wherein —according to Mrs. Ebright who made the rounds of the igloos in her capacity of nurse—sexual activities had been suspended. She said many of the newborn babies perished within a few weeks, and lack of sunlight made all the women wan and listless.

But now, the Eskimos had all been liberated from their foul underground dungeons by the coming of spring. They squatted atop the igloos soaking up the warm, all but continuous, sunshine of early May. Vitamin-packed fresh seal meat, freshly shot birds, fresh fish, green shoots, and roots from the edges of receding snow banks were padding their bones. Bright spots of color began appearing on the cheeks of the women, and they began making eyes at their men again. All about them the awakening tundra echoed with the amorous squawks and trills of newly arrived bird couples, and in fine attunement with the wildlife about them, the Napakiagamute Eskimos responded to the mating urge.

Though a favorite trysting place was in the high, dry grass on the hill around the schoolhouse, we members of the Brandt-Conover-Bureau of Biological Survey expedition had precious little time to observe the romantic rumpus nightly taking place just outside our windows.

For us there were not enough hours in the day to complete the job we'd come so far to do. Every morning at three o'clock, Brandt, Conover, Murie and Warwick piled their paraphernalia on my dogsled and I freighted it three slushy miles to Point Dall on the edge of Bering Sea where we were privileged to witness one of the grandest spectacles in all the north—the coming of the birds in the spring.

Beyond the extreme outer tip of the point a few huge, green icebergs, high as three-story buildings, had grounded on a low sand island, and these became our lookouts for field-glassing, photographing, and collecting a long list of birds wanted by Dr. Nelson for completing the Bureau's scientific series in Washington, D.C. Late in the evening I mushed a sledload of downed birds; mostly early migrants like gulls, terns, jaegers, loons and cormorants, back to the schoolhouse. While the Napakiagamute maids giggled and cavorted with their dusky lovers outside, we worked until midnight removing bird skins, cleaning the feathers with corn meal, salting, and shaping them into specimens. To each bird's crossed legs was attached an India-inked label bearing such notations as No. 718 *Gavia stellata,* (red-throated loon) ♂ (male) Point Dall, Alaska, May 4, 1924. O. J. Murie."

We were barely snuggled into our sleeping bags after our bird-skinning binge when the alarm clock and tireless leader Brandt roused us out for another 21-hour day. At this crucial period in the Hooper Bay waterfowl migrations, our sleep came only in short cat-naps, often out on the icebergs in the warmth of the midday sun when the flights slacked off for a few moments. We'd nod our heads, our eyelids would droop, then suddenly the argus-eyed Brandt would sound off like a steam calliope and we'd jerk ourselves awake just as a sky full of birds blocked out the sunlight. Some of us would snap pictures at high speeds of one-thousandth of a second when the viewfinders of our cameras were black with wings. Others would try to pick off wanted specimens with the shotguns. By the time we finished our chores of developing film and pelting birds that night at the schoolhouse, it would be almost time to head back to Point Dall again. The Napakiagamute Eskimos stared at our frenzied carryings on and shook their heads. They watched us lavish attention on the bird skins and discard the meat, and they told the Ebrights they thought we were all sick in the head. I was not far from agreeing with them when the whole show came to a grand finale.

The spectacle had been progressing steadily toward this high point ever since the first of May. As the open leads grew wider in the melting sea ice, more and more birds flew over our lookouts on the stranded bergs. A channel of Bering Sea now separated the mainland from the jagged ice slabs and it was necessary to paddle to our lookouts in skin boats. The gulls and loons were joined by eider ducks, returning from wintering waters off the Aleutian Islands to their nesting grounds along the Arctic coastline of Alaska, Canada, and Siberia. Every flock appeared to be driven by a compulsion to pass directly over the bergs off Point Dall like baseball players touching third base on the way home.

Of all the waterfowl, the eiders were the most exciting to watch. The drakes were strikingly marked on the upper parts with white and pastel shades of blue and green, and some of the feathers were fine as hair. The king eider sported a fatty orange-colored knob at the base of its bill. The spectacled drake wore a ring of delicate creamy feathers around each eye, and the handsome Steller's male looked as if it had skidded on its belly across a patch of brown mud. For several days as the channels of sea water widened and spread northward like spider webs, across the rotting ice, flocks of low-flying, densely-packed eiders dominated the aerial show, pushing ahead as each gleam of green water appeared on the white surface of the sea. In a single day we saw countless thousands wing past our perches on the grounded bergs, their pinions clapping and sideswiping other birds, the growling calls of the fancy-paint-job drakes and somber brown hens swelling to a dull roar as they hurtled over our heads close enough for us to rise up and grab at their legs. We thought we were witnessing the ultimate in massed bird migrations. But that was before the climactic spectacle of May 17.

On that morning soft, pressing zephyrs came puffing out of the south pushing summer ahead. The open patches in front of us began spreading. The floating ice-cakes, now so honeycombed we dare not set foot on them any more, started nodding to one another, milling and grinding their corroded edges into billions of small pieces glittering in the sunlight like precious stones on the green velvet of Bering Sea. We heard crashes like far off gunfire as the vast ice pack wrenched free from its winter shackles. My dogs, staked some distance back on the tundra howled open-mouthed at the zenith as if some mysterious inherited sense had told them that winter had come to an end, that something close to a miracle was about to occur on the shores of Hooper Bay.

A sea lane, growing wider with every passing moment, started flowing like a river into the northern ice mass, farther than we could see with our binoculars, and suddenly the gateway to the Arctic was flung open to a pot-pourri of waterfowl utterly without parallel in all our combined experiences. A band of handsome, slate-blue emperor geese with rusty-white heads cocked to look us over came close enough for me to scale my fur hat among them. Flights of Canada geese, snows with black-tipped wings, garrulous specklebellies, and black brant started showing up, all drawn as if magnetized to the pinnacle ice slabs on which we were perched unnoticed in our white-drill parkas. Then came flocks of pintail ducks, baldpates, scaups, scoters, golden-eyes, buffleheads, whizzing green-winged teal, harlequins color-daubed like circus clowns, and enormous numbers of long-tailed old squaw ducks whose musical "*ah-AHN-uk!*" calls pealed like organ notes in the sky.

The flocks were like skeins of lace drifting across the blue. They came swinging in from the open sea, and zooming down from the heights to whistle wings across our watchtower as we shot film like mad. We had already given up any thought of trying to estimate the mounting thousands, even before the cliff-nesting marine fowl loomed like clouds of smoke on the southern horizon—auklets, murres, murrelets, puffins, kittiwakes—fighting for air space to beat their wings as they merged with the migrating hordes. With them came shorebirds like curlews, plovers, phalaropes, dowitchers, godwits, and swarms of sandpipers flashing silvery in the sun as they banked and wheeled in perfect unison. As the pent-up migrants—all crying out in the ecstasy of what for them as well as us must have been the most exciting day in the year—streamed across the broken barriers to the north, it was like the bursting of a dam; a feathery deluge no witness would forget for as long as he lived.

Late in the evening when the low sun, riding the rim of the sea, had turned the ice-dotted expanse all deepening red and purple, we started back to the schoolhouse with enough birds and exposed film to keep us working all night. It was our last and biggest day at Point Dall. The big flights were over. Our next theater of operations would be the tundra, which in a single day had purged itself of snow. Already, thousands of birds had veered inland to start building their nests. The most important, the most incredible adventures of the summer still lay ahead.

14 The Medicine Man

When the tundra threw off its white winter mantle, we looked out the schoolhouse windows on a scene of far away beauty and nearby ugliness. Beyond the shining bergs off Point Dall, Bering Sea stretched in pastel greens stippled with sunlight until it curved over the western horizon. Twice each day on the high tide it flooded the bay and sent saltwater fingers exploring through the flatlands. Between times the water ebbed into a narrow slough, and the shoreline in front of the village became a slimy, filth-laden expanse of clay in which the Eskimo hunters struggled crotch-deep as they dragged up their kayaks at the end of the day. The children, most of them clad only in skin shirts reaching to their belly-buttons, frolicked in the foul muck and became so plastered as to be barely recognizable as humans. Afterwards, they squatted on the igloo tops until the clay baked dry, then knocked off the pieces and became cleaner than they'd been all winter.

Beyond the sand dunes on the beach spotted hair seals and pure white pigmy whales gathered off the mouth of the slough, while over their arching backs wheeled flocks of screaming gulls, terns and jaegers. The presence of these predators was clear evidence that one of the biggest events of the Napakiagamute year—second only to the annual spring mating season—was about to occur. It was the coming of the salmon, the bountiful migration of silver hordes from the pale green mystery of the sea into the muddy slough which coursed between the village igloos. No power on earth could stay the salmon instinct to fight their way through this delta outlet and on to their natal spawning streams far up the Yukon River. Yet, an Eskimo character by name of Oomalik, the medicine man of Hooper Bay, *claimed to be responsible for the run, and collected a tithing for his efforts*. The shenanigan was supposed to be a tribal secret, but Brandt's boy Tommy spilled the story, and when the medicine man went into his act down at the slough mouth we were all at the schoolhouse windows spying through our bird-glasses.

The sly old rogue had been observing the salmon for several days as they milled outside the river bar, exactly as other schools had done in years past, and he couldn't help noting that the highest tide of the month was due to cover the shoals and lift the giant king salmon over into the slough. Of all this, the other natives must also have been fully aware, but they all tried very hard to believe their medicine man because, according to folk tales, that's the way it had always been at Hooper Bay. The salmon would come only if their leader had strong enough power, and as far back in their history as any of them could remember, Napakiagamute had always been blessed with such a man. Now, they stared in wondrous awe while the current man of magic followed the ritual prescribed by legend. They saw him build a bonfire on the shore and prance wildly about as though being pronged with spear thrusts from the devil himself. Now and then he'd fling his arms in the air, and bound nimbly across the bonfire through flames so close they must have singed the hair off the seat of his pants. The show reached its climax when the tide rose full and salmon began pouring through the wave tops into the slough. At this moment the medicine man heaved an armful of grass on the fire to send a column of smoke into the sky. That was the signal! The Napakiagamute Eskimos rushed from their igloo tops down to the shore of the slough and began stretching their gillnets in the eddies. It wasn't long before the floats began tugging under, and prolonged cheers sounded all over the village. Oomalik had brought the salmon! Oomalik had kept faith with his forefathers! Great was the power of the medicine man!

We members of the bird expedition were inclined to regard the medicine man as a goofy crackpot until Tommy gave us the facts of his life. Oomalik was the kingpin Eskimo in Hooper Bay, and contrived to control most of its humble assets. He had a bigger and better igloo, more sealskins, more children, more of everything, than any other native in the village. We watched the gillnetters bring their fattest salmon to his door. Women came crawling out of the tunnels to split them and hang the slabbed sides on his private rack to dry in the wind. They dug a pit in the salty clay into which they tossed the severed heads to cure into a delectable product known as *titmuk*. When the flesh had attained a degree of ripeness so that it could be sucked freely off the bones, the medicine man would feast in elegance. Concluded Tommy, "Him only man in village got two wife."

All around Napakiagamute the land was a trembling morass bisected with sloughs which filled and drained with the tides; pocked with bogholes where a misstep could plunge a man up to his armpits. The vast, wild region between the mouths of the Yukon and Kuskokwim Rivers was bigger than my entire native state of New Hampshire. The low, crawling scrubs, bushes and profusely growing grasses of the previous summer, now matted and wind-flattened, were perfect places for the birds to hide their nests. Even before the first green shoots appeared, there was food in abundance.

I had but to drop down to my hands and knees, bird's eye level, to note the full wonder of it; to discover a Liliputian "forest" of willows and birches that stood only inches high; to see tiny "orchards" still loaded with dwarf fruits from the previous summer, preserved through the winter by natural deep-freeze. Sweet blueberries hung like plums from 4-inch "trees." Red lingonberries were like miniscule apples, and the ground under our boots became stained with the purple juices of pin-head size crowberries as we walked upon them. Grass seeds and fallen grains from dozens of alpine plants could be scooped up by the handfuls; all of them, when later subjected to laboratory analysis, proved to be packed with concentrated vitamins.

When the birds arrived in the spring to build their nests, the tundra was like a miniature Garden of Eden, a land of plenty for small creatures.

There was something for every kind of bird, including the birds of prey. A week earlier as I sat among the grounded bergs off Point Dall I had been witness to a strange migration of rodents. Fat little mouse-like creatures known as lemmings had come swarming blindly off the tundra to scurry across the beach sands and launch themselves into the sea. They climbed out on the stranded berg with me and covered it with a creeping brown carpet. Some of them nibbled boldly on my mukluks, others crawled in and out of my velvet-lined camera case, and rested without fear in the palm of my hand when I gathered them up for close examination. But they were restless and didn't remain long. Driven by an unexplainable madness, they slid off the berg like tiny zombies and started swimming out through the waves to their certain doom. Many reasons have been given for the lemmings' massed suicide migrations which have been observed to occur periodically around the Arctic zone in Europe and Asia as well as North America. The most logical explanation, that the lemmings are seeking new food supplies, did not seem to fit the circumstances at Hooper Bay in 1924.

Not only was the tundra they had vacated loaded with food, there were also endless thousands of rodents still remaining there after the lemming migration. Walking the area with Brandt and his boy Tommy, stooping over to watch, the stumpy-tailed creatures reminded me of wee brown bears in an ankle-deep "forest." Among them, Tommy's quick eyes spotted a tiny animal remarkably like a thumb-sized polar bear. Although I recognized it at once as a species of lemming with the Latin designation of

Dicrostonyx, the only mouse to develop a white coat in the winter, Tommy supplied a more interesting bit of natural history. He told us that *ki-lug-u-mi-u-tuk* lived in the sky, but sometimes got swept down to earth by snowstorms. "Never see in summer," he pointed out, and of course he didn't, because then they were brown like the other rodents.

For the fish-eating birds there was an endless supply of food, too. Brandt and I were munching mid-day sandwiches when Tommy pointed to a slight movement in the water-soaked tundra at his feet, then scraped an opening in the floating vegetation. While the roiled water cleared, the Eskimo lad took from the folds of his parka an exquisitely woven fine-meshed piece of netting which he said had been made by his mother from hair plucked out of her own head. Spreading the gossamer square between his fingers, he slipped it under the water and lifted it out full of silvery-blue fishes each about the size of a kitchen match.

"Now, *me* eat," declared Tommy, and began tossing the flopping fishes into his mouth, the bladders popping between his teeth. "Good this way," grinned the boy as he observed our shudders. He added that the tiny fishes (they were nine-spined sticklebacks) were so fat that if left in a wooden tray for a day or two they would dissolve into almost pure oil. The Eskimos dipped green shoots into the stuff to make a sort of salad, used it for flavoring, and drank copious quantities neat from the tray. Loons, grebes, gulls, terns, and other fish-catching birds had but to submerge their beaks in the brackish pools to stuff their craws.

At this season the birds were silent. Their mating antics over, the males had stopped singing and displaying and now were humped quietly among the tussocks while their mates brooded over clutches of eggs. Eggs! It was the biggest word in the language to leader Herb Brandt. For the joy of hunting birds' nests in the Yukon-Kuskokwim Delta he had vacated an important business in Ohio, left a beautiful home to dwell among a primitive people, and laid at least $10,000 on the line for expenses of the party. Eggs? Brandt collected them with the same fervor that sent archaeologists digging among the pyramids of Egypt, like other people hunted sea shells, pored over old coins, or saved postage stamps. His private wild egg collection in Cleveland already contained thousands of sets from all over the world, and now he hoped to cap it with wholesale numbers of rare specimens from the solitudes of Hooper Bay.

It was by no means a one-man project. It was more like an every man-woman-child-in-Hooper Bay effort. In the summer the Eskimos spent hours combing the tundra for eggs to eke out their existence. Brandt quickly managed to organize the entire village as his helpers, to have all the eggs routed through him for blowing. All he wanted were the empty shells; they could have the contents, and everybody would be paid. Convinced that they were dealing with the silliest white man ever to visit Hooper Bay, the Eskimos agreed on a price for their co-operation, and the grand egg hunt was on!

Tommy with his ability to use both Latin and Innuit names for the birds, became Brandt's shadow as they set up a chain-line production unit in the schoolroom. A dozen of the village women were taught how to drill a small single hole in the end of each egg with a dental burr. Then a fine stream of air was blown into the same hole with a rubber squeeze bulb to force out the contents. Naturally adept, the Eskimo ladies were soon blowing eggs faster than Brandt could identify and catalog them. Every night the matrons returned to their mud igloos clutching to their bosoms packages of tea and cubed sugar. We would hardly have time to crawl into our sleeping bags when we'd hear them outside the schoolhouse door again, tongues clacking eagerly, ready to start another happy day in the egg factory.

There would be "tea" breaks during the day. A plate was always kept filled with hardtack for them to nibble on, and Mrs. Ebright's especially trained maid, an incredibly sloppy, cross-eyed girl she's named Sadie, would dish out scrambled eggs. It didn't make any difference what kind of eggs, or how badly incubated, Brandt's employees loved them all. As he moved up and down the long table supervising production, hugely enjoying the spectacle, Brandt would reach playfully into a bowl with a pair of tweezers and lift out an owl embryo mostly all head and a staring outsize eye.

"'ere, old chappie," he'd sing out in Cockney accent to Tommy, "'ave an 'ighball!"

We members of the bird party also shared in the egg festival. Whenever completely fresh sets were processed, the contents would be blown into a special bowl. In the platter placed on the breakfast table each morning by Mrs. Ebright, there might be yolks and whites from red-poll eggs tiny as lima beans, up through an olio of sandpiper, phalarope, plover, curlew, loon, eider, gull, and hawk eggs. We never knew what kinds, and though the yolks varied in hue from tomato red to bilious green, they all seemed to taste about the same. Compared with the commercial dehydrated eggs of 1924 Mrs. Ebright's scrambled wild eggs were, in fact, pure ambrosia.

For a period that early summer the village reveled in such prosperity as it had never before known. Men and boys scouting the tundra with flagged sticks for marking nesting sits were given finders' fees for every one they located on Brandt's wanted list. The women were then paid for blowing out the shells, and carried most of the contents down to the igloos to share with their stay-at-home sisters. On her rounds as nurse, Mrs. Ebright reported that the egg-blowing ladies were forming an upper crust in the native society. They were starting to give tea parties in their igloos, the first sign of aristocracy to rear its head in Napakiagamute.

Women of proper ages were contentedly pregnant; all, that is, except the unlovely Sadie. As nearly as we could assess the condition without appearing to pry into their sex life, the men of Hooper Bay took to wife without further ceremony the first girl who carried their unborn child. If the first mating flurry didn't show results, they were both permitted by tribal custom to try again elsewhere. Sadie's troubles were that after numerous tests involving practically all the village swains she could prove no evidence of conception. She had lost caste, and was fervently seeking a potent sire. It was no wonder then that Sadie, in her desperation, began putting the cross-eyed whammy on members of the Brandt-Conover-Bureau of Biological Survey Expedition.

None of us escaped, though we were never quite sure whether her hot stares were directed at us, or at some other member across the schoolroom. Before we learned which one of us was the intended victim, a fortunate development occurred in Hooper Bay. All over the tundra fledglings started filling the bird nests, and suddenly the great egg hunt was over.

Brandt stowed away his egg-blowing gear, and his female workers went back to their igloos to return no more. With them went the amorous Sadie. With her dowry from Brandt's generous payments, she had become the richest unattached female in the village, and we hoped she would have better luck on her next tour among the menfolks. Several weeks later we heard the good news.

"Sadie, she got big belly," remarked our boy Tommy one day. "Medicine man, he make-um."

15 Exploring the Delta

Onset of the hatching season quickly separated the members of the Brandt-Conover-Bureau of Biological Survey Expedition. His project completed, Brandt wrapped his hundreds of blown eggs between layers of cotton and sphagnum moss and packed them snugly in wooden boxes for the long shipment to his home in Cleveland. With his usual foresight, he had long ago made arrangements for a gas-boat to come down from the Yukon to pick him up on a designated day, and it came chugging into Hooper Bay right on schedule. Without so much as an hour of lost time, the very efficient Brandt and his stacked crates of eggs were on their way to catch an upriver sternwheeler to the railhead at Nenana. Shortly afterwards, the Ebrights and fur warden Warwick boarded the only trading vessel of the summer, and suddenly our party was down to three members.

H. Boardman Conover of the Field Museum remained behind to make a collection of downy young specimens. Olaus J. Murie, who was later to become President of the Wilderness Society of America, and I still had to carry out our principal assignment on the Yukon-Kuskokwim Delta. By whatever means of travel we could devise, we had to make our way among the interminable maze of sloughs that spilled out of the main Yukon and spread like cobwebs through thousands of square miles of primitive marsh to Bering Sea. We had to find out whether or not this enormous wild delta was as productive as it had been a half century earlier. Was it still the greatest waterfowl nursery in all of Alaska? Dr. Nelson wanted to know.

A stroke of rare good luck launched us on the undertaking. All through Dr. Nelson's detailed reports covering the years 1877–1881, he had made frequent mention of a valued guide and companion, a trader named Captain Peterson of Andreafski married to an Eskimo woman. Among the captain's sizable brood of dusky children there had been a son whom he called Charley, now grown to middle age, an inventive genius with a born love for boats. When Conover and Murie and I saw his latest creation—a house complete with smoking stove-pipe—floating serenely toward us across Hooper Bay in water scarcely a foot deep, we knew we must charter it at any price.

It was easier than we thought. By "mukluk wireless"—a method of transmitting news between Eskimo villages no white man will ever really understand—Charley Peterson had heard about the visitors sent into the delta by his father's old friend, Dr. Nelson, and he was eager to help. With the same feverish scramble that had kept us jumping day and night ever since we reached Hooper Bay in a battle against the too short Arctic summer, we piled aboard the *Flounder* with camera, guns, sleeping bags, and food items. Then with the morning sunrise in our eyes, we headed northeast into a series of fantastic discoveries and mishaps.

Though he couldn't know them all because they were constantly changing, Charley Peterson came as close as any man to qualifying as a pilot for the twisting channels in the delta. His boat, bottomed with thin, limber boards, buckled and slapped its way across the shoal spots like a flounder stranded on the tide flats, and I kept waiting for it to spring a leak. That it stayed reasonably dry was a triumph of Charley's expert calking learned from a seagoing father. The one-cylinder gasoline engine went *chunk-a-lunk* day after day on less than a pint of fuel an hour. The schoolhouse at Napakiagamute faded below the tundra skyline and we pushed deep into a flatland swarming with bird life.

Not all the delta water was roily. The huge loads of mud carried down the rampaging Yukon each summer gradually settled to the bottom along the tortuous sloughs in the alluvial fan, building more and more land and extending its silt bars farther and farther out into Bering Sea. In places the sloughs backed up to create shallow lakes pure as crystal with rich growths of pondweeds and sedges. Young waterfowl fed around the clock in the all but continuous daylight to develop into maturity in a miraculously short space of time. With a short skein of net strung across the sloughs in the brief hours while the rest of us slept, Charley Peterson kept the boat supplied with fat whitefish and sweet grayling. We saw them schooling on the clear lake bottoms, and one morning I spotted what I thought must be the biggest fish that ever swam in the Yukon. It was resting alongside a grassy bank with its back awash of the surface. With infinite stealth I wormed my way to the edge. When I lifted my head to peer through the grassy fringe, I could scarcely believe my eyes. This was no fish. It was a whale, in fact, two whales!

In water little more than knee-deep a beluga cow and calf were as perfectly defined as though under glass. The larger one was the usual pure milk-white of this pigmy, 12-feet long species. Resting alongside was her slate-blue calf. Safe from the bloodthirsty killer whales of Bering Sea, the mother had chosen this sequestered spot to bring forth her young. I had happened along in the rare moment when it may have been taking its first drink of warm milk. As I watched, the yard-long baby swung around broadside to the cow and its blunt nose started bumping against her body. Under the urging, the cow rolled over on her side to expose a vertical fold which opened to disclose a nipple at the surface. The lake water became cloudy with discharged milk and it appeared to me as if the calf was wasting more than it suckled. Air sighed and whistled from the blowholes in the tops of their heads as the calf drank its fill and fell away satisfied for the moment. When I slipped away, the mother beluga was nudging her newborn with affection. Their stay among the weeds would not be for long. No more than ten days later we began to see the white cows and their blue calves out in the tidal basins, mingling and romping with the waiting bulls.

Strange names began appearing in our field notes as we probed the unknown delta: Igiak, Kokechik, Chevak, Kgun, Chowhoktolik, and dozens of other mouthful-of-potatoes names supplied by Charley Peterson but which we could neither pronounce nor find on our maps. Everywhere the *Flounder* twisted and turned among the snake-looped waterways, the surface ahead was lathered with the foam of flapping waterfowl; pintails, mallards, widgeons, scaups scoters, golden-eyes, buffleheads, eiders, and green-winged teal; white-fronted, emperor, lesser, and cackling geese; whistling swans. Gaunt sandhill cranes stalked across the tundra. The air was dinned with trilled alarms of curlews, godwits, plovers, yellow-legs, turnstones, jacksnipes, sandpipers, and clouds of mewing gulls and terns. For every young bird we could catch we had a band to fit its leg, and they were later to reveal that the Yukon-Kuskokwim Delta not only sent its winged bounty down to supply the western states with the bulk of their migratory bird shooting, but some of its species passed on to the Gulf of Mexico and down to Central and South America. Some notable varieties like the cackling and blue-scaled emperor goose nested almost exclusively on the delta. There wasn't any question but that this wild, enormously rich tundra was all that Dr. Nelson had long ago declared: a region vital to the preservation of the waterfowl, shorebirds and many other birds of the New World, and today as many of our northern marshes are being overrun by civilization is even more important.

Some of the sloughs up which the *Flounder* pushed its way on the rising tides were no more than muddy trickles during the low water stages, and our house-boat settled to the sticky bottom until another flood tide lifted it off. At such times the bared flats around us became densely covered with thousands of bright plumaged males of many duck species. The drakes—like the men of Napakiagamute—deserted their females after the mating season and paid them little attention during the period of incubation and family raising. The only faithful male we observed—and I think he rather overdid the job—was a snipe-sized bird called the phalarope. The female was larger than the male, more brilliantly colored, and very much the aggressor during the courting season. She pursued the drab little male relentlessly from one tidal pool to another, fluttering eagerly before him, prostrating herself invitingly, only to have the reluctant fellow turn his head and fly away. Finally, he succumbed, and for the fleeting second of conjugation, he paid the price all the rest of the summer. Not only did he have to build the nest for his domineering mistress, he also had to sit on the eggs until they hatched, and he alone fussed over the babies while his tyrant wife gadded about with other females.

To escape the fury of a savage storm which smote the *Flounder* in midsummer and threatened to turn it upside down, Charley Peterson ran it far up a tide-filled estuary beyond reach of the ocean swells. While the rain poured down on the canvas top and kept streaming right on through the spark-holes into the cabin, Charley made the *Flounder* fast to an oar jammed down into the soft bank. We crawled into our sleeping bags to ride out a night that turned out to be a lot wilder than we'd figured. While we slept, the tide ebbed stealthily away and when there was no longer enough water to buoy up the stern, the *Flounder* pulled tight against its tie-rope, teetering on the edge of the cut bank, and eventually pulled the oar loose. The *Flounder* shot almost straight down into the half-filled slough, and suddenly we were struggling for our lives in the icy water.

Buckled in our sleeping bags struggling like maniacs in straightjackets, we might have all been drowned immediately except for two factors. The force of the inrushing waters washed us forward and upward into the pilot house, and there was enough imprisoned air in them to float us at the surface. With one another's help we pulled loose from the bags and scrambled out on the bank. To keep the *Flounder* from being carried away on the next rise of the tide, we reset the oar and once more cinched up on the tie-rope. Clad in our sopping wet longjohns we began diving into the waterlogged craft in an effort to save some of our most needed possessions. For Murie, Conover, and me this meant film, cameras, field notes, and collected specimens. For Charley Peterson it was a matter of trying to save the boat, itself, because without it our chances for survival were none too good. In and out of the water like a seal, Charley managed to strip off the canvas top which, with oars for upright supports on the bank, became a windbreak against the wet gale. Next, he submerged long enough to wrench the sheet-iron stove loose, and in some miraculous way involving the liberal use of gasoline managed shortly to have it rumbling hot in the lee of the flapping canvas. We hung our garments and sleeping bags to dry, then returned to our diving chores. Our camera and gunnery equipment, stored in the forward end of the *Flounder,* came through the wreck in usable condition, but our food supplies were a sodden, sorry mess to be dredged out of the water in squishy handfuls. There was almost nothing in edible condition. For Conovor, a confirmed tea-sipper, there was a special shock when he found his precious store of tea leaves tainted with spilled gasoline and salty bilgewater.

While we waited for the tide to go completely out so we

could walk around the boat and assess full damage, I shot down a passing eider duck and fried it in its own grease. It was tough and rank, but we chewed it down gratefully. "Might as well get used to eating the blasted creatures," observed Conover sourly. "Looks like we'll be living like savages before we get out of this mess."

The tide level dropped around the *Flounder,* and we kept pace with bailing buckets, so that when it rested on the drained bottom of the slough, the hull of the *Flounder* was also dry. By prying and propping with lengths of driftwood as the tide started running in again, standing in rising water up to our necks to heave with all our strength, we managed to float the flimsy craft to an even keel and push it up on the grassy bank where it wouldn't take another stern dive when the tide went out again. Charley Peterson started tinkering with the engine which had been under water for several hours. Nothing happened. We suggested that we might as well give up and start drifting down to the bay on the next outgoing tide, then rig a sail from the old canvas top and try working our way back to Napakiagamute, or somewhere.

Charley Peterson wasn't listening. He was taking the engine apart, wiping each piece and swabbing out the cylinder and crank case. The magneto and spark plug received special treatment. Charley shoved them into the camp stove oven to bake completely dry. Hours later when he reassembled the engine and gave its heavy flywheel a heave, I held my breath in suspense. But the engine didn't. It gasped with life. Charley twisted valves, pulled wires, turned petcocks, advanced the throttle, and the old one-lung sang a beautiful song of *chunk-a-lunk.*

"If we go back to schoolhouse for more grub," warned

Charley then, finally answering our question, "lose too much time. Must go on from here."

We agreed. We couldn't afford to lose a day. We'd been living on restricted rations aboard the *Flounder,* anyway. Now, we'd cut down some more and try to make out on birds and fishes and tundra berries. To our surprise but not that of Charley Peterson, who considered it no hardship at all, we thrived on the diet.

Charley had a special reason he didn't tell us about for continuing on with the *Flounder.* A few days later we chugged into the small native village of Kashunuk just in time to take part in one of the oddest of waterfowl hunts—a hunt without guns. It started when Chief One-Eye came padding down the bank to board the *Flounder* and beg for *chi* and *tabac.* Before I had a chance to foul the operation by saying that our trade goods had all been ruined by dunking in slough water, Charley fetched the sodden remains of tea and twist tobacco and engaged the chief in swap talk. It went on for hours, and we stared in fascination at the Eskimos in their bedraggled, clay-smeared patchworks of sewn skins stripped from geese, eider ducks, and loons. They wanted that *chi* and *tabac,* but Charley wanted something in exchange. Finally, he turned to let us in on the secret.

"All fixed," he explained. "Village make goose drive. They take old ones for eating; you have little ones for banding." Charley hesitated a moment, then added, "They think you too much koo-koo in the head."

We assembled a few miles from the village and Chief One-Eye sent most of his boys sneaking low to form a hidden line across the tundra. The rest of us strung a line of fish-nets in the shape of a small corral with a V-shaped lead-in, crawling on our bellies while holding sections of net ready to be lifted on signal. The chief stuck a long pole into the mud to give the beaters a target, and they jumped to their feet and started driving the birds our way. For a while all we could make out were the beaters, scurrying back and forth, themselves looking like overgrown birds. Then we began sighting the small dark heads of the real birds bobbing up here and there above the grass tops. We remained hidden until the line of drivers converged to within arms' length of one another; then on signal we stood up with our sections of the net to form a funnel and holding pen.

Almost no waterfowl had flown away during the drive, and when we sat down among the massed birds with our banding equipment we saw the reason why. The young had not yet attained flight status. The parents had shed their wing feathers. When the last of the haul went dashing away wearing its aluminum bracelet, we had made an important contribution toward tracing the migration routes of the Yukon-Kuskokwim Delta geese and ducks. Through Charley, we explained to the Eskimos what it was all about and they nodded their heads with understanding. They were all squatting in their feather parkas along the bank of the Kashumuk like outside birds, grinning from ear to ear, happily chewing their *tabac* when the *Flounder* chugged out of their lives. Soon we were breasting the undulating swells of Hooper Bay, headed north on the final leg of our journey back to the schoolhouse at Napakiagamute.

There the Brandt-Conover-Bureau of Biological Survey Expedition split up again. Charley headed for his home on the Yukon with his *Flounder*. Olaus J. Murie announced that he was meeting his future bride on the lower river and they would spend their honeymoon aboard a sternwheeler as it churned upcurrent to the railhead at Nenana. To celebrate the coming nuptials and to show proper appreciation also to the valued services of Charley Peterson, Conover and I prepared a banquet from our stored supplies in the schoolhouse. I washed the mold off a ham with vinegar and baked it in the oven with the last of the canned yams. Not to be outdone, Conover manufactured some pies from our only dried fruit.

"There's covereds, cross-bars and opens," he announced grandly as he brought them to the table, "and prunes in every one of them."

It was an evening of good fellowship, but for Conover, Murie, and me it made the succeeding days that much harder to bear. We had been five months in the wilderness. We had lived like primitive people. The big job was over and all the other members of the party were on their way home. There was little for us to do except study the early fall sky through our binoculars as the nesting birds of the Yukon Delta began taking to wing with their broods and moving down to the shores of Hooper Bay to form up for the massive migration to the south. Conover sipped his tea and watched them enviously from the schoolhouse windows. "I wish the hell I was a goose," he said. "They can take off any time they feel like it. But how about us?"

The same question had been occurring to me. All Dr. Nelson had told me was that I would be picked up at the end of the season and brought back to Nome. Already, the first chill nights were upon us, and soon there would come ice on the tundra pools, and snow flurries to send the winged hordes on their way out of the country, and then Hooper Bay would be a desolate place, indeed.

We began spending more and more of our time watching the sea for signs of a boat. One evening as we were watching, without much appreciation, the gorgeous colors off Point Dall a triangle of white flashed on the pastel-colored waters, then turned red in the sunset as a schooner swung about and headed straight into the bay. Inside the sandspit it dropped canvas, and we saw the splash of an anchor. I waited no longer, but slid a kayak across the mudbank and started paddling down the slough. The name I'd read on the schooner's bow was the *Hazel,* of Nome, and the chunky little figure who tossed the anchor overboard was Napook.

16 The Many Sides of Nome

As I drew alongside the *Hazel* more figures joined Napook on deck, and the hands of total strangers reached over the rail to help me aboard.

"I'm Henderson," said a gray-haired scientist whose blue eyes twinkled behind octagonal spectacles.

"I'm Le Bourdais," added a tall young fellow with a slight trace of accent and a slightly receding hair line.

I started to say, "And I'm the Medicine Man of Hooper Bay . . ." when Napook, friend and buffoon with whom I'd shared many an adventure on the *Hazel,* flashed his big white teeth from ear to ear and seized my hand in both of his. "Hello, Prank! Long time no see! By golly, you smell alla' same Eskimo!"

Napook rowed the dory ashore to fetch Conover, and Murie, and next morning we finished ferrying our paraphernalia out from the schoolhouse. On the final trip we brought my sled dogs which the native boy Tommy had kept in prime condition all summer on a diet of skinned bird carcasses. The *Hazel* slipped out of Hooper Bay on the turn of the tide, and as the schooner rounded Point Dall I stood silently at the stern for a final look at the squalid, primitive, God-forsaken, fascinating village of Napakiagamute.

I was aware that the man Henderson had been eyeing me curiously for some time before he led me aside to finish introducing himself. He said he was the Assistant Chief, Bureau of Biological Survey, and that Dr. Nelson had sent him all the way from Washington, D.C. to run a check on the bird expedition. He told me that the good doctor had wanted more than anything else in the world to pay us a personal visit on his old stamping grounds, but had been counseled against it by his physician. Dr. Nelson was thirsty for every possible bit of information we could relay him through his assistant. All the way into the port of St. Michael where Mr. Henderson had to transfer to an upriver sternwheeler, he kept up a running fire of questions, and at the end talked me into giving him my report which was still in the rough, longhand stage. When we parted at St. Michael, Mr. Henderson said cryptically, "If ever I saw a man made for the north country, you're the one." It was a remark to be interpreted in two ways. It could mean I might be slated for some kind of promotion. It could also mean they intended to station me in the Arctic boondocks forever.

Conover decided to travel on the *Hazel* all the way to Nome before catching an ocean steamer south to Seattle, and then by train to Chicago with his cases of downy young specimens for the archives of the Field Museum. D. M. Le Bourdais, who turned out to be a Canadian newspaper correspondent, had a tragic subject on which to report before leaving the north country. After Assistant Chief Henderson and Murie departed at St. Michael and the *Hazel* was sailing across Norton Sound to Nome it was Le Bourdais' turn to question me. Did I, he asked casually, know Alan Crawford, Lorne Knight, Milton Galle, Fred Maurer, and the Eskimo woman known as Ada Blackjack? And by this question I guessed the object of the Canadian journalist's mission. He was here to learn what he could about the four men who had been put ashore on Wrangell Island in the Siberian polar sea at the instigation of Vihljalmur Stefansson, the lecturer, to boost sales for his book about the *Friendly Arctic*.

"Everybody in Nome knows them, or knows *about* them," I answered. "And nearly everybody who met them pleaded with them not to offer themselves as guinea pigs on so foolhardy a stunt, relying only on the word of a man who. . . ."

Le Bourdais interrupted to say he'd better let me know that he had for several years been Stefansson's secretary and lecture agent; that he was not inviting criticism of the "great man," but only wanted to have the facts which might explain why the "friendly Arctic" had proved to be such a death trap. Why had three of the nature students sent by Stefansson to Wrangell Island vanished without a trace? Why had the fourth man died in the agony of scurvy?

Wrangell Island was one of the coldest spots in the entire world, and by continguity a part of Asia. It was more than 400 miles northwest of Alaska's Cape Prince of Wales, and only 100 miles off the Siberian coast. Whalers knew that it remained locked behind mountainous ice barriers for several years at a time. Only occasionally and somewhat unpredictably would it be open to seagoing ships. It was beset with boreal winds of unimaginable violence. Enormous, churning icebergs guarded it fiercely against human intrusion. When Nome veterans—who themselves knew a thing or two about cold weather perils —tried to dissuade the Knight-Crawford-Galle-Maurer party from being marooned on this frigid prison with barely enough supplies to last out a single winter, their advice was scoffed at. "That's the very idea," said one of the members. "We're going to live off the country."

They had it all figured. They were going to shoot polar bears and seals for food, use their blubber for oil lamps, and Ada Blackjack was going to tan the hides and sew their clothing. They were going to trap white foxes, and return famous and wealthy.

Everybody in Nome knew the cruel results. *It was three long years before another boat could land on Wrangell Island.* When the gas schooner *Donaldson* out of Nome finally bucked through, it found only the Eskimo woman Ada Blackjack still alive. The white leader Lorne Knight's skeleton was in the sleeping bag where he had wasted away from scurvy. According to the terrified Ada, the other three members of the Party—Alan Crawford, Milton Galle, and Fred Maurer—had made a desperate bid for life by striking out over a hundred miles of jumbled ice cakes and salt water channels for the Siberian mainland, and she had never seen them again. In a local camera shop I had been privileged to examine secretly some of the gruesome photographs and ghastly remains of the ill-fated, hushed-up attempt to support a lecturer's theory.

Earlier in that summer of 1924 journalist D. M. Le Bourdais had himself made a harrowing trip to Wrangell Island on the whaler *Herman* to interview yet another trapping party sent there the year before to get rich and lay claim to the place in the name of Stefansson. They were unable to penetrate the icy barrier and had to return to Nome with no news of the trappers. *Later it was learned that the men had already been removed from the island—by the Russians!* All thirteen trappers had been taken prisoners and loaded aboard the ice breaker *Red October*—the same Russian patrol vessel which had once given me such a bad time around Big Diomede Island. Their furs had been confiscated and the men taken 2,000 miles to Vladivostok, some of them never to be seen again. By this act the USSR made it plain that Wrangell Island was their property, as it is to this day, and that they did not take kindly to colonization attempts by Vihljalmur Stefansson or anyone else. From these incidents and from the blunt remarks he heard around Nome, I would have been surprised if the confidence of Le Bourdais—himself a sincere, high-grade man—in Stefansson's "friendly Artic" had not been somewhat shaken before he departed from Nome.

Months before when egg collector Brandt left Hooper Bay for the "Outside," I had entrusted him with a letter to Klondy Nelson, the pretty co-owner of my dogteam, promising to have the team back in Nome for her to drive on the first snow of the winter. But when I sorted through six months' accumulation of mail at Nome, the answer was not very encouraging. She was busy with her violin studies in Seattle, wrote Klondy; she was leading a string quartet in one of the large hotels; she was doing some concert work; she had no plans for coming back to Nome that winter. That was all, except a brief footnote: "I still hope to see those dogs again some day, so please take good care of them."

It was the one thing I didn't do. On my first winter patrol, a grueling, 1,700-mile, 80-day trip covering the entire length of the Kuskokwim River, the team was struck down with distemper and every one of Klondy's dogs were wiped out by the pneumonia-like epidemic. Gloomily aware that I was probably severing the last thread of interest between us, I penned her the bad news. Much to my surprise, she answered promptly, and this time I read her footnote over several times: "If you ever get down to Seattle, I'll be glad to see you."

Klondy Nelson wasn't the only Nomeite deserting the old gold camp. In the four years I'd been there, the steamer *Victoria* had been steadily draining away its inhabitants, and the time was near when only a few diehards and a spate of summer tourists would walk its rickety boardwalks. It was still unique in a bleakly barren sort of way. It would always bear the charm of utter isolation from a crowded world. Its red sunsets slowly fading into the pastel green of Bering Sea would always be glorious. But now I had carried out most of Dr. Nelson's assignments and the data had been incorporated in a bill before Congress to give Alaska its first game law. In another sense, too, I'd accomplished what the gold rush pioneers had done. I'd mined out the rich pockets of adventure and discovery.

I began to wonder about the rest of Alaska I'd heard about—the birch and spruce wilderness of the interior, the giant moose, the moss-carpeted plateaus where caribou grazed by the hundreds of thousands, the highest mountains in America, the southeastern rivers teeming with salmon and brown bears, the mysterious Aleutian Islands stretching to Japan, smoking with volcanoes and trembling with earthquakes, their fog banks possibly still shielding the last of the rare northern sea otters. Would I ever get a chance to see the rest of this great Territory? Or when Mr. Henderson told me he "never saw a man better fitted for the north" was he trying to say that Nome was the end of the line?

If I needed any further confirmation that the once wildest gold camp in Alaska was skidding downhill to the obscurity of a ghost town, it was supplied by an old timer who claimed to know all the signs. Big Hans, growing new whiskers to replace the ones he'd shaved off for the funeral of a painted lady, came right to the point.

"I seen it happen in the Klondike an' ag'in at Rampart," growled Big Hans, "an' now its happenin' here. We're losin' our girls." The giant bit a corner off his tobacco plug and chewed it morosely until he could work up an angry spit. "Hell, there ain't hardly any of 'em left behind the boardwall any more. A man could freeze to death on a winter night an' no place to go."

I said I guessed I knew what he meant. On the last sailing of the *Victoria* there'd been quite an exodus of "girls."

"That ain't the trouble," cut in Big Hans. "Them were just young fly-by-night, summer time floosies that come an' go like the tourists. I'm talkin' about the real old time dance hall girls, the ones who made this camp a fit place to live—Sourdough Gertie, Deepwater Dorah, Halibut-face Mary, Dawson Kitty and the Oregon Mare. We're losin' them, too."

Big Hans brought me up to date on what had been going on during my absence in the Yukon Delta, and it was a sad story he told. Frenchy Joe, no friend, had started it all by marrying Sourdough Gertie and taking her out to live in his cabin on the Kougarok. Right after that, Charlie the Bear made off with Halibut-face Mary. A stinker named Misery Chris eloped with Toodles, and the King of Denmark stood up before the preacher with Deepwater Dorah. There were more marriages in the offing. The camp had shrunk too small to support a red-light district and the ladies were up for grabs. Big Hans gave me the shocking news and spelled out the meaning.

"Son, any time the girls begin comin' out of the cribs an' livin' private, the camp is goin' to hell!"

That winter the Nome gossips had so many true stories going they couldn't make up any better lies. The camp was split right down the middle of Front Street on whether to invite the newly married "girls" into their social gatherings, or hold their noses in the air. The fact of history is that in almost every case the old dance hall habitués became the strictest sort of wives. They didn't play around, nor allow their spouses to stray, a few even bore children in their late years, and in time were accepted and their primrose past forgotten.

In the lengthening daylight of February, Napook came around one morning with a proposition I couldn't resist. Would I like ketchum hunt Eskimo-style out on Bering Sea ice? Dr. Nelson had wanted me to make a report on winter wildlife on Bering Sea, and that night we bivouacked alongside an open lead far out among the sapphire-tinted bergs. Napook shot a ring seal and cut its blubber into strips for use as fuel in a stove made from a 5-gallon kerosene can. We ate seal ribs boiled until the dark flesh fell away from the bones, naturally salted in sea water. I melted ice, which is always fresh even at sea, and made a pot of coffee. We huddled in our furs in the lee of an upthrust slab until darkness settled, watching the glistening heads of seal popping the surface, and listening to the crash and ringing reports of the ice field splitting around us. Then with rifles handy in case a polar bear might come prowling in for a visit, we crawled into our sleeping bags stretched inside the kayaks we'd hauled out to retrieve game. I slept profoundly as the wind howled eerily across the white wilderness of the frozen ocean.

Even in the coldest days of winter the swirling currents and gale-force winds kept the ice pack grinding out open channels, and as I lay on my stomach at the edge of the floe I could make out tiny shrimp-like forms clouding the green water, and among them enormous schools of 6-inch fishes. Food was here in massive abundance for hardy diving birds like guillemots and murrelets, and for great herds of whales when the spring breakup made room among the floes. The presence of eiders indicated that not far below were beds of bivalves on which these hardy ducks mainly live. And as always, the moving edge of the ice field attracted seals. Napook's rusty old .30-.30 rifle cracked steadily during the day, and though he seemed to be scoring mostly near misses, the flat ice pan around our "camp" became heaped with carcasses. Contemplating them brought me to the biggest discovery of the trip. It was the realization that Napook had hornswoggled me again. He'd tricked me into going on the ice hunt only because he needed my dogteam to haul his blubbery plunder back to Nome.

I was no sooner back in the Survey office when Big Hans came thumping across the high drifts in his mukluks. Things were going from bad to worse behind the boardwall. The compound was in darkness most of the time, and hardly any girls around to open the doors to a man on a cold night. Snarled Big Hans, "Damnif I don't quit this camp!"

Me, too, I told Big Hans, and showed him a wireless message just delivered by the Signal Corps Station: CONGRESS TODAY PASSED FIRST ALASKA GAME LAW BUREAU BIOLOGICAL SURVEY OFFICE NOME BEING ABOLISHED END THIS FISCAL YEAR LETTER FOLLOWS E. W. NELSON.

ℚ17 Last Days at Nome

Morale in Nome always sunk to its lowest ebb in the month of March, and the one I spent waiting for Dr. Nelson's letter to drop the other shoe on my career was the worst of them all. Blizzard after blizzard screamed off Bering Sea to pound the Bureau of Biological Survey headquarters. Powder fine snow came spitting into the office through the tiniest cracks, and an open keyhole in one of the back rooms let in enough snow to fill it to the ceiling. It seemed at times as if every building in Nome must collapse before the battering-ram of the wind, and bury its inhabitants alive. Most of the sod-roofed shacks could be located only by stovepipes sticking up through the drifts, with only the heat of red-hot stoves below to keep them from clogging tight.

For days on end, sometimes not knowing whether it was night or day outside, the residents cowered in their homes with nothing to do except stoke their fires, read their old books over again, and suffer sour stomachs from a gas-forming diet of beans, rancid bacon, and sourdough flap-jacks. Twenty years earlier, as the then budding novelist Rex Beach huddled alone in his cabin on Dry Creek wrapped in blankets while he penned the first rough draft of *The Spoilers,* he had moaned, "The real *Call of the Wild* is not a wolf howl. It's the dyspeptic belch of a miner."

One day as I sat with queasy stomach skinning a Pacific eider drake I'd shot during the ice hunt with Napook, wondering what kind of scientific research I might under-take to help while away the tedium, an inspiration came to me. Why not count the feathers on a duck?

It took me a week to pluck and tally the wings. The re-sults were confusing. There seemed to be 43 more feathers on one wing than the other. I started patiently to recheck, but the feathers blew all around the room and I had to give it up. Also, there was a problem of even greater magnitude. How to tell feathers from fuzz, especially at the butt end of the duck! As the storm screamed outside, I wrestled alone with this crucial question. It was too much for me. Suddenly, I hurled the whole feathery mess into a corner and contented myself with a guess of 5,000.

I wasn't even close. Somebody else, with more fortitude than I, later stayed with the job until the last pinfeather was jerked free. A lady by name of Phoebe Knappen, em-ployed in the Research Section of the United States Fish and Wildlife Service, persevered to tweeze the plumage off a mallard. Her count rocked the bird-lover's world. It was an utterly incredible 11,903! Such an astonishing achievement deserved a better fate than to be eclipsed soon afterward by a gentleman named Pierce Brodkorb. With the assistance of a duck of the pintail species, he set a new record of 14,914. There had to be an explanation for this discrepancy of 3,011. At first I was inclined to accept the theory that a pintail simply had more feathers than a mallard. But on maturer thought, I was driven to the conclusion that as Mr. Brodkorb worked on the butt end of his duck he inadvertently mixed more fuzz with his feathers.

Seeking relaxation from our separate frustrations, Big Hans and I sought surcease in Billie Code's Theatre one roaring March night to watch a streaked and flickery movie depicting an elephant hunt in Africa. To help brighten the moments while the operator spliced and rethreaded film and corrected arc-light flame-outs, Big Hans had fetched along a small demijohn of local moonshine. By the time the film fluttered into its climax, the whiskered giant's head had dropped on his chest. His eyes were closed and he was snoring blissfully. As a charging bull elephant with enormous flapping ears filled the screen and came charging straight at a man aiming a rifle, I prodded my sleeping companion awake.

"Look!" I yelled.

Big Hans threw back his head, cocked a bleary eye open for a second, then collapsed again. "Who the hell," he mumbled, "couldn't hit an elephant?"

A month later, *I couldn't!* It happened in the foothills back of Nome during a rabbit hunt; not for the common varying hare one kicks out from underfoot all through the interior bush, but for a special pure-white giant with black ear-tips found sparingly beyond the limit of trees in Alaska. The huge Arctic hare was wild as a mountain sheep. It could sail like a bird over the hardpacked drifts, and if you missed the first shot you might not approach within range again all day.

In the lengthening sunlight of April, I drove my dog-team thirty miles into the Sawtooth Mountains to an abandoned prospector's hovel to establish rabbit headquarters. Next morning before skirting along under a great snow cornice hanging high overhead I took the usual precautions of a man in strange, wild country. I made a careful survey of the camp location to orient its position in the folding hills, because this tar-papered hut was the only shelter for many miles. Before I passed out of sight on a ridge, I took still another long look, and it was well that I did.

A blob of snow in the shadow of a drift suddenly came to life and vaulted away over a hog-back as if it had wings. My first shot kicked snow behind it, and I began trudging along on its trail. The spring sun had put a sheen on the snow surface. The glistening hills were bouncing reflections into my eyes, and after an hour or two they began to sting as though they were full of sand. I fished in a pocket for my smoked-glass snow-goggles. I'd left them in the cabin! But somewhere ahead I spotted two dark spots marking the ear-tips of the ghost hare and I thought I could get by without snow glasses long enough to shoot it and get back to the prospector's shack. But unaccountably the rabbit ears floated off into space and vanished. The hills and the sky blurred into total whiteness. After a while I couldn't have hit an elephant, or anything else, because I was snowblind!

I'd had touches of it before. Snowblindness, I knew, was sunburn of the eyes. Normal overhead sunshine caused no trouble because the pupils were protected by hat visors and jutting eyebrows. The damage had been inflicted on my eyes on this trip by the rays of the sun mirrored off the dazzling surface of the melting snow shooting directly up into the retina. The dangerous violet rays had actually scorched the unprotected under side of the eye, and the effect had been like a flash burn from a welder's torch. Prolonged exposure could result in more than mere temporary blindness; it could even bring on permanent loss of sight. I realized that I must somehow grope my way back to the hut.

Though I'd made many turns in pursuing the big rabbit, the situation was not hopeless. There was no call to panic. The weather had turned mild. I could tell when I was facing the full heat of the sun, which in midday would be due south. There had been a slight breeze against my left ear when I left the cabin. Now, if I put the other ear to it and held a steady course it was bound to take me back in the right general direction. The rest would depend on how well I could play my memory tape backwards, reversing the ridges and gulches. Finally I would have to rely on a trick which I must save until the time was ripe to try it.

The agony of hot ashes in my eyes was not quite so severe when I kept them tightly lidded, and in this way I stumbled like a blind man uphill and down, sometimes bumping full face against a wall of snow, or skidding into a ravine bottom. I was moving down what I hoped would be the last long slope leading to the hut when one of my snowshoes felt as if only the tail was resting on snow, and the forward part on nothing at all. Lying flat on the surface I reached forward to feel with a mitted hand. There was nothing but sheer emptiness. It could mean only one thing: that I had reached the dizzy overhang high above rabbit headquarters; that I was at that moment on the very edge of the snow cornice I'd looked up at in the morning before starting out. One more step would have launched me on a world record snowshoe jump!

Scrambling back out of danger, I probed gingerly along the ridge until it sloped down into a snow-filled draw which should lead past the prospector's shack. Now was the time to play my ace in the hole. Cupping hands, I shouted at the top of my voice, calling out the name of each sled dog in my team.

I'd hit it closer than I'd dared to hope. What I heard first was the faint jingling of chains as the dogs roused from their naps and stood on their feet. I yelled again, and there came a chorus of howls. Guided by the serenade, I climbed out of the gully and skinned my nose squarely against the tar-papered wall of the hut. Applications of wet tea leaves and the blessed cool darkness of the cabin eased the pain, and restored enough sight to let me make a night time drive back to Nome.

While I was treating my eyes with a boracic acid solution prescribed by the little white-haired doctor in Nome, my devious ally Napook regaled me with a grisly account of a terrifying little monster which lived out on Bering Sea, and darted through the water faster than the human eye could follow. I didn't let on, but I'd already heard about the dreaded U-gu-gin-uk from the Eskimo Tommy of Hooper Bay. According to legend, the tiny, sharp-muzzled terror was likely at any time to drill a hole up through the bottom of a seal-hunter's kayak, enter his bowels, and run riot all through his alimentary system, even popping out his ears to catch its breath before diving back in again. This much was folklore, but Napook had a twist of his own. During my absence on the ghost rabbit hunt, he was quite sure he had been pursued by one of these living drills, and had barely escaped being reamed out like a swiss cheese. He was afraid to go back to the scene alone, but if I would drive my dogteam out there to the edge of the ice, he thought he could point out U-gu-gin-uk and maybe the white man's magic could destroy it.

He almost took me! For a moment I teetered on the edge of the pitfall Napook had dug for me, and then I pulled back. While I would be hunting for a sepia-colored thing no more than 2½-inches long and no bigger around than a pencil, and which would undoubtedly key out in my guide book as nothing but a common shrew, Napook would be shooting another slug of seals for me to freight back to town.

Though Napook took huge delight in pulling my leg with his sly stunts, and trying to make me a patsy for his operations, he was completely honorable. He'd dicker by the hours on a swap, but under no circumstances would he cheat me, or pilfer even the smallest object. In his vocabulary there were no obscenities. He accorded the same unfailing courtesy and happy smile to the lowest drunk in town as to the highest official. The color of a man's skin meant nothing to him. He was humble to all, subservient to none. Long before the rest of us had to face up to the problem of integration, Napook had settled it in his own way. There was one Negro in Nome, a deserter from a whaling ship. Napook called him the "black white man."

Napook's bronze face was generally wreathed in a wide grin, displaying the biggest and whitest teeth I ever saw on a human. His usual expression was one of sublime, contagious happiness, though I remember a time when he couldn't smile. When Dr. Nelson's lettered instructions finally arrived, Napook was one of the first to hear about them. After I'd explained to my old shipmate that this meant I would be leaving Nome and not coming back, Napook stared into space for several moments, tight-lipped and silent, his brown eyes clouded with sadness.

"Me talking sorry inside," he said at last.

I wrote Klondy about the new assignment and promotion; that I'd be making $16.67 more a month at Fairbanks. It wouldn't be quite so isolated as Nome: two days' train ride to Seward, and then only five more days on the steamer to Seattle. I said I might even try to take a leave of absence and go down there to look her up if the invitation still held.

There would be many more miles of game surveys to be made in the great birch and spruce forests of interior Alaska, so the new sled dogs I'd acquired, since losing the other team to distemper on the Kuskokwim, would be taken to Fairbanks on the river steamer right after the breakup. I told Klondy that the new team was one of the finest and handsomest ever assembled in the north. Every dog was a Siberian Husky racer; every one was pure white with pointed ears, blue eyed, and carried a bushy tail curled over its back. The leader's name was Jack Frost and his mate's name was Snowflake, and they were housebroke and gentle as kittens. When all twelve dogs were wearing their new harnesses decorated with red pom-poms of dyed reindeer hair, I took a photograph of them and sent it to Klondy along with the reminder that, of course, half of them belonged to her. And how would she like to be standing at the handlebars behind this string of beauties?

But after the letter had been posted, I realized it wasn't much to be offering a beautiful, talented girl, and my hopes weren't very high that I'd ever see her again.

¶18 Decision at Fairbanks

Like most Alaska gold strikes, Fairbanks was largely accidental. In the fall of 1901 when stampeders were deserting the Klondike to drift down the Yukon River on their way to the golden sands of Nome Beach, another group of adventurers headed upstream to open a fur trading post among the Tanana Indians. Heavy laden with wares and building materials, the sternwheeler *Revelle Young* thrashed full speed against the muddy currents of Tanana River, hoping to reach its headwaters before the freeze-up. But the pilot made a wrong turn at the mouth of Chena Slough and within a few miles the ship's paddles were flailing helplessly, and the hull was aground in rapidly falling water which always precedes the beginning of winter. In order to float free and escape downriver, the *Revelle Young* hastily off-loaded cargo on the bank of Chena Slough and left it in charge of the Northern Commercial Company's leader Barnette.

In those days everybody carried a gold pan, and to help pass the days several of the stranded men started out prospecting. It wasn't long before Felix Pedro came rushing back to the Chena Slough bank with the news that he'd hit it big. Colors were running a fabulous 50 cents to the pan! Racing madly against time, the men started shoveling gravel into hastily erected sluice-boxes, and until they clogged with ice it was a poor day if they didn't clean up a hundred dollars' worth of nuggets. On the first snowfall of the winter when dogteams came to visit them, the secret leaked out. Word was flashed to the world that another gold strike had been made in the very center of the Territory, and the name of the place was Fairbanks.

Though the Fairbanks boom days were over when I arrived in the summer of 1925, it was a well-to-do community of 2,500 people, and was calling itself "The Golden Heart of Alaska." It was second in size only to Juneau in the Southeastern Section, and had several hundred more inhabitants than the village of Anchorage on Cook Inlet, 300 miles to the south. While Fairbanks was 14 miles farther north than Nome, its summers were much warmer, sometimes soaring into the 90°s. The river-bottom soil was incredibly rich and the vegetation was lush. The all but continuous sunlight from mid-May to September sucked moisture up from the permafrost to form a perfect irrigation system, and cultivated plants grew to astonishing sizes in record time.

I found a huge, jovial, hollering Dutchman named Van Bibber to board my sled dogs on fish netted out of the slough behind his cabin at the going rate of five dollars per month. Van Bibber loved dogs, but lavished even more attention on his garden patch. He showed me the biggest cabbage I'd ever seen, and said it would probably go 50 pounds!

"Have to hire me a bulldozer to harvest it," roared Van, "An' I'll need a stump-puller for m' carrots an' rutabagas." A jungle-like mass of enormous, serrated leaves towered over our heads in a corner of the garden. "Rhubarb, son; three pies to a stalk!"

Most of the Fairbanks residences were log-cabin types made from spruce trees felled not far from where the *Revelle Young* had dumped its freight a quarter century ago. With Van Bibber's help I started hunting for a vacant building I could use as a combination home and office. Several were for sale for no more than $1,000 each; neat one- and two-room log bungalows with moose or caribou antlers nailed over the doorways; shaded with white birches; banked around the sides with gorgeous displays of blue delphiniums, iris, pansies, peonies, and petunias, with trellised sweet peas of extraordinary size and brilliance. Some of the cabins behind the white-painted picket fences even had adjoining greenhouses in which I could see tomatoes and cucumbers hanging from the vines.

I typed a note to the Bureau of Biological Survey to let them know I had arrived in the new headquarters, ready for assignment. Then I wrote a much longer letter to Klondy Nelson in Seattle, telling her about this exciting new part of Alaska; that I had rented a beautiful, flower-banked log cabin right next to Ernest Patty, dean of the college that was being built on a hill four miles out of town.

Dean Patty drove me to the site of the college in his T-model Ford and introduced me to a man in carpenter's apron helping nail up siding on a two by four framework. "Meet Judge Bunnell," said Patty, and the President of the farthest-north college in the world set aside his hammer to shake hands.

Among the projects being tackled by the sprouting college was that of trying to develop special types of livestock for future settlers in that part of the Continent. In charge of the work was my old friend L. J. Palmer with whom I had shared office space in Nome when he was surveying the reindeer herds of the coastal tundra.

They were bringing in buffalos from the National Bison Range in Montana, and muskoxen from Greenland. They were cross-breeding Alaska's wild white mountain sheep with domestic woollies from the States. Long haired Yaks from Tibet had already been mated with hardy Scotch Galloway cattle; the progeny was called *Galyak* and it was hoped they would be able to forage for themselves all through the rigors of the Fairbanks winters. A special experiment was that of breeding the long-limbed, much heavier, native caribou with the dwarfed European reindeer, teach them to eat hay, and perhaps develop a milking strain such as the Laplanders had already done in Arctic Scandinavia.

President Bunnell, who looked like Robert Benchley and possessed some of his puckish humor, told me he had a special request from a cranky old sourdough to turn some African gorillas loose in Alaska to cross with the grizzly bears, because "there's too dam' many cheechakos gittin' away from the grizzlies by climbin' trees."

The cross-breeding experiments weren't all as crazy as they seemed, argued Judge Bunnell. In ages past, Alaska had produced much odder creatures than he dared hope to duplicate at the college. The President led me downhill to an open shed to witness the evidence, and to meet the little German scientist, Otto Geist, who was going out of his mind trying to sort out the tremendous masses of material being dumped at his outdoor laboratory. They'd heard about my "old bones" pickups in the surf below the ice cliff in the Arctic Ocean, and now they showed me fossil finds of a thousand times greater magnitude. In the new era of big-scale mining being initiated in the Fairbanks gold fields, giant hydraulic nozzles were shredding away a hundred feet of frozen muck to lay bare the earth surface of 50,000 years ago, exposing a game field the like of which did not exist anywhere in the present world. Truckload after truckload of prehistoric remains had been carted from the ancient bedrock to the college and piled in enormous heaps. There were bones from toothpick size up to tree trunk dimensions, teeth big as cobblestones, ivory tusks 15 feet long, skulls, horns, swatches of reddish hair, and hides showing the claw marks of long gone predators. All around the college the earth had once shook with the tread of mammoths, mastodons, supervisons, ton-sized bears, giant elk-moose, lions bigger than any existing forms, and savage bob-tailed tigers with 6-inch stabbing teeth. There had been yaks, antelopes, camels, horses, hyena-like wolves, titanic ground sloths . . . the list went on and on, with new species being discovered from day to day as an overburden of 300 centuries accumulation was washed away by streams of water from the nozzles.

Sighed Judge Bunnell, "What a wildlife paradise the campus must have been before the Ice Age!"

I said this part of Alaska was still a great game country, perhaps the best in North America, and the proof was all around us. Spruce and sharptail grouse clucked in the bushes, and snowshoe hares hopped about on the new lawns. There were moose tracks in the willows, and black bear were frequently sighted from the dormitory windows. Not long before my visit a great migration of caribou had swept across the dirt road between the college and Fairbanks, tearing down fences and clothes-lines and trampling fields of experimental wheat. The students could go big game hunting between classes.

The very abundance of the wild game around Fairbanks put me off to a poor start with the recently appointed game commissioner who was to represent this region of the Territory under the new Alaska Game Law at the annual meetings in the capitol city of Juneau. When old timer Doc Whitney drove me out the narrow dirt road to show me the surroundings and do a little hunting, we were hardly clear of the town when caribou stragglers started showing. They paid almost no attention to the occasional car that chugged out to the placer gold claims, in fact, tried to race us across the road. The bag limit was five and you could shoot bulls, cows or calves.

The sourdough Doctor drove me to a high ridge where antlers on the skyline looked like waving brush tops. He had an old tunnel in perpetually frozen ground not far away where game would keep hard and sweet for months.

"We'll load up and head for the ice shaft," he said. "Don't shoot any young ones. They're stringy as snowshoe webbing. You want good eating, pick the biggest bull in the herd. Catch one before the rut, like now; there's no better wild meat."

We came around a steep knob and there was a hog-fat, white-necked monarch with antlers that belonged in a museum. It was standing spraddle-legged in the middle of the road, panting like a dog. I jumped out of the car, levered a soft-point cartridge into the firing chamber of my .30-40 Krag and looked up in time to see the bull poised on the break of the highway, ready to ramble some more. Just as I squeezed the trigger it jumped. I heard it crash-land and roll fifty yards almost straight down into a white birch thicket at the bottom of a gully.

We scrambled down over rocks and fallen trees to where the bull was wedged between two saplings. It looked as if it might weigh 400 pounds, and I was feeling quite satisfied with myself until Doc Whitney, knife in hand and ready to operate, felt called upon to deliver a lecture.

"The next caribou you kill on the lower side of the road, you'll tote uphill by yourself," he began sternly. He looked over his shoulder at the steep cliff up which we'd have to haul the carcass. "I hope none of my friends come by and catch me down here, because this is what I call a tenderfoot stunt." With knife blade between his fingers, Doc Whitney ran an incision neatly from vent to brisket. "If you don't know what I mean, you better let me take the next one."

We must have passed up a couple of hundred caribou before the Doc spotted a bull to his liking. It was staring down at us from the edge of an overhang no more than sixty feet away. When Doc eased the car to a stop, stepped out and let fly, the white-necked bull rolled gently down the gravel slope until it thumped against the rear fender of the car, kicked a couple of times, then stiffened with all four feet in the air.

"See what I mean?" said Fairbanks' first Game Commissioner, Doc Whitney. "Never shoot a caribou on the downhill side of the road."

I did some hunting on my own a few evenings later in Van Bibber's backyard. To save his super-colossal vegetables from the shuttling jaws of the wild rabbit hordes, Van Bibber patroled the edges of his garden in the evening with a .22 rifle, and I followed with a pair of tweezers to pluck the ticks off the long-eared pests. I had a hunch that these ticks not only carried germs of epizootic diseases that periodically reduced the snowshoe hare populations to the vanishing point, but also transmitted the dread disease of tularemia and even spotted fever. There had been several cases reported from Alaska. The Bureau of Biological Survey laboratory had sent out a call for its field men to make a sample collection of ticks found on wild animals.

I was squatting beside a pile of shot rabbits, transferring the all but invisible ticks to a vial when I became aware of Van Bibber looming overhead, straining his eyes, but apparently seeing nothing. He straightened up after a while to stare at me incredulously. "Young feller," he bellowed, "one of us has got to be crazy, an' it ain't me."

My next salary check was postmarked Juneau instead of Washington, D.C. and an accompanying letter conveyed the unwelcome information that while the Washington Bureau would continue to exercise certain controls over the new wildlife setup, henceforth my immediate supervision would come from the Juneau office of the Alaska Game Commission.

There was only one part of the letter I liked. It was the footnote: "Dr. Nelson has instructed that copies of all your reports go to him, and that any orders by him will have precedence over those of the Juneau office."

I could sense the tension of dual authority in the air, and I knew it wouldn't be long before I would face trouble because of it. Not long afterward it flared with dramatic suddenness, and the spark that set it off was an exciting letter from Klondy in Seattle. "Fairbanks," she wrote, "seems a very nice place and if you ever get down this way I'd love to hear more about it."

I hadn't taken a day off since joining the Service, but now was the time! I wired the Juneau office to request a month's leave of absence, and on second thought sent a duplicate request to Washington, D.C. Juneau replied first. The telegram was signed by someone I didn't know and it was to the point. The man said: REQUEST FOR LEAVE NOT GRANTED THIS TIME.

I took the message over to the Signal Corps Station to make sure it hadn't been garbled in transmission, and then I sent out two more telegrams of my own. The first one was to Klondy in Seattle telling her I would be arriving there on the next southbound steamer. The second wire was to the Juneau office. It consisted of four words: RESIGNING EFFECTIVE THIS DAY.

ℚ19 Honeymoon Below Zero

It was a two-day ride south over the 411-mile narrow gauge tracks from Fairbanks to the seaport at Seward. As I mounted the gangplank of the steamer for Seattle, the purser met me with another telegram from the Juneau office of the Alaska Game Commission. The message said that if I wished to withdraw my resignation they would then grant me the leave of absence I'd requested. All I had to do was report to the headquarters office and sign some papers. I crumpled up the yellow sheet, tossed it over the side, and told the purser there would be no answer.

The next development came three days later when the steamer was moored alongside the dock in Juneau to let off and take on passengers. A carrot-topped young fellow who looked like a bank clerk but who said he was the assistant executive officer of the game department, looked me up with some papers to fill out so they might give consideration to furlough on pay. Again, I refused. I'd been doing a slow burn all the way across the Gulf of Alaska, and the earlier injustice of denying a short leave to a man who had spent five unbroken years of service in the far north, still rankled in my mind. Also, there seemed to be something odd about their conciliatory attitude. I told Carrot-top to report back to his superior that my resignation was final. He shrugged his shoulders, spun on his heel, and I gained the impression that so far as he was concerned it was good riddance to a troublesome character. In my mood that suited me fine, too.

But other forces were in motion. That evening as the vessel twisted and slued through the famous Wrangell Narrows, I was accosted by a small, studious-looking, impeccably-attired gentleman who had come striding up the steamer gangplank just before it left Juneau. He measured me up and down through his pince-nez glasses, and evidently decided to make a head-on charge: "See here, Dufresne, I want an end to this talk about resigning."

I felt like an overgrown lout of a schoolboy being dressed down by a little professor, and for a moment failed to catch the significance of his next words. "Go ahead with your leave," he snapped, "I'll cover as much of it as I can on expense-paid status. But report back to Fairbanks when it's over."

It was fair enough, I guess, but I wasn't even thinking about Fairbanks now. I was thinking about Seattle and the blue-eyed beauty I would soon be meeting. The steamer had entered the quiet waters of Puget Sound and was rounding Magnolia Bluff at slow bell ready for warping into the wharf at Seattle, when the Juneau man came around for a final talk. After making sure no one else was within earshot, he handed me a telegram he'd been carrying around in his pocket for several days. It was addressed to him from the Washington office of the Bureau of Biological Survey. It was a sort of ace-in-the-hole he was most reluctant to expose. As near as I can recall the words after forty years, it said: SHALL HOLD YOU PERSONALLY RESPONSIBLE IF DUFRESNE ALLOWED RESIGN, and it was signed E. W. NELSON.

Again the great wildlife scientist who had influenced so much of my life—the good doctor I had never met nor was ever destined to meet—had come to my rescue. Only this time I wasn't sure I wanted to be saved.

Nor was Klondy sure she wanted to go back to Alaska. There wasn't any question about our love for one another. We knew that in the moment we met again. It was there in both of us, deep and abiding, and I guess it had always been there since our first meeting. Wherever the future took me, I knew there must be room at my side for this strikingly handsome, talented, strong-willed girl of the north.

The decision was much more difficult for Klondy. She was launched on a promising career with her violin, she had more jobs than she could handle around Seattle, and had just been offered a contract to appear as a soloist on the Orpheum Circuit from coast to coast. But something transcending this opportunity was troubling Klondy, and after a while she told me what it was that held her back.

It was her father; a father she hadn't seen since she was a little girl. He had been what the old timers in Alaska called a "real stampeder." He had found gold in the Klondike and Alaska camps. Each time he had left his family to rush to some rumored bigger and better bonanza over the next hill. With him, as with many other footloose pioneers of the early days, it wasn't really the gold they wanted. It was *finding the gold*. Klondy had seen her roving parent only at intervals in her childhood. The family had gone from rags to riches and back to rags again and again, and then there had been the final embittering blow when her mother was deserted in penniless condition and died of grief soon afterward.

"You know, you could be my father all over again," she said one night as we visited in the apartment she shared with a lady pianist. "Father and his gold over the next hill; you and your wild geese calling; both of you chasing something as illusive as a rainbow." She considered her next words carefully. "I couldn't go through the lonely days that my mother had to suffer. I couldn't stand the terrible disillusionment of watching you drift away like my father did."

It was then I confessed to Klondy that I had quit my job with the government and might not be going back to the north again. "Right now, your career down here looks a lot more promising than mine will ever be in Alaska," I said. "Maybe I can stay here and try to fit into a new line of work." During the past three or four years I had placed several feature articles with Seattle newspapers. Maybe they could find a place for me on their regular staff.

Klondy studied me carefully through the long lashes of her half-closed eyes, then interrupted. "Tell me more about our white dogs," she said, and before I realized it I was pouring my heart out about the part of Alaska she had never seen.

I was painting a picture of the Fairbanks log cabins shaded with white-barked birches and banked with flowers. I was unrolling red carpets of lingonberry vines across the nearby hills, and dotting the autumn landscape with groves of quaking aspen turning gold in the first frost. I was filling in the background with snow-chiseled peaks rising so high they seemed to melt away in the blue space of the heavens. I was telling her about the incredible herds of caribou and moose and mountain sheep. The fall skies, I said, would be alive with the sound and sight of migratory water-fowl winging south out of the Arctic. I tried to describe the exhilaration of standing at the handlebars of a dogsled racing over pure, new snow in the profound stillness of the Alaska forests, the good neighbors, the challenge of it all . . .

Klondy stopped me with a hand on my arm. "*Why don't you show me the rest?*" she asked.

She added something about the north country being in my blood, and what was the use of pretending anything different? She said she knew, because it was in hers, too. "Somehow, we'll manage."

We spent the first part of our honeymoon on a steamer ploughing through the big seas on the way back to Alaska. Dr. Nelson had sent us a warm message of congratulations, and the Juneau office had also wished us well. But when the train puffed to a stop at Fairbanks and we stepped out on the station platform, the subzero cold was like a shock. The air was filled with frozen mist, and the streets so dimly lighted I could hardly find the log cabin I'd rented. It didn't look pretty any more. The bright yellow leaves had fallen from the white birch trees, and the beautiful flowers were all dead. When I pushed open the slab door, the interior of the cabin seemed crude as a trapper's hovel compared with Klondy's nice apartment in Seattle. I muttered something about maybe we ought to go to a hotel until I got a chance to fix it up and buy some decent furniture.

"Nonsense," said Klondy. "This will do just fine. Now, let's get a fire going. We'll fix it up together . . ."

The next day Dean Patty's jolly young wife came over to greet her new neighbor with a friendly hug. I heard the booming voice of Van Bibber at the door with an armful of his supercolossal vegetables. Game Commissioner Doc

Whitney delivered my share of the caribou meat he'd been holding for me in his ice-tunnel cold storage. They all stayed for coffee, and Klondy said it was like the good old days at Nome; everybody so hospitable, and she knew she was going to love it here in Fairbanks.

A couple of days later the weather softened. With our heater rumbling and the flames glowing through the isinglass front, the sweet scent of birch wood perfumed the old cabin. Klondy and I looked out the window at the first snow of the season sifting down; not with the winds and bluster of Nome but in silence so calm that the big flakes formed a mushroom on top of every fence post, and clung to the tiniest twigs on the leafless birches.

"It's like a Christmas card," said Klondy. "It's what I've been missing."

Her words stabbed my conscience. How could I break the news that this first snowfall meant something else to me, that I must leave on a dogteam patrol into the Indian country along the Yukon?

That November was one of the coldest in central Alaska history. After two feet of snow had fallen, the mercury plummeted downward to dangerous levels. By the time I had finished my meetings with the Fort Yukon trappers it was 65 degrees below zero and most dogteam travel along the Yukon River ice had been suspended. Only in the direst emergency would a man subject himself to its perils, and I didn't meet another musher on the trail all the way back to Fairbanks. When I came bursting anxiously through the slab door into our cabin, I saw at a glance that I wasn't the only one who had suffered.

It had been almost as cold in Fairbanks. The stove-pipe leading from our heater up through the sodded roof had clogged with soot and creosote. In trying to clean out the old pipe Klondy had broken it in two, scattering ashes and soot all over the cabin. Dressed in fur parka and mukluks to keep from freezing, she was trying to restore order. Her face was smudged, she was gasping with fumes, she was angry, and when she first saw me she was ready to declare war. Her second look saved me. My face was purple from frost-bite, and I was staggering from fatigue. Without a word we fell into each other's arms, and suddenly in our shared misery, we were laughing.

Having done its worst in November, the Fairbanks winter became surprisingly mild during the month of December. Though the sun appeared above the distant Alaska Range for only three or four hours in the middle of the day, at night the moon shone with silvery brilliance in which we could read the print in the *Daily News-Miner*. Warmly clad in furs, we drove our team of white Siberians almost nightly around the outlying country. We could see snowshoe hares bouncing across the way in the bright moon rays. Several times the dogs surprised horned and great gray owls as they fed on killed rabbits, and it was a common occurrence to spy red, cross, and sometimes pure silver foxes, as well as tassel-eared Canada lynx prowling along the edges of the brush.

One night we had a race that nearly ended in disaster. Ahead, a huge, gaunt form blotted out the moonlight. The dogs were almost upon it when the bull moose stopped chomping willow twigs and took off straight down the trail, flinging clods of snow back at us from its flying hoofs. Klondy, at the handlebars, jammed on the foot-brake to no avail. Jack Frost, the team leader, was snapping at its hamstrings and his mates behind him had reverted to their wild ancestry as they howled for blood. Suddenly, the bull turned, plunged headlong through a thicket of willows and down over a steep cut bank into a frozen slough. The brakes finally snagged at the edge of the drop-off and the dogs hung in mid-air by their collars, choking and strangling while the moose made its getaway.

Dr. Nelson had routed a letter through the Juneau office expressing interest in a midwinter survey of mountain sheep in the Wood River Mountains some 40 miles south of Fairbanks. Van Bibber, who had built a trapper's hut in the last timbered draw leading up to the peaks, offered it for headquarters.

"Want to come along?" I asked Klondy.

"Try to stop me," she retorted. "If we freeze, at least we'll freeze together."

We established base camp in the snow-buried hovel, and then toiled higher up the slippery incline to pitch a small tent in a patch of scrub willows among the crests. There were mountain sheep on all sides. Wearing white drill parkas, we scaled the snow-covered crags, and by stalking cautiously against the wind were often able to approach within camera range. The white Dall sheep seemed to prefer the bleakest, windswept spurs for feeding. It was here that the snow cover was lightest, and only a few strokes of their sharp hoofs were needed to expose the short tufts of sweet mountain hay upon which they were feeding. Several times we spotted timber wolves against the blue skyline. As it had been since the beginning of time, these predators were levying toll among the game animals. Most of the sheep were too agile for the wolves to catch, but the old and weak ones in the herd were being pruned away by savage killers, and when we saw bloodspots on the snow we knew what had happend.

December was the mating season among the mountain

sheep. Sometimes, even before we could see them, we could hear their heads cracking together like rifle shots. We witnessed the smaller rams battered into retreat until only the lords with great full-curled horns were left with the females. Each monarch amassed a harem of twenty or more and began sniffing eagerly among them, riding ewe after ewe until it came to the end of the flock, then starting all over again with undiminished virility.

Under the magical radiance of the full moon, high in the cold, pure whiteness of the mountains, we crawled into our double sleeping bag for our last night in the tent. Streamers of northern lights played their changing colors across the canvas. Now and then the perfect silence of the peaks would be broken by the far away ululations of the wolves. There was the eerie feeling of remoteness, of being the only two people in the world. I mentioned something to Klondy about this being a night that would live in my memory forever . . .

She interrupted. "I'll give you something else to help you remember," she murmured drowsily. "I think I'm going to have a baby."

20 Life along the Yukon

From their earliest infancy, the two babies who came to bless our marriage—a girl with Klondy's light golden hair and later a boy as husky as a cub bear—shared our travels and adventures. They spent hours in dogsleds all bundled in furs. They slept soundly in river boats which were screened to keep the mosquitoes out and the babies in. They gazed out of tents at herds of caribou and moose. Before they were school age they had seen more wildlife than most people would see in a lifetime.

As I traveled and observed I became convinced that while the Alaska hinterlands had been explored for gold, the greater wealth of its fur and game and fishes had received little attention. It seemed to me that these renewable assets, which everybody took for granted, could be managed to yield an annual harvest of considerably more value than the gold.

Most abundant of all the big game resources were the caribou, outnumbering the combined totals of the moose, mountain sheep, wild goats, deer, and the bears. I remember a September morning when I ran our gasboat ashore on the upper Yukon River and climbed a nearby knoll overlooking a series of hills where the Circle Indians had reported an enormous migration of caribou. At first I saw nothing but the usual moose or two browsing on the willows, and a few black bears grubbing on the flame-colored patches of lingonberries, and of course the streamers of cranes and waterfowl from north to south across the autumn sky.

I must have dozed in the warm sun, because when I lifted my binoculars again a thicket of dead brush seemed to be spilling over the rim of a plateau and sliding out of sight into a gully. Suddenly, I realized that what I was seeing were the massed antlers of moving caribou. The big, clove-colored deer were spewing out of the crevices in the hills and marching along the skyline, more and more of them, hundreds and then thousands. Showing no fear of me, the hoof-clacking herds passed within a few feet and went skidding down a steep, clay bank into the muddy Yukon on both sides of our gasboat. Klondy and the youngsters were almost within touching distance as the animals plunged into the swirling flood and started for the other shore. Buoyed by their hollow hair, they swam with surprising speed, almost as if they were running half out of water.

A band of five hundred strikingly marked, silver-necked bulls split ranks around my knoll, emitting odd coughing sounds and dog-like barks. Their wide-spreading antlers, newly stripped of summer velvet, gleamed blood red in the low rays of the Arctic sun. Behind the herd sires came thousands of cows with smaller tines, and a traffic jam backed up at the river bank when some of the mouse-colored calves balked at taking the icy dive. As the pressure of onrushing animals shoved them helter-skelter down the slick ramp, I saw a very small young one being swept away in the rapids and heard Klondy cry out when it appeared to be doomed by the whirlpools below. Suddenly, a cow detached herself from the swimming herd and went racing downstream in pursuit. We saw her catch the little one against her flanks and prop it against the current until they reached the safety of a sandbar.

Farther up the river in the mountains behind the border village of Eagle, Jack Warwick, who had been with me on the 1924 expedition to Hooper Bay, was making a separate survey of the migrations. "I saw 50,000 caribou in a single day," wrote Jack, "and the run was on for 12 more days."

All up and down the Yukon the Indian smoke racks hung heavy with rib slabs, shoulders, and haunches of caribou meat dry-curing for their winter food supply. Hides were nailed on the sides of the log cabins and then stacked on the roofs and high-pole caches waiting to be tanned and sewed into moccasins, mitts, parkas, and sleeping bags. Because these restless animals were here today, gone tomorrow into the wilderness, nobody blamed the Indians and white settlers for slaughtering the caribou in wholesale quantities when they had a chance. There were times when it wasn't easy to come by these ghost deer.

During the same migration, for instance, a group of gold miners in a nearby diggings laid down their shovels and picked up their guns to lay in a stock of fresh meat. They were carrying every firearm in camp when they drove their trucks to a summit a few miles away. For two days they waited there for the fat bulls to walk into their guns, and then they returned to their mining. They hadn't seen a caribou, and that was only half the story.

The camp cook told me the rest of it. During the miners' "hunting" trip, the entire caribou herd had passed squarely through the center of the diggings. The excited beasts had knocked down jim-poles, bumped over sluice-boxes, carried away hung-out washing on their horns, and left an aftermath like a stampede of buffalos. The cook said all he could do was flap his apron to keep them from making off with the cook tent.

Mainstay of life along the Yukon was not the crazy caribou, nor the endless millions of snowshoe hares and ptarmigan. All the way up from Bering Sea 2,000 miles into the Canadian headwaters of the great river, the most important food product was salmon. As we chugged the lonely stretches of the gray flood—so thick with silt that the settlings in a glass of water would be one-third solid matter—it didn't seem possible that fish life could exist in important quantities. Yet, the salmon with marvelous stamina and instinct were able to find their way, blindly and without food, for hundreds of miles to reach the exact tributary where they had been hatched several years before. There, sometimes in the very riffle where their own life had started, they would deposit their pink roe. The timing would be so exact that within the hour they would gasp their last. In the strange life cycle of the salmon, it was doomed to be born an orphan and to die childless.

We could always tell when we were nearing an Indian village by the fishwheels slowly turning in the current, scooping out the fish from the turbid river and chuting them into holding boxes. During the summer the Indians cured tons of salmon, splitting each fish along the backbone and hanging it on a covered rack with just enough smudge from the constantly burning fires to ward off the bluebottle flies. Sometimes we could smell the pungent smoke long before the colorful red scaffolds came in sight.

At the end of the summer season the baled fish were as good as cash at the trading posts. Most of the dried product would be used to feed sled dogs, though the finer flavored king salmon species were often cut into narrow strips, brined and smoked with special care to become the mouth-watering "squaw-candy" of the Yukon.

The owners of the fishwheels would always invite us to help ourselves out of the holding boxes, and we would have our choice of flopping fresh whitefish, northern pike, grayling, red-meated salmon of two or three species, or giant sheefish. We would tie our gasboat alongside the little docks and spend the evening visiting with the friendly natives. Our youngsters would play with the Indian tots. Klondy would strike up conversations with the women and soon they would all be laughing hilariously over this blue-eyed girl's strenuous attempts to speak their language. This would give me a chance to visit with the men, to get their ideas on the kind of game laws which would be useful to them in safe-guarding their living.

They learned how to understand our problems in the matter of wildlife protection, and what was far more important, I learned to understand theirs. My reports to the Juneau office were many times in sharp contrast to the white man's rigid ruling, but I kept stressing the point that successful management of Alaska wildlife must be dovetailed with the ability of the native people to obey them. I learned that when an Indian was hungry he would kill to eat; that he had been doing this long before the first white man moved into the north country, and that he would continue to do so. More than once I expected to have my bluntly-worded reports greeted with a call for my resignation, but the worst I ever got were reprimands. Finally, even these tapered off. Instead, I received a formal notice that the head man at Juneau had been transferred out of Alaska. Coupled with this news was a rumor that Dr. Nelson might soon be retiring as Chief of the Bureau of Biological Survey and moving to Arizona for a worsening lung condition.

Meanwhile, life along the Yukon had its lighter moments. There was the saying we heard over and over again at every trading post and white village. It had to do with the definition of a "sourdough." There were variations, but the favorite version went like this: *A "sourdough" is a man who has seen the ice come and go in the Yukon, has shot a caribou, and slept with a squaw.*

The final fillip was added by a salty individual who was then governor of the Territory. At a banquet in Seattle he recited the sourdough definition, upon which a pert young miss seated at his elbow asked, "Governor, are you a sourdough?"

"No, my dear young lady," retorted the Alaska dignitary, "*I have never shot a caribou!*"

Each spring the Yukon ice went roaring out to sea in a catacylsmic spate of melting snow water. The gray flood dug new channels as it gouged deep into the bends to undermine the forests. Cabins and sometimes sections of old villages were toppled into the river and went churning away among giant ice slabs and uprooted trees. For every acre of land it claimed on the one side, the great river gave up equal parts of its old bed on the other side. A log cabin with the current swishing past its door in the fall might find itself far back from the river's edge after the high waters of next spring subsided. In a year or two sprouting willows would hide it from view.

Some of the old timers along the Yukon reminded me of their cabins. The river had shunted them into a sort of oblivion. Unseen and alone they smoked a few salmon, trapped a few beavers and muskrats, panned a little gold, and watched the Yukon ice come and go through the quiet years. Because nothing much worth remembering had happended since the gold rush, they recalled as if it were yesterday the hectic days of their youth: the Soapy Smith gang waylaying them with its crooked shell game at Skagway; the deadly toll of Chilkoot Pass; the whipsawed boats at Lake LeBarge; the strike at Klondike; the dance halls; the exodus from fading Dawson downriver toward a place called Nome where the beaches were said to be lined with gold!

Somehow, they'd drifted off the mainstream of the stampede. Some of them had succumbed to the charm of the native belles along the Yukon. Some had fallen under the lure of the great river itself and decided that here was where they wanted to live out their days. Some had found just enough gold along the Yukon tributaries to keep them looking for more. Now it was too late to move anywhere else, and for most of them their only fortunes were their memories.

Wally Laboski at Rampart had shared a cabin one long ago winter with a ruggedly handsome blond youth named Rex Beach who scribbled with a pencil and left Wally to cut all the firewood. He'd bought whiskey from Tex Rickard and Wyatt Earp in their tent saloons. He'd served on the vigilante committee who stripped the clothes off a thief and set him adrift on a raft for the mosquitoes to eat up. He'd seen a man shot dead over a card game.

The "Stepladder Kid," had traveled on a paddlewheel steamer with a famous writer of the period. "Feller named after a city," he reminisced. "Wait a minute, I'll think of it." He combed his whiskers thoughtfully. "Jack London!"

The Stepladder Kid, now pushing seventy, also remembered other river travelers. He'd seen a couple of prospector partners pull into the bank of the Yukon with their long poling boat, cut it in two with a crosscut saw, seal up the open ends, divide their possessions, and start out again each in his own half of the boat. "Cabin Fever got 'em," explained the Stepladder Kid. "God never meant fer two men to live together. That's why I don't want nobody else around here very long." I took the hint and moved on.

Old Alec Whately, dreamy in his dotage, couldn't seem to think of anything special about the gold rush. He'd hung on in Dawson quite a spell after most of the stampeders were gone, and he'd boarded with some folks called the Fischers. There'd been another fellow who ate there regular, a bank teller who wrote little skits for local talent shows, then finally started mailing his poems out to a publisher. The writing man's name was Robert Service. "Never seen a feller so crazy fer blueberry pie," said Old Alec.

At a bend along the Yukon he'd christened Purgatory, was a Swiss woodcarver who whittled out clocks for a pastime. When I stepped on a board across the pathway leading to his steep-roofed cabin, a wooden bear popped up in front of me. Nearby was a grave marked by a white cross, and the owner chuckled gleefully when he told me about it. The deputy marshal from Fort Yukon had made a special trip down to investigate the death. He'd dug up the grave to uncover a shoe-box in which reposed the remains of a bird called the Canada jay, but better known in the north country as the Camprobber. And then it was all clear to the deputy that he'd been hoaxed, because the epitaph on the white cross had read: *He Robbed my Cache.*

Another pioneer genius along the Yukon in later years made the town of Eagle a "must" stop for tourists and columnists, for here lived an old time resident who shot a bear to make himself a set of dentures, then used the teeth to eat the bear.

Still farther up the Yukon, enjoying good health thirty years after he'd been burned to ashes in the furnace of a river steamer, was a man by the name of McGee. The explanation was that Robert Service had chosen his name for its phonetic value in "The Cremation of Sam McGee." The man actually cremated had been an anonymous prospector.

In the final days of summer when the hills were aflame with color, and the blue smoke curled lazily upward through the red racks of drying salmon, a small airplane zoomed low over our houseboat, then cut across the hills to Fairbanks. In an hour it would be home. It would take us two weeks. Joe Crosson, the pilot, waved a gloved hand out of the open cockpit and in that instant I realized that gasboats and dogteams were doomed to obsolescence. Like the old gold rush characters they'd served, they'd had their day and would soon be fading away into the past. That night after we'd pulled in to shore to spend the evening, an old settler put it into words for us.

"The blasted things'll be buzzin' up an' down the river thicker'n mosquitoes," he predicted sourly. "Everybody'll start rushin' from one place to another. There won't be no time fer livin', an' I don't like it!"

Klondy and I felt the same unreasoning resentment. It marked the end of a golden era along the Yukon, and we didn't like it, either.

❡21 New Horizons

Dave, the colored man who served food to dogteam and auto travelers at a log cabin stop on the way from Fairbanks to Circle on the Yukon River, had a knack for turning the products of the north country into meals to remember. One fall when Klondy and I stopped our T-Model runabout in front of Dave's hostelry, he had a special treat for us. He'd been rambling over the hills and he'd found a giant puffball mushroom the size of a basketball. He'd gathered a bucket of tart lingonberries which he called "low-bush cranberries," and he'd shot a wild beast from which he had sliced a couple of "mystery steaks."

Klondy watched, big-eyed, as he pounded the thick cuts full of salted flour, brown sugar, ginger, and other spices and "yarbs." But when the hammered steaks came smoking off the grill they were tasty and hot as mince pie—and defied identification.

"Don' nobody knows what dey's eatin'," grinned Dave. "Dey on'y knows its good."

Afterward, he let us in on the secret, though I wished he'd kept it to himself. Out in the cache Klondy took one look at the hung carcass of a cub bear and winced. With its cinnamon-colored hide removed, the pink body was strikingly like that of a small disemboweled human hanging by its heels. "I feel like a cannibal," she wailed. "It looks just like a skinned baby."

Another one of Dave's specialties was moosehead cheese. It was so delicious that Klondy took out her notebook and demanded the recipe. The directions started by chopping off the horns and stripping off the dark hide. Then before boiling the long skull (which looked like a horse's head) in a big iron pot to loosen the flesh and cartilage from the bones, Dave had some preliminary instructions to impart: "Yo' cuts out de eyeballs, lady, an' yo' washes out de ears an' de nose . . ."

I looked across the luncheon table at Klondy. She'd stopped writing, and we never did find out how to make moosehead cheese.

As with all Yukon country cooks, Dave's cuisine was based on the liberal use of beans; the big red kind they called "Alaska strawberries." Even with this lowly fare, Dave contrived a dish fit for nobles. In each heaping plateful placed before a hungry traveler, reposed the boned breast of a ptarmigan simmered to lip-smacking goodness among the "strawberries."

To less imaginative old timers of the region, the porcupine was a ubiquitous pest to be booted out of camp. It chewed axe-handles for the salt left there by sweaty hands; it ate up table-tops and outdoor toilet seats; and it lashed poisonous darts into the faces of sled dogs when they tried to interfere. But Dave welcomed all quill-pigs with a butcher knife and a skillet. He sauteed the surprisingly large and mild livers in butter and sliced onions. I counted myself lucky when my game patrols took me by his log-cabin cafe on such a day.

The Yukon fishwheels provided Dave with the raw material for much of his culinary art. We will never forget his way with a plump king salmon. He began by making a skin-deep incision around the body just behind the head, then pulled the hide down over the tail like stripping off a wet sock. With the skill of a surgeon he removed every bone, and wielded a hand-chopper to mince the red flesh in a big, wooden bowl, into which he blended finely diced onions, dill, salt, pepper, eggs, cracker crumbs and canned milk. When this mixture was fluffed by long chopping, Dave poked it all into the salmon skin until the fish looked pretty enough to hang on the wall. Instead, it received a brushing of bacon grease and went into the oven of Dave's woodburning stove to bake for several hours. Now and then he'd pull down the heavy iron door to take a peek, and the escaping aroma was almost more than the waiting patrons could bear. When the salmon had been browned to Dave's liking, and not a second before, he bore it to the table on a great slab of charred birchwood.

It was a sorrowful day for all backwoods gourmets when Dave sold his log-cabin eatery and headed home for Memphis. For thirty years he'd followed the gold stampeders, and though he'd never panned an ounce of yellow dust, he left Alaska with a nice fat poke.

But only violence and tragedy rewarded another fine cook in the Fairbanks country. At his bunkhouse and eating-stop on the old winter trial to Chena, Slim featured sourdough-buckwheat flapjacks drenched with his own blueberry syrup, flanked with patties of sausage ground by hand from cuts of caribou and pork. Slim was one of the gentlest of old timers. The aging bachelor fairly worshipped our towhead youngsters. To this day, as I write these lines, I can see "Uncle Slim" down on his hands and knees playing "horsey," the toddlers mauling and spurring him and the old bunkhouse shrilling with their whoops of delight. It was the last time I ever saw him alive.

On our way back to Fairbanks that afternoon we were stopped on the trail by a swarthy, bearded foreigner whom I knew only as the "Bolshevik." He'd deliberately halted his small string of malemutes to block the way, and I had to turn our white team out into the loose snow to get around him. As I swung back onto the beaten trail behind his sled, he snatched the sleeve of my parka. In broken English he made an obscene remark about Klondy. I was about to respond as any man would under the circumstances when Klondy shook her head and cried, "No! No!" With two little children asleep in the sled, I realized I had to hold my temper. Besides, there was something very wrong about this man. His talk was incoherent, raving, and his eyes rolled up in their sockets until I could see only their whites. It was a sign of dementia, or at least a badly unbalanced mind. Without a word, I tore my arm loose. My white Siberians raced back to Fairbanks, and that evening I paid a visit to the United States Marshal's Office and told them about the incident. They said they would get right out there in the morning and bring the man in for a sanity hearing.

The officers were too late. The madman had already struck, and the victim of his senseless attack had been mild, lovable old Slim. Because Slim had been one of our closest friends, and because I thought I knew the location of the murderer's cabin, I joined the posse to search for him.

When we reached Slim's bunkhouse it was clear enough what had taken place. The crazed man had stopped there overnight. Plainly, Slim had sensed something wrong. He had not slept in his regular bed, but had lain down on a cot in a back room which could be barred from the inside. In the morning, evidently somewhat reassured, Slim had come out of the locked cubby-hole and started to make his usual breakfast of sourdough flapjacks and sausages for his unwelcome guest. Then it had happened. The murderer must have leaped upon him without warning. The bowl of batter had been spilled across the floor. The untended sausages had burned to a crisp in the skillet. Chairs and furniture had been flung about, evidencing that old Slim had tried to defend himself against the burly maniac. An officer pointed to the slot where Slim kept his meat cleaver. It was empty. We found the murder instrument all covered with blood beside Slim's dead body.

The mad killer was not at home when the posse surrounded his cabin and moved in, though he could not have gotten very far. His sled dogs were still chained to their stakes. Two men to a dog team, we began spreading out to locate his snowshoe tracks. When we found them, they led us cunningly back to the broken trail where we lost them among the tracks of the posse members, and for several hours we played a dangerous game of hide and seek among the spruce thickets. We knew that the insane man had armed himself with one of Slim's rifles, but he would be cornered sooner or later.

The end came abruptly. Just before darkness fell, one of the deputies shouted. We drove at full speed to where he was standing on a narrow, swaying bridge where the dog trail crossed a steep ravine. The deputy gestured in silence. Far below on the ice sprawled the broken body of a man. It was the same crazed creature who had accosted Klondy and me on our way from Slim's place to Fairbanks on the day before. He had committed the ultimate act of violence by hurling himself to his death.

During our final years in Fairbanks Klondy was finding it increasingly difficult to share my journeys into the Yukon wilderness. It wasn't the children who held her back. Any time we wanted to leave them behind, they thrived under the indulgent care of a jolly, fat native woman who went by the unlikely name of Mrs. Callahan. She was a sort of Indian "Hazel." She had a way of fascinating the little imps, and they flourished under her watchful eye. So, it wasn't the children who cramped Klondy's travel. It was her violin.

A modern theatre had been erected in Fairbanks to show the latest motion pictures shipped weekly from Seattle. The owner had learned about Klondy's professional record, and made her a standing offer to play a few numbers of her own choosing between films. On such nights the manager would set out sandwich boards in the open lobby. The theatre would be packed, and I would get in for free. It wasn't long before she was being begged to appear at all social functions, and receiving rave notices in the *Daily News-Miner,* and for all the rest of our days in Fairbanks, I took second billing as "Klondy's husband."

In her spare daylight hours Klondy would often take the children out with the Siberians on the nearby trails. Sometimes she would mush them through the middle of the town at breakneck speed, and the merchants would stand with noses pressed against their windows to watch the beautiful white dogs racing past. One night they asked us to attend a town meeting in the Court House. I thought it was to be about game matters, but it was something else. They wanted our help in organizing a winter celebration, the feature of which would be an invitation for dog owners up and down the Yukon to compete against our team of white Siberians in a series of dog races.

The downriver dogteams not only arrived in large numbers to challenge our white dogs, they won their share of the races. The Ice Carnival with its Snow Queen dressed in beautiful white furs became one of the biggest events of all future Fairbanks winters.

The excitement of the first winter carnival was barely past when another grand spectacle took place. They called it the Nenana Ice Pool. Nenana was only a little railroad stop where the sternwheelers loaded supplies for distribution up and down the Yukon, but for a couple of weeks each spring it was the most important place in Alaska. A tripod was anchored in the ice in front of the depot and a slack wire led from the tripod to the town clock, which was connected by another wire with the railroad-yard whistle. The contraption remained in place like a trap ready to be sprung by the elements while everybody waited for the breakup of the river ice. Tickets were sold at a dollar each, and each holder made his own private guess on the exact minute, hour, and day of the month when the moving ice would shift enough to tighten the wire, blow the whistle, and stop the clock. A Signal Corps operator sat at his key, ready to flash the news to every settlement and trading post in the Territory; the winners split a bonanza worth several thousand dollars and the losers tore up their tickets and tossed them into the river.

One spring when a sole winner was announced, all the residents in Fairbanks groaned. The lucky guesser was the local garbage collector, the one indispensable man in town. Just as the good citizens feared, he immediately bought a ticket to Seattle to celebrate, leaving trash to accumulate in back alleys and doorways. It was a day of rejoicing when he returned, chastened and broke, to take up his old duties again, and the cheery clanging of garbage cans once more resounded throughout the town.

Right after the rivers opened in a raging jumble of broken ice, high water, uprooted trees, dumped garbage and torn-up Nenana Ice Pool tickets, it was time for me to launch our gasboat *Beaver* for another summer-long patrol. For the first time since coming to Fairbanks I did not look forward to it with much enthusiasm. I'd been here five years—the same length of time I'd spent in the Nome country—and I began to feel the need to widen my horizons. There was so much more of Alaska to explore: the dark green forested islands of the Southeastern panhandle, soaked with steady rainfall, which I had seen but briefly from the deck of a steamer; the Kenai Peninsula, rated the greatest big-game hunting region in North America; the Valley of Ten Thousand Smokes; the Kodiak and Alaska Peninsula, habitat of the largest bears on the planet; the green-grassed Aleutian Islands strung like emeralds across the North Pacific Ocean to link America and Asia.

It wasn't just my curiosity, or mere thirsting for more adventure that impelled me. Rather, it was a sort of premonition, or possibly only hope, that if I could learn conditions in all the game fields of the Territory I might some day be in a stronger position to give them the protection they would surely need in the years to come. It was that simple, that sincere.

I told Klondy how I felt, and then I wrote a long letter

to Dr. Nelson outlining what was on my mind and asking his counsel. When his reply came, it was somewhat of a setback. The Doctor's age and failing health had at last forced him to resign as Chief of the Bureau of Biological Survey, and he was living quietly in Arizona. In his bold handwriting, noticeably shakier now, he expressed complete approval of my hopes and regretted very much that he was no longer in position to help me carry them out. I read his letter over several times, then started outfitting the *Beaver* for another summer of Yukon travel.

But, somehow, he must have made known his wishes. On the next train from Seward came a message from the Alaska headquarters of the Game Commission saying that my future assignments would be based out of Juneau.

22 The Bear Man

The region known as Southeastern Alaska, with its several hundred green-timbered islands strung southward to those of British Columbia and Puget Sound, is like the wet tail of a sled dog dangling in the ocean. When I first saw it in the 1920's the only way to reach it from the great mainland mass of the Alaska in the north, or from Seattle in the south, was by steamer. The first port of call was Ketchikan where Siwash Indian women in baggy dresses squatted miserably on the wet planks of the dock among their proffered seal-skin slippers. In this drizzly setting the traveler heard his first typical Alaska story.

It seemed that one of the Indian matrons bore on her back an infant with flaming red hair which so titillated the curiosity of a tourist lady that she could not refrain from asking, "Did the baby's father have red hair?"

The Indian woman's reply was to the point. "Me don't know. He don't take his hat off."

The story is allegorical, because the parentage of Southeastern Alaska itself is as cloudy as that of the Indian babe. The islands were "discovered" by the ships of many exploring nations in the late eighteenth and early nineteenth centuries. Native Indian damsels were courted through the years by bearded Russians, Spanish, French, English and red-headed Scotch sailor men. For a long time the residents of this mild, sopping-wet region couldn't make up their minds whether to claim kinship with the snowbound giant neighbor or point with pride to their closer blood ties with the States, and didn't do a very convincing job of being either. The truth is that Southeastern Alaska possesses unique features found in no other part of our country.

Early day travelers who saw it from the decks of the steamers marveled at the nearness of the trees reaching out from the islands as their vessels twisted and turned through the narrow "Inside Passage." They swept past Indian camps and fishing villages close enough to shout at the natives; they felt the current of gushing rivers, and looked up steep-walled inlets at rumbling glaciers. With its abundance of water pouring down from the gray skies and coursing through virgin forests into the sea, Southeastern Alaska supported an enormous fishery peculiarly its own—salmon, trout, halibut, crabs, shrimp, clams. The island wildernesses were inhabited by deer and bears and wolves. Pure white mountain goats looked down from mainland peaks. Nothing I had learned while evaluating the living wealth in the open spaces of central and northern Alaska could be applied to the jungle growths of Southeastern Alaska. I found this out very quickly when my first assignment took me to the grizzly-infested rain forest of Admiralty Island where a bear the size of a horse could hide within twenty feet.

Captain Talmadge of the *Sea Otter* let me know right away that he would assume no responsibility for my actions once I left the deck of his 40-foot patrol vessel. After we dropped anchor off Admiralty he helped me lower a skiff into the water, then uttered brief words of advice.

"Don't ever go ashore on this island without totin' a rifle."

The time was late July and the stream at the head of Mole Harbor was beginning to fill with spawning salmon. They finned in the current from shore to shore, thrashing the riffles into foam with their tails as they scooped out beds for their pink eggs. Downstream where salt and fresh waters met at the river mouth, more and more thousands of migrating fish from the sea struggled to join those on the already crowded spawning beds. Their flurries rocked the skiff and I could feel their bodies drumming steadily on the plywood bottom. There was not room to dip an oar into the water without striking a fish, and the spoiling carcasses of those already spawned and died littered the shorelines. The air was dinned with crying gulls, croaking ravens, and the shrill screaming of bald eagles disturbed at their gorging. When I pulled ashore I saw that the sandbars were punched deep with enormous bear tracks.

I dragged the light skiff across slimy kelp bulbs and over windrows of bleached clam shells to the high-tide line and made it fast to a snag. Ahead, where the river issued from the dark gloom of the forest, I saw the only evidence of human life in the entire bay: a tiny, box-like structure with a wisp of smoke curling into the trees. It was the homestead of Admiralty Island's hermit Allen Hasselborg who nursed a choleric dislike for other people, especially those on a government payroll. But I was willing to risk his wrath, because this short-fused old recluse was said to be the greatest living authority on the grizzly bears of

Admiralty Island. He lived among the fierce beasts by choice, and when he stormed out of his cabin he looked like one. A huge black beard hid most of his face and covered his green-checked wool shirt to the belt line. Big, piercing eyes under jutting brows stared with animosity as, rifle in hand, he blocked the trail to his door.

"Who the devil are you?" he demanded to know. "And who sent for you?"

I told him as best I could. I said I'd been assigned to patroling Admiralty Island and hoped he might give me some hints on how to get along with its grizzlies, that I neither wanted to shoot a bear, nor be chewed by one, either. What I didn't tell him was that I'd been asked by Washington to join with the Forest Service in "counting" the Admiralty bears, and that I didn't have the faintest idea how to go about it.

Hasselborg's retort was deliberately taunting. "Go on back to your swivel chair with the rest of the government parasites!"

I rose to the bait angrily, and said that whether he liked it or not I was going to have a look at the bears along his river.

For some reason my display of temper seemed to amuse the old man. He cocked his head to study me carefully. Slowly, the whiskery mass on his face parted to reveal a row of teeth, and the wild look faded from his eyes. He'd been testing the new game man, and now his mood made a right-about-face.

"Well, don't stand there jawing," he scolded. "You want to see grizzlies; follow me."

The way led along a bear-made trail beside the river bank through spiny devil's-clubs and salmonberry briars into a primeval forest of giant moss-draped evergreens to a pool well-filled with salmon. The sunlight flashed on fish leaping against a waterfall and scooting up the thudding white water to a quiet stretch above. But many were failing to clear the barrier and were tumbling back into the pool. Hasselborg, whispering now, said the river was too low; it needed some rainfall to help the salmon.

I hadn't seen a bear. "Don't seem to be many around," I ventured to say.

The old man swung around to glare at me through his whiskers as he hissed, "Good God, man, we've passed more than a dozen!"

He said that it was the middle of the day. The bears had filled their bellies in the morning and now most of them were lying all around us in the timber, and then he added pointedly that I'd do a sight better if I could manage to keep my eyes open and my mouth shut.

We squatted behind an uprooted windfall overlooking the pool while Hasselborg pointed out the several species of salmon fighting for swimming space—big calico-colored dog salmon with their hideously hooked jaws, developed just before they spawned and died on their natal stream beds, small black humpbacked salmon, and silvery-bright cohoes forging powerfully upstream to tiny tributaries in the mountains, while among them all darted schools of red-spotted Dolly Varden and black-speckled cutthroat trout.

I felt the hermit's hand pushing me down behind the log. A rust-colored bear had shoved out of some high ferns across the river. Behind her bounced three cubs of cocker spaniel size. The youngsters loped ahead into the shallows and began batting playfully at salmon. The mother waded out beyond them, plunged her muzzle into the water and lifted it out with a flopping fish in her jaws. She was halfway back to shore when she rose to her haunches, spun about, and stared straight at our log. Instantly, all three cubs were also standing on their hind feet, noses quivering and pointing our way. I didn't need Hasselborg to tell me that the situation had all at once become explosive, that no grizzly is more likely to attack a human than a mother in defense of her young.

The old man had frozen into immobility behind his whiskers and a slight screen of hemlock foliage. From my position below the top level of the windfall, I mirrored the action through his eyes, and after a moment or two saw his hard glare soften. "That's my pal Susie," he whispered out of the corner of his whiskers. "She's gone back into the brush with her salmon. We'll have no trouble with her."

But I don't think the old man was prepared for the next performance at the waterfall. Soundlessly, as though they had been waiting for the female and her cubs to leave the pool, four more grizzlies came easing out of the dark timber across the narrow river. I started to ready my camera for action, and felt Hasselborg's hand gripping my arm and again pushing me down. A grizzly, larger than any of the others, had come out of the forest on our side of the river, and when it padded past the front of our log it was no more than fifteen feet away! Hasselborg waited until all five bears were up to their chests in the pool, their heads lowered into the water to grip a salmon, then backed away from the log to the trail that led back to the cabin.

When we were at a safe distance, I asked, "How come they didn't see us?"

Once more the old hermit shriveled me with a look. "Every one of those bears knew I was behind that log," he said, "same as I've been most every day since the salmon run started." He paused to accent his next words. "It's the alien smell of a swivel-chair character like you I was worried about. They've accepted me."

But on the way back to the cabin we ran into a bear which I thought had a strange way of showing its acceptance. It reared out of the river like a monster out of the prehistoric ages, water dripping off its claws, moaning and groaning belligerently as it trundled our way. When it reached a waterlogged snag on the bank, its teeth began clicking, and it hauled off and started cuffing chunks off the rotted stump.

Shaking his outthrust black whiskers like an enraged billy-goat, Hasselborg stepped forward to meet the dare. "Get the hell out'a here!" he ordered as one would talk to a fractious dog. "Get back in the creek where you belong!"

The bear did even better. To my surprise, it turned slowly away, sloshed back across the creek, and with upraised shoulder hackles sauntered on upriver. The old man said he hadn't seen this particular grizzly many times because it mostly came out to the river for its salmon after dark.

"But it's here every night," he declared. "I can tell by its tracks."

We went down to the river's edge where the bear's pad marks were deeply imprinted in the damp sand to reveal every detail, and the old man spanned the tracks with outstretched thumb and little finger. "Ten inches across the front paw," he called out. "Hind foot close to thirteen-inches long." He added there wasn't another grizzly on the river with those exact proportions, and then he showed me something even more important. The pad prints were dotted with irregular pores and bore their own peculiar pattern of wrinkles, whorls, cross-hatchings, twisted or missing toenails, and scars. When he straightened up from his scrutiny of the tracks, Hasselborg made a casual statement worth my entire trip into his bailiwick.

Every bear track, said the old man, *is as individual as a human fingerprint.*

He walked me down to my skiff and helped me drag it across windrows of kelp and beach rubble to the water. He said it had been a good day and danged it he hadn't enjoyed it—especially when I'd kept my mouth shut and used my ears and eyes. But if I'd had any hopes that I might have broken through the old man's crusty shell it was dispelled at his final remark. "Good-bye. If I ever want to see you again, I'll send for you."

With the key supplied by Hasselborg's keen observations I was able to open the door to bear populations all over the island. By mounting a camera tripod over a track, hooded by a black cloth to let in only a narrow strip of bottom light across the pad print, every wrinkle and pore was revealed on the film. We made scores of plaster casts of the bear footprints for comparative purposes, and we measured hundreds of others with steel tapes and entered the measurements on a tally sheet. Almost daily showers during the period gave us fresh sets to work with, and we made occasional trips to the mountain tops to spot certain bears who seemed to favor blueberries to salmon. It took a forest ranger and me, each with his own patrol vessel and helper, just a month to make our survey of the Admiralty Island grizzlies. The results were headline news of that period. The beautiful, park-like island was revealed to harbor the greatest known concentration of big bears in all the world, approximately one grizzly for every one of its 1,600 square miles.

Our final anchorage was in front of Hasselborg's cabin. I couldn't resist an attempt to row ashore and thank him for the tip which had made our census-estimate possible. The bearded hermit wasn't home. Instead the place appeared to have been booby-trapped, and there was a chilling sign nailed to the door. NO TRESPASSING! SET GUN INSIDE! I peered through the small window gingerly. His rifle and packsack were not in sight, and I concluded that he'd gone off on another of his lone trips into the hills to commune with the bears he liked better than people.

I started to pin a "thank you" note on his door, then decided against it. The old man would like it better if I just got the hell away from there.

23 The Lights of Juneau

On my return to Juneau I learned that our small daughter Ginny had featured in a bear story of her own. Once on the Yukon River she had watched from Klondy's arms while I leaned over the bow of our gasboat to snatch a black bear cub out of the whirlpools and hold its head above water until I could turn it loose again in shallow water near shore. When her first grade teacher read a local news story about her father *counting* the grizzly bears on Admiralty Island, and asked Ginny if that wasn't rather dangerous, our little towhead set the whole class at ease.

"My daddy," she piped out, "just grabs them by the ears!"

Klondy and the children were adjusting to Juneau better than I dared hope. Alaska's capital in the early 1930's was the largest and most modern city in the Territory. Its population of 5,000 lived partly in homes built on pilings driven into the mud flats and surrounded by water at high tide, and partly in houses hung on the steep sides of the mountain. The narrow gravel streets were so steep that automobiles labored uphill in low gear, and the drivers had to ride the brakes all the way down again. We had found a good residence at the top of Main Street from which our bay window gave us an eagle's eye view of the harbor and the remarkable lights of Juneau. Every night the waterfront was lit up with green and red signals to guide incoming steamers which probed the darkness with searchlights as they warped in to the docks. Every porthole flashed with light, the social hall at deck level was ablaze, and when the wind was right we could even hear the ships' orchestras playing the popular Alaska song of the period, "I love Humpback Salmon, Caught by a good Swede Fisherman!"

Small seiners and trollers and longliners coming in to the cold storage plant loaded to the scuppers with herring, salmon, and halibut, winked their lights on the velvety black surface of the water; the ferry boat which plied from Juneau to Douglas Island across Gastineau Channel every hour on the hour was a cluster of colored brilliance. Along the planked streets of crowded downtown, auto lights dodged and twisted. Well up the mountain side above town were the bright lights from Juneau's famous AJ gold mine as it ground hard-rock ore to paste and sluiced it through the cyanide tanks. Strings of lighted dump cars loaded with tailings roared down a steep railroad to the waterline to dump their rock, automatically carrying the empties uphill on an adjoining track; all tooting whistles and flashing endless lights. But I thought the lights of Juneau put on their best show of all when the miners came off shift at midnight. As they single-filed out of the tunnel and doubled back and forth down the switchbacks of the mountainside in a sort of snake dance, the carbide lamps on their hats blinked like fireflies against the total blackness of the night.

Klondy's extraordinary ability with the violin soon put her in the thick of the social swim that characterizes a capital city. She played engagements at the two local theatres, led the orchestras at numerous balls, and appeared often at the Governor's mansion. Even so, we made it a point to get out in the forests and along the beaches regularly with our small children, sleeping outdoors overnight, fishing the trout streams, clam-digging on the tide flats, and cooking over campfires.

My zeal to have my boy catch his first salmon almost ended with a salmon catching his first boy. Frank junior was only three years old when he sat in my lap while I rowed a skiff along the edge of the kelp beds trolling a spoon hook on a handline. The youngster had the heavy cod line gripped in his chubby fingers when, suddenly, there was a terrific strike from a salmon heavier than the boy. I thought the fishline would slip through his hands; instead, with that unbelievable strength of an infant's finger, the tad hung on like grim death and the first thing I knew he was sailing off my lap. I grabbed him just in time to keep him from flying overboard.

I could hear Klondy ordering both of us to come ashore at once, but pretended not to hear while my toddler and I subdued the battling giant. Then, with our 40-pound king salmon spanking the bottom of the skiff with a tail the size of a snow shovel, we rowed proudly ashore to take our scolding.

In spite of Juneau's 83-inch rainfall—5 times more than Nome and 7 times more than Fairbanks—its summers were generally fair and there was much opportunity for the outdoor living that Klondy and the children enjoyed. They settled into the new community and soon were surrounded with new friends. The unhappiest member of the family was I, especially when my duties forced me to spend protracted spells in the headquarter's office of the Alaska Game Commission. Like most field men I had little understanding and less sympathy for "pencil-pushing," filling out printed forms, the red tape, the onerous, useless, and sometimes misleading reports, the mounting correspondence between outlying residents from the huge land mass to the north who didn't like the new game rules, and the cubby-hole office in the tail of the Territory trying to wag the big Alaska dog.

Because neither the new executive officer nor his assistant had ever traveled in central and northwestern Alaska, the irate correspondents in these regions addressed many of their letters to me, personally, and I would be required to comment on their complaints before replies were sent out. More often than otherwise I would note on the margin of the letters, "I think this man is right, and the law is wrong."

These frank opinions did nothing to enhance my standing around the headquarters office, and it was a relief to escape the stuffy atmosphere and smell the fresh salt breezes from the deck of a patrol vessel. Every trip ashore on a new island was an adventure. As I padded silently along the game trails in the gloom of the moss-draped trees I would sometimes catch glimpses of black and gray timber wolves slinking along a parallel course. Although there had never been a proven case of wolves attacking a human in Alaska, I had seen the grisly remains of a lost beaver trapper on a nearby island. It had been stripped of flesh and some of the bones crunched, and wolf tracks were punched in the mud all around the spot. However, the pad prints of a lone black bear were also discovered at the site, and they tended to fog the circumstantial evidence against the wolves.

The incident was fresh in my mind when I was tramping across a wild section of Kupreanof Island across the channel from Petersburg and heard a wolf howling in the distance. Giving way to an impulse, I let go with my best imitation. Instantly, the foggy forest around me echoed with lobo ululations, and I realized the brutes had been keeping me stealthy company for some time. There wasn't the slightest shred of evidence to prove they had been planning an attack, but I couldn't help wondering what the unfathomable brutes had in mind.

There was no doubt about the danger of molesting the huge brown and grizzly bears of the ABC islands—Admiralty, Baranof, and Chichagof—in the upper part of the archipelago. Mostly, they would leave you alone if you kept out of their way, though there would be the occasional rare cases of attack without discernible provocation. Most every village in Southeastern Alaska had its maimed victim ready to show off his terrible wounds. Whenever I walked their dark trails alone, my rifle was cradled across my arm ready for instant action. Sometimes, I could sense the unseen presence of grizzlies on all sides, and I could feel the hair rising on the back of my neck. I knew that a bear who really intends to attack usually wasted no time in preliminaries, but closed in with a furious rush on all four feet; nevertheless the sight of a grizzly rearing out of the undergrowth to look me over at close range never failed to lock the breath in my throat, and I would have the unpleasant sensation of adrenalin fairly oozing out of my pores. Even so, I was never more startled in the Southeastern Alaska forests than when I came face to face with my first "wild" totem pole.

I was pushing through a jungle-like growth of alders, devil's-clubs and new growth evergreens at the head of a hidden bay when I had the odd feeling of being watched. I stopped to look about me carefully, and after a while I saw it: a huge carved head of Abraham Lincoln, complete with beard and tall stovepipe hat. The Great Emancipator was gazing benignly down at me from the outstretched wings of an eagle, which in turn was standing on the nose of a killer whale whose tail was caught in the mouth of a bear. Supporting the bear was a red-eyed raven, and low man on the totem was a blue-spotted toad. As I stood rooted to the spot, slowly swiveling, I discovered several more similar tree carvings looming above the brush. Though there were no houses in sight, I realized I had blundered on a lost Indian village, abandoned and rotted into the ground several years before, with only the everlasting cedar totem poles, their garish colors faded and chipped, left to mark its quondum existence.

I was still shaking my head over the strange discovery, when the *Sea Otter* dropped anchor off a village of living Indians, and a fresher collection of totem poles. Here, I learned that the carving of these weirdly-daubed monuments was by no means an ancient form of expression but had apparently begun within the past century when a carved palm tree trunk from somewhere in the South Pacific washed ashore on one of the Southeastern Alaska islands. For a while the art of totem-pole making had flourished, though the Indians were never quite sure what it was all about. The ravens, toads, whales, eagles, and their entwined attitudes on the poles had a vague relationship with marriages between clan members, peace treaties, potlatches, and other events. Having served their contemporary purpose, the hacked cedar trunks possessed no permanent value and were readily acquired by merchants for the main use to which they are put today—to attract tourists. Some people who pretend to understand the Thlinget totem culture claim the poles are really like a file of old newspapers, depicting outstanding happenings dating as far back as a century or more, though they did not always agree on the story they told.

Near the old village of Howkan, now all but reclaimed by the forest, stood a pair of totem poles quite alike in general appearance, except for the placement of a purple-spotted toad. On one totem the monster appeared to be grinning expansively from the top of the pole. On an adjacent totem the toad not only cowered in fright; it was also upside down at the bottom of the pole. I would not have given the matter a second thought had not a rheumy-eyed old chief taken it upon himself to interpret the story told by the two totems. Each had been carved by a rival brave shortly after a bear hunt. Each had claimed credit for bravery and accused the other of cowardice.

"Same hunt, two poles," said the Indian. "Somebody tell big lie!"

Maybe it was the old chief.

White settlers in the Alexander Archipelago also had their own evanescent culture, more fleeting even than that of totem-pole carving among their Siwash neighbors. It was the great blue-fox pipe dream: a plan to live-trap the small maltese-colored foxes of the distant Aleutians where they were indigenous, and turn them loose on the smaller, timbered islands of Southeastern Alaska which was not at all a natural habitat. Like many other cases of transplanted creatures, the experiment seemed to go well for a while. The foxes multiplied, the demand for breeding stock kept pace. Men moved their wives and children to lonely, wave-pounded islands many miles from the nearest villages and led a sort of Swiss Family Robinson existence among the foxes, tame goats, dogs, and other family pets which came to include native deer and sometimes bear cubs. Every time I came ashore on one of these isolated islands I could see children, unaccustomed to visitors, scattering like quail for the cover of the timber. The goats would blat their alarms, the dogs would bark, and the savage, little blue foxes would squall hideously from the mouths of their burrows.

On every island the story was similar. As long as the ranchers could find a market for high-priced breeding stock to outfit still more adventurers, they could earn a fair living. But when they were forced to dump surplus pelts in the fur markets the prices were disappointingly low. To the Swiss Family Robinsons it became evident that they could not expect to keep peddling brood stock at inflated prices forever; that sooner or later the bubble would burst in their faces.

But what finally pricked the bubble on island blue-fox ranching in Southeastern Alaska was not inflation. It was infection. It was a microscopic parasite that spread diseases through the animals as they ranged at large where they could not be treated. While the real killer remained unseen, the islanders blamed their decreasing litters to bald eagles making off with the young foxes and won their demands to put a bounty of one dollar on our national bird. When they saw that this did no good, a few ranchers tried to modernize by confining their foxes in pens and resorting to hand-feeding. It was no use. The boom days were over. In the few years I traveled among them, the island blue-fox ranches joined the Indian totem poles as another passing phase in the history of Southeastern Alaska.

The exodus of the Swiss Family Robinsons from island log-cabin homes was sometimes sudden, frequently dramatic, and always sad. I visited one family just as they were preparing to start back to the States. Their gasboat was dangerously overloaded with household effects. I could see little tear-stained faces peering out of the portholes, and there were more children out on deck beseeching their parents to make room for their pets; please not to desert them on the island. Before I realized the complications, I had promised to find a home for a rollicking mongrel pup named Pooch. I would see that Daisy-Belle, the milk-goat, and her newborn kid Pansy were properly taken care of; that a gorgeously plumed Rhode Island red rooster who had been living a celibate life in the house ever since the vicious blue foxes ate up his wives, would once more command a harem. I would even provide nursing service for a wee bear cub called Topsy, whom the rancher hadn't discovered until he'd shot the marauding mother.

The government patrol vessel *Sea Otter* looked like Noah's Ark when I left the island, and with the children's wails ringing in my ears, started out to search for some animal loving, kindhearted homesteaders. A cannery watchman took the lumbering mongrel Pooch off my hands. A fisherman's wife welcomed Daisy-Belle and little Pansy with open arms. She further promised to provide the amorous red rooster sultan with some hen-folks, and never, put an axe to his neck. But no amount of persuasion could induce anybody among the islands to adopt Topsy, the bear cub. I still had her when the *Sea Otter* docked at the finish of the patrol. The bright lights of Juneau terrified her and she clung to me piteously. She was cuddling on my lap when I drove my pickup truck out to our little beach cabin where Klondy and the children were spending the weekend.

It was love at first sight between Topsy, Ginny, and young Frank. They romped wildly around the cabin, raising the merry devil. Afterward, Klondy fixed a nursing bottle with evaporated milk, warm water, and sugar, and the children took turns holding it for Topsy until it was sucked empty. Instantly, then, Topsy collapsed with fatigue. They carried her tiny form to the couch; Ginny and young Frank wrapped themselves around her and soon they were all fast asleep.

Klondy and I looked at each other and threw up our hands. We'd have to put up with it. Topsy had a home until she could fend for herself, and Ginny had for her schoolmates another bear story.

24 The Indestructible Mountain Goat

One would have to visit Greenland or a Canadian polar island like Baffin Land to find a northern ice mass comparable to the 800-mile long blanket that covers a large part of the Southeastern Alaska mainland from British Columbia to the head of Prince William Sound. From this Ice Age terrain, glaciers push their white fingers down steep-walled valleys, shoving millions of tons of icebergs into the sea. The movement has been going on for countless centuries, and no one can predict when it will stop. Measured against the briefness of our own lives, it is forever.

The vertical canyon sides, scoured by eons of avalanches, polished smoother still by windblown sleet in winter, appear at first glance to be devoid of living things. Yet, when the very hostility of the region invited challenge; when I dug fingernails into the fissures along its sheer walls and risked my neck scrambling along its slippery ice falls, I found a surprising variety of plants and animals.

There were tufts of wiry mountain grass and fern clumps sprouting from the crevices. In the hidden gullies not visible from below, I found stunted berry bushes and flowering shrubs, almost like cultivated rock gardens with their bright splotches of color. Looking up from the deck of the *Sea Otter* I had seen no evidence of fauna, but as I clawed my way toward the clouds, I became aware of bird songs from sparrows, wrens, finches, thrushes, and juncos. There were the odd frog-like croaks of white-tailed ptarmigan all about me. Red squirrels chattered and scolded from every cone-bearing dwarf spruce, and fat hoary marmots shrilled their alarms ventriloquially from hidden den mouths. I found the tracks of marten and wolverine, and once I spotted the rare and beautiful Emmon's Bear, found nowhere else in the world. The small, maltese-colored phase of the black bear seemed almost to melt into the blue shadows of an overhanging glacier. Platforms of sticks piled on rocky knobs where only winged creatures could reach attested the presence of peregrine falcons and eagles.

One of the most astonishing discoveries had to wait until I had worked my way to the top of the bluffs, a mile or more above the fjord. There in cloudland, tiny rills flowed out of melting snowbanks, coursed across green meadows for short distances, then leaped dramatically out into space, spinning into liquid lace, shimmering against the rocky palisades to fall like raindrops into the ocean. The unbelievable feature of these wispy waterfalls was this: *Above them in the mountain plateaus, the tiny glacial streams were filled with red-speckled trout.*

At first no logical explanation of the phenomena occurred to me; there seemed no possible way for the small, handsome trout to have reached there from the sea. Then, it came to me! In ancient history these fjords had been filled to the brim with salt water. Proof of the ocean surging among the peaks was all about me in marine shells still encrusted in the rocks, and fishes, perhaps of many varieties, could have finned here. Of them all, the hardy Dolly Varden had been the one to inure itself to existence in the ice-cold trickles among the glaciers as the ocean level slowly fell away during the centuries. A similar natural wonder also had taken place in the high ranges of western Mexico when the Ice Age of 50,000 years ago enabled rainbow trout to fill the mountain rivers, and where they still occur at lofty altitudes in streams which fade into the desert sands and no longer reach the sea except as underground seepages.

But for me, the most unusual attraction of the Southeastern Alaska mainland with its cracked-open mountains and its snail-paced rivers of ice inching down to saltwater, was a white beast with stubby little black horns and a brave heart. It was the indestructible mountain goat.

One afternoon I looked up from the *Sea Otter* on ice-filled Tracy Arm fjord and saw, through my binoculars, a tiny, snow-white creature teetering on a dizzy mountain ledge. It was a mountain goat kid no more than a few days old. The ledge was so narrow that the slightest misstep would send it plummeting to its death. While I was watching the wobbly little beast, an eagle suddenly dropped out of the heights. Its plan was clearly to snatch the kid loose—an old eagle trick—and let it fall hundreds of feet to the rocky shoreline below. There, it could feed at its leisure.

But at the first screaming dive of the eagle, the mother goat materialized on the crack in the granite, and began working her way out to her kid. Before she could reach her baby, the eagle struck. It was a glancing blow; the great bird of prey's talons raked the kid's side, but they did not dislodge it, and before the bird could mount the air currents for another strike, the nanny reached her wounded kid and laid her head across its body to shield it.

The eagle was not through trying for its dinner. On its next stoop, the she-goat felt the full force of the eagle claws biting into her shoulders. She stood unflinching under a third attack. Then, on the fourth swoop, the nanny made her move. Suddenly, she slashed upward with perfect timing. There was a collision of talons and black, dagger-sharp horns. The eagle was flung off in space, tumbling down the chasm wall for many feet before flapping heavily away, losing altitude. It did not return.

Holding my breath with the anxiety of it, I watched Nanny nudge her hurt baby inch by inch along a gray wall higher than the Empire State building. With infinite care, stopping often to study the way ahead, she maneuvered it to a sloping ramp of green grass which looked no larger than a postage stamp pasted against the hard granite, and began licking its wounds. Then I heard myself cheering. The little kid had swung about and was punching its head against Nanny's udders. For this courageous mother another crisis had been resolved.

The mother goat's own lacerations would soon heal, and the scars would be added with scores of others she had been acquiring since her birth among these perilous pinnacles. Her life had been marked with one hairbreadth escape after another. Many times in the past she had deliberately pushed a kid out onto what looked like a sheer palisade, then turn to stand off a bear or wolverine, her head lowered between her front legs, ready to stab out with her black stiletto horns. An Indian told me he had once seen a nanny charge a wolf and send it spinning into a gully.

For its steeplejack existence, nature has given this animal we call a mountain goat some very special equipment for staying alive. Its hoofs are small, vertical, oblong-shaped, with chiseled edges that bite into sloping glaciers like a pair of mountain-climber's crampons. They are strong enough to wedge footholds in the smallest cracks along a steeply slanting rock wall. When a goat puts its full weight on its hoofs a spongy pad comes down to form a suction. Its bones are oversize, the joints wrapped with heavy gristle—nature's way of protecting its framework in spills and tumbles. The average female weight is 150 pounds; the billy can weigh from 250 to 300 pounds. Their bodies are slabsided, the rib cages flattened so they won't need as much room to get around narrow ledges which often overhang dizzy drop-offs of a mile. Nanny's big brown eyes are unflinching in the face of danger, and their lenses give her telescopic vision about equal to that of a man with 8-power binoculars. But I think the greatest of her natural gifts are calmness, unhurried judgment, and valor eclipsing that of any other American animal in the wilderness.

Her mate has his remarkable traits, too. Later in the summer when I revisited the Tracy Arm fjord, I saw the "head man" in Nanny's family perform a gravity-defying trick unbelievable in a hoofed beast. Billy had undoubtedly heard the pop-pop of our engine exhaust. He came strolling nonchalantly to the very edge of a jutting spur; then he stretched his head and shoulders far out and looked straight down a quarter mile on the *Sea Otter's* deck. The sight was so unnerving that I instinctively clutched at a guy line. But Billy thought nothing of it. As casually as a wealthy club member in a penthouse, he settled back on his haunches against the canyon wall and began chewing his cud. Gazing serenely down from his skyline perch, white chin whiskers trailing in the breeze, Billy was the "old man of the mountain."

I kept my binoculars focused on him as we proceeded up the fjord. He eyed a wheeling eagle until it returned to its aerie. His head turned to follow a pod of killer whales hunting hair seals among the floating bergs. For a few moments he gave his attention to a glacier at the head of the fjord while it put on its daily spectacular. With the special privilege of a grandstand seat-holder, he watched an emerald-green slab as big as a battleship split off and topple, slow-motion into the sea. Moments later came a thunderous detonation echoing forth and back across the fjord, followed by a tidal wave that heaved our little *Sea Otter* high on its crest. When the turmoil had subsided and I dared take another look upward, there was old Billy still reclining in the mountain sunshine, still grinding his cud with lofty disdain, still keeping a lookout on the proceedings of us lesser creatures below. I did not sight Nanny on this trip, though she and her kid were undoubtedly in a hidden gully under Billy's watchful eyes.

Unlike the mate-and-run tactics of most other big-game animals, the mountain goat billy was a good family man. While the nanny tended their single youngster, he topped out on the highest eminence and posed like an icy statue against the puffy clouds and blue sky. In the fall mating season, I watched him issuing his "Keep Off—Private Property" warning to all cliff-hopping swains. At the base of each 9- to 12-inch horn was a rubbery boss from which he was able to exude a musky scent as he thrashed the bushes in a perimeter around his homestead. Seldom did actual duels take place. They were too dangerous. With Billy's ability to vanquish predators as big as bears, the slamming together of the 250-pound gladiators armed with ebony-black bayonets would certainly have resulted in the death of one or both rivals, and they seemed to know it.

Descended from primitive old world antelopes, the Goral and the Serow, the animal we call a mountain goat came originally from Asia across the Bering Straits land bridge that once connected Alaska and Siberia. At that time their coats were probably dark gray or black, but over the generations as their search for food took them higher into the Alaska mountains, their coats turned gradually white. It was nature's way of adapting them to a snow-field habitat, though traces of dark hairs may to this day be seen on some individuals.

Even now they still wander down into the valleys from time to time. In decades past, they were hunted by the Indians for their wool which was mixed with inner bark of the cedar to make the now rare Chilkat blankets. Trophy hunters are not greatly attracted to the narrow face with its small horns and ridiculous goatee, and an old goat's flesh, as might be expected, is about as tender as a boot heel.

So the mountain goat's worst enemy as I observed its way of life along the Southeastern Alaska mainland was the land itself. In spite of its built-in safety features, it suffered many bruising falls. Avalanches were a constant threat. It was an avalanche, in fact, that gave me an ending to this chapter on the indestructible mountain goat.

Late in the following spring, almost a year after I had watched Nanny fight off an eagle, an Indian seal hunter was cruising among the floating ice-bergs of Tracy Arm when a snow slide thundered down from the crags and roared over a precipice. When the niagara of slush, boulders, and uprooted trees had subsided, the Indian spotted a goat swimming feebly in the flotsam and hauled her aboard his gas-boat. As Nanny lay flattened on deck like a watersoaked heap of rags among the seal carcasses, her sides heaving as she fought for breath, the Indian's first impulse was to put her out of her misery and salvage the hide. Then he remembered that we of the Alaska Game Commission were offering a special reward for every mountain goat delivered alive for shipment to Washington. Maybe Nanny could be kept among the living long enough for him to pocket a check for $400.

We crated Nanny at Juneau and put her aboard a steamer going south. At Ketchikan, part way to Seattle, the local game warden came on ship to report on her condition. His wire back to us was not very encouraging. It said that she was bloating badly and showing signs of acute distress.

There was no more information until the steamer docked at Seattle two days later. There a veterinarian was called in to do what he could to save Nanny. His cablegram explained everything. Nanny was no longer bloated, it said; she had given birth to a kid en route to the local zoo. The message finished: MOTHER AND CHILD DOING FINE.

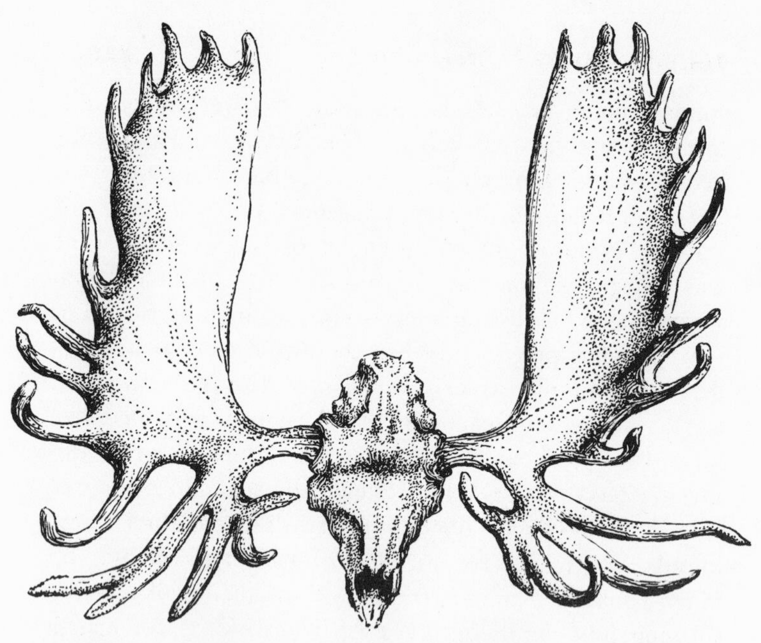

¶25 Campfires on the Kenai

Though they have long turned to ashes, I can still smell the campfires—the sputtering birch bark igniting a handful of crushed twigs and a tongue of flame licking its way through a tepee of split spruce. Beyond the curling smoke I can see a bull moose shouldering out through the alders to stand motionless, black and huge against the red twilight. Of all my adventures in the far north, I remember best those hours spent around the campfires on the Kenai.

Alaska's most famous game field, the Kenai, is a 300-mile long peninsula of towering mountains and ice hanging pendant in the North Pacific below the present city of Anchorage; all but pinched off by the waters of Prince William Sound and Cook Inlet so that it is almost an island. East of the narrow-gauge, government-owned railroad connecting the seaport of Seward with the northern terminus at Fairbanks, 411 miles away, the Kenai was in the early 1930's a pristine jumble of rocky spurs and eternally frozen alpine lakes above which jagged white pinnacles spired into the clouds like inverted icicles. Glaciers rumbled like thunder as they dumped endless ice-tailings into the sea. It was a forbidding region man would not know well for years to come, if ever; a setting from the Ice Age inhabited mostly by the snow-white mountain goats and sheep and ptarmigan.

The western half of the Kenai, on the other hand, was a paradise for wild game of many kinds. It sloped down from its 10,000-foot peaks into a series of scenic table lands, then lower still to a million potholes thicketed about with willows and birches and dwarf spruce before it finally flattened out against the swirling gray flood of Cook Inlet. It was rich with the browse preferred by horned game, and for the bears there were vast berry patches, and streams abounding with salmon and trout. It was the game field I wanted most to explore, and when the Kenai guides asked the Juneau office to send me up there to help them work out a management plan for their world-famous moose herds I was aboard the next northbound steamer.

My first campfire on the Kenai was an old hunting site on the bank of Funny River between Skilak and Tustumena Lakes. With me were two of Alaska's best known guides: Andy Simons, holder of Alaska Registered Guide Badge No. 1, and his lean, little partner Hank Lucas. To reach the heart of the moose range, we had carried heavy packsacks across the Moosehorn Trail, named from heaps of shed antlers stacked along the way by earlier explorers to distinguish the route from a network of paths made by the wild game.

Hank Lucas climbed a notched log to a high-poled cache

to toss down a canvas tent to fit a standing frame left from the previous season, and soon our bedding was unrolled across a mattress of fresh spruce twigs with the sharp ends pointed down into the earth so that the soft tops felt like feathers under our blankets. It was then that Andy Simons lit the first of a hundred Kenai campfires. Afterward, he reached up to a spruce limb to unhook a blackened 2-pound can which he'd hung there a year before at the end of the fall hunt, filled it from Funny River, spooned it generously with coffee, and when it came to a frothing boil, he doused it with a dipper of cold water to settle the grounds. Meanwhile, Hank had brought down from the cache a skillet into which he sliced some ham, then added a handful of desiccated (he called them "congratulated") potatoes, and we finished the first of our many open-fire meals with hardtack spread with canned jam.

The guides hadn't spoken a dozen words all day, but now as Andy tamped his big curved-stem briar with plug whittlings kneaded between his palms, and Hank rolled himself a brown-paper fag between the fingers of one hand and lit it with a brand off the fire, they were ready to talk. Their first subject was not moose, but bears. Being right on a salmon stream, our campsite was a thoroughfare for grizzlies—the Alexander subspecies, biggest in all the world since the extinction of California's golden grizzly—some of them weighing well over a thousand pounds and with cantankerous tempers to match. A female with two cubs had left their sign at our camping grounds within the hour. There'd been hat-size tracks of an enormous bear on the trail sloping down to the water. We'd have to watch our steps, and the guides said they didn't want me straying off by myself with a camera. Hank gave me a good reason why I should stay in line.

A few months earlier when camped at this very spot, he had been walking along under a steep sidehill, not hearing nor seeing any sign of bears until, suddenly, a shadow blotted out the sky above. Instantly, he dove headfirst to the ground. His stetson hat was batted off his head by the paw of a grizzly as it sailed over his prone body. Hank said he sat up in time to shoot the bear as it came clawing back up the hill to get him, and he was sorry about it because the grizzly really hadn't meant to kill him at all. "It thought I was a moose calf," shrugged Hank. "But if I'd been carrying a camera like yours instead of a rifle like mine, it wouldn't have made any difference."

While Andy and Hank reminisced around the campfire, a gangling young bull moose with bulbous antlers in the velvet came shoving through a screen of birches, and after standing in silent appraisal for several minutes, flopped its long ears, spread its lanky front legs wide apart and began cropping grass like a domestic cow. In the ruddy afternoon light more moose materialized along the ridge tops: cows, bulls, a few yearlings, but no calves.

"You see anything today?" Andy asked me. I knew what he meant, and I said it looked very much as if this part of the Kenai moose range, at least, might be overgrazed. The willows, essential food of the giant deer during ten months of the year, had been nipped down to the stubs; the coppice-growth of new suckers wasn't supplying enough new food, and the undernourished cows might be expected to produce some runt, or even stillborn, calves. We'd have to study the conditions over a wider area of the Kenai to be sure.

While we talked, the evening sun sank slowly down behind the far away volcanoes across Cook Inlet, their wisps of smoke like dark plumes on white peaked hats.

The red heavens were deepening around us, and soon the gray moose turned black and became invisible against the ebony of night. The moving tip of Hank's brown-paper cigarette and the round, bright glow of Andy's pipe vanished in turn as the guides knocked off their bedtime smoke, and the only light now came from the dying embers of the campfire.

The guides, with rifles close at hand, crawled under their Hudson's Bay blankets and drifted off to sleep. I stayed awake listening to the rasping of bark on a spruce trunk and guessed it was a porcupine. But the stealthy crunch, crunch of gravel at the river's edge surely was no quill-pig. Before I could decide what it might be, the exertions of carrying an enormous backpack and heavy Graflex camera all day caught up with me, and I joined my snores with those of the guides.

We had no more schedule than a jackrabbit that long ago summer on the Kenai. We siwashed under the open skies wherever night overtook us. We built our campfires and we lived "off the country" on trout, small game, wild berries, and an endless succession of mushrooms that sprouted along the moose trails—dainty morels in the spring, then pink-gilled field mushrooms, shaggy-manes, golden chantrelles, and boletas—augmented by carefully husbanded staples like flour, salt, bacon, coffee, sugar, and canned milk. We grew pinch-gutted as coyotes, stubble-faced as Airedales, and because I chose to carry my bulky camera in lieu of a rifle, I developed a positive radar for detecting the yellow grizzlies of the Kenai before they detected me.

One day we were following a series of switchbacks high above timberline where some of the biggest moose bulls liked to spend the summer under the melting snowbanks where the browse and grass grew tender and green. Black bears dotted the open lingonberry and blueberry patches, sometimes a dozen in sight at one time, grubbing with such concentration that Hank crept almost close enough to slap one on the rump. But neither he nor Andy took any liberties with the big yellow grizzlies. Every year somebody on the Kenai was mauled, or killed, by one of the dish-faced giants, and none of us cared to join the statistics. On one of the few times when I wandered away from camp with my camera, I peered over a gully rim and there not fifty feet below me was a huge Alexander grizzly ripping apart the carcass of a mountain sheep. I backed away in a hurry, and when I reported back to Andy and Hank they said that unless we wanted to be forced into killing a bear—which we didn't—we'd better be getting out of there, which we did.

Still higher in the mountain peaks, on a spur between the blue tongues of a glacier where an ice-water spring bubbled from the rocks, we built our campfire for the night; a fitful, crackling flame fed with resinous junipers. From this lofty eminence the entire slope of the peninsula stretched before our eyes, and it was here we came as close as we were going to to understanding the ecological history of the Kenai.

Prior to 1900 the plant life on Kenai Peninsula had been an Ice Age aftermath of primitive gray lichens known as "reindeer" or "caribou" moss, and the dominant animal forms had been herds of caribou and their timber wolf predators. Then, in the late 1880's, a gold miner's campfire got away from him and started a conflagration that raged for months. When it finally burned out because there were no more oily lichens to feed it, the caribou were forced to migrate and with them went the wolves.

Slowly, over the charred landscape in ensuing years, the next stage of plant life began to sprout—willows, birches, aspens, alders, berry bushes, and other deciduous browse favorable to a new succession of big game like moose and mountain sheep and bears. Now as we looked down from our juniper-fed campfire, we saw the vegetative chain on the Kenai moving to its climax—evergreen forests all but useless to big game.

Dark splotches of scrub spruces were spreading like scabrous growths across the plateaus and swamplands beneath us to choke out the willows, forcing heavier cropping on those that still found the sunlight to thrive. Andy and Hank knew, as I did, that when the spruce trees claimed the Kenai soil, as they were now in the process of doing, the great moose pastures would deteriorate. It was that logical; that inescapable.

"What we need," said Hank, "is another hell of a big forest fire."

Miles away down on the placid lower curves of the Kenai River where it flowed into Cook Inlet, there was a tiny smudge which Andy had been studying through his powerful Zeiss glasses—the ones he used for spotting mountain sheep rams and estimating the trophy value of their curled horns. After a while he handed the glasses to me.

"Like that one down there," he observed mildly.

We took turns watching a low ring of smoke edging away from a salmon fisherman's campfire on the river bank, fanning out with the wind, eating its way across sered grasslands and dry peat beds into the timber, and then leaping from spruce to spruce as from one lighted torch to another. It was the first of many such blazes we saw during that hot, thirsty summer. They charred miles of the Kenai forest, and from their ashes sprouted revitalized willows needed by the moose. In succeeding seasons as settlers started clearing roads and building their log cabins on the peninsula there were enough wild flames to keep the big deer in fresh browse.

From our eagles-eye view in the mountains we could see it all now. Burning had not only created a perfect habitat for the moose, but must continue to play the major role in maintaining it. All the laws and regulations we could devise would be far less important to the giant bulls than the runaway campfires of the Kenai.

¶26 The Mysterious Aleutians

From the year of 1741 when the Russian vessel *St. Peter* foundered on the rocks during its voyage of Alaska discovery, and its Danish commander Vitus Bering died in the agonies of scurvy with most of his crew, the Aleutians have been the scene of shipwrecks, debauchery, and murder. No other part of Alaska—nor of America—has witnessed more treachery and violence. When I explored behind the Aleutian fog curtain in the summer of 1931, another sinister development was taking place under the very noses of our government; the islands were being infiltrated by Japanese spies in preparation for the first full-scaled enemy attack and occupation of American soil in our history.

Beginning at Isanotski Straits at the end of Alaska Peninsula, roughly 800 air-miles west of Anchorage, the Aleutian chain is strung out in a thousand-mile arc, washed on the south side by the warm currents of the Pacific and on the north by the cold turbid waters of Bering Sea, and it is this collision of ocean currents which produces a curtain of almost perpetual mist. The largest island in the chain is 68-mile-long Unimak. The smallest are countless, dagger-pointed rocks that show above the surface only at low tide, and at high water lurk below the wave-tops to shear the bellies out of passing ships. To confuse the navigator even more, some of them materialize, and vanish, every time there is an earthquake or volcanic eruption from one of the 20 active "smokers" in the chain. Beyond the farthest west island of Attu, hidden in the fog, is Russia's Kamchatka Peninsula and Japan's Kurile Islands.

Ever since 1867 when we acquired the Aleutians with the rest of Alaska from the Russians for about two cents an acre, the sparsely peopled islands had been blanketed under a Federal bird refuge and the chief business was the ranching of blue foxes on a turn-loose, run-wild basis under special permit good only from year to year, and revocable at the whim of the government. It was a tenuous project at best, poorly supervised, and it was no great wonder that abuses developed. It was, in fact, suspected skullduggery among the leaseholders that sent me out there in 1931.

I had made no effort to conceal my identity as a government agent when I boarded the trading vessel *Aleutian Native* when it left Seattle loaded to the portholes with trade goods, and carrying an enormous deckload of lumber. The small ship was perilously over-weighted and top-heavy for a 3,000-mile voyage on the high seas, and every little slop of water from a passing vessel in the harbor washed in and out of its scuppers. I wouldn't have been surprised if it had turned turtle the moment it backed away from the dock. I waved good-bye to Klondy and Ginny and young Frank who had come down from Juneau to see me off, and I guessed that the tears in their eyes were born of terror as much as from the sorrow of parting.

We were hardly out of Seattle's Puget Sound and into the Straits of Juan de Fuca when the first ocean swells came smashing over the bow to splatter the pilot house windows, and I had to don rubber boots and time the ship's roll so I would be on the high side before breaking out on deck and making a dash for the galley at mealtimes. I hoped we would have ten days of smooth sailing to the nearest shelter in the Aleutians, but what we got were gale strength winds and mountainous waves in which the *Aleutian Native* wallowed like a harpooned whale. The captain, of all people, came down with seasickness. The first mate, a happy-go-lucky red-faced giant called "Tiny," took over and I was pressed into service as a crew member as the vessel sloshed and bucked, shivered and groaned from stem to stern, and plunged almost out of sight into every curling green sea. When I staggered, drenched, to my stateroom for a rest between bouts with the steering wheel and slammed the door shut, every wild roll of the *Aleutian Native* sent a stream of icy brine shooting through the keyhole until I plugged it with a wad of toilet paper. It was the roughest ocean ride I'd ever had, and worse was coming.

We ran out the calculated days and hours which should have brought us under the lee of the Alaska Peninsula, but after a week of savage pounding, there was no land in sight when the eighth black nightfall came. Then in the first gray light of the next dawn we woke on the brink of disaster. Suddenly, we were almost in the same predicament that had wrecked the Russian vessel *St. Peter* 190 years earlier. The trading vessel had been driven far off course by winds and currents and was trapped in a maelstrom of rocky reefs and tide rips. Pinnacles were popping out of the wave troughs all about us, missing the bottom of the *Aleutian Native* only by a succession of miracles. Bells jangled furiously, and through the ship rang the cry "All Hands on Deck!" Crewmen in oilskins rushed to the lifeboat davits, and hung on desperately to the block-and-tackle ropes as waves and tide rips buried them in foam and green water, while they waited for the call, "Abandon ship!"

There was no sign of the seasick captain. He stayed in his bunk, fortunately, because in our midst that desperate morning a hero was born. It was Tiny Campbell, the devil-may-care mate, who bawled orders, took the steering wheel in his enormous hairy hands and under slow bell began dodging rocks. It seemed like an eternity, but gradually the brawny Scot worked the vessel back into open water again. Once in deep ocean we bucked past the whaling station of Akutan where eleven years before I had climbed into the mouth of a whale, and hours later made our first stopover of the trip in Dutch Harbor, Coast Guard base on the Island of Unalaska. But as the *Aleutian Native* backed and filled at the dock, it wasn't the trim white cutters that caught my eye. It was a rusty old hulk with strangely uniformed sailors lining its rails to look us over. The word *Maru* was painted on its bow, and flapping in the wet wind at its stern was a coal-smudged Japanese flag.

A Coast Guardsman explained its presence. The *Maru* was here by permission. The Japanese had started what they called a "Tokyo-San Francisco Good Will Flight." An aviator of the Rising Sun was about to attempt an overseas flight in a single-engined pontoon plane via the Aleutians, and the *Maru* had dropped what they said were "watch-service" parties of Japanese here and there along the entire length of the Aleutians with caches of gasoline for refueling the "good will" flier. The Coast Guardsman said the project had the blessings of our Washington top brass, so I gave it no more thought—not until the *Aleutian Native* plowed on westward and I began to observe the strange activities of these "watch service" sons of Nippon.

The Aleutian Islands weather forecast usually showed seven or eight clear sunny days a year, though I remember none at all during my six months of investigation; just rolling curtains of fog and storm clouds. Even in summer the temperature seldom rose above 50 degrees, and as I tramped across the islands I never knew what moment I would be blasted by the williwaws—winds of mysterious origin that suddenly shrieked straight down out of the overcast to strike the earth with cyclonic force and go howling off in all directions.

There weren't any trees, only a few willows along the creek banks, and the rest of the islands would be all violently-waving grass tops, glass-sharp black obsidian that cut my boot-soles to ribbons, and porous lava rocks spewed out by the volcanoes. The shorelines were mostly sheer stone walls, their tops shrouded in mist, shelved and wind-carved to provide perches and nesting sites for millions—make it *billions*—of auklets, murres, puffins, cormorants, screaming gulls, kittiwakes, and bald eagles. Along the wave-pounded beaches huge Steller sea lions weighing up to a ton each, slumbered like yellow slugs, and the bays were dotted with the glistening heads of hair seals. I looked in vain for a sight of the fabulous sea otter, presumed to be extinct.

The only land mammals on most of the islands were foxes, though on one group of surf-beaten rocks shown on the chart as the Rat Islands, a sinking vessel had been deserted by its rats and they had swarmed ashore over heaps of kelp and flotsam to battle the foxes for their existence. From this incident had sprung the legend of the self-sustaining fur farm—the foxes living on the rats, and the rats living on the skinned carcasses of the foxes.

Almost as astonishing was the scheme devised by the master of the *Aleutian Native* to skin the untutored Aleut villagers out of their co-operatively owned stores. Every man, woman, and child owned a share of these co-ops, and were supposed to share in all the profits. Unfortunately, there had been none because the fox trappers hadn't paid their bills. They all owed themselves money, which was like their left pants pocket being in debt to the right pants pocket. But it worried them, so when the clever white trader made an offer to buy them out, he remembered the good old "fox-eat-rat-eat-fox" formula. He solemnly promised the natives—most of whom could neither read nor write—*that his first act as store owner would be to cancel everybody's debts. Not one of them would owe the new store so much as a dime!*

But what he neglected to tell the Aleut people was that prices would be raised on nearly every commodity; that they would all be in debt again shortly; that they might have to sign their government fur farm leases to him, and that a state of peonage that hadn't existed since the cruel Russian rule might soon be reborn among the long-suffering natives.

It had taken some time for all these implications to sink into the Aleut mind, but they were finally beginning to see the light. They had been holding secret meetings in the beraberis, and when I arrived they were only too glad to make revealing affidavits and scrawl their "X" marks. It wasn't long before my brief case bulged with enough statements to bring a halt to this "stealing candy from babies" swindle, and I found time to delve into another subject; that of the Aleut people themselves.

What was the racial background of these strange little people, isolated on a few islands in the Aleutian Chain? From whence had they come, and how long ago? Their family names—Gregorioff, Snegaroff, Pleshnakoff, Stepatin, Zaochney, Hodikoff—meant only that they had survived a century of pillage and brutality; that their forefathers had been murdered wholesale; the women seized and made to bear the children of their Russian lords, and the existing offspring made to carry the names of their oppressors. The Aleuts of 1931 were neither white, nor Eskimo, nor Indian; neither yellow nor brown, but a stunted, polyglot mixture of oriental and slav. What their ancient background had been may never be known, though there is one indisputable fact of their early history: They—not Columbus, nor Cabot, nor even Leif Ericson—had been the true discoverers of America. They had come out of Asia to cross the Aleutian Chain almost two thousand years before the time of Christ. They had moved century by century across the face of the new continent, slowly evolving into the copper-faced people who gathered along the Atlantic beaches a hundred generations later to watch the first Europeans land.

The earliest known culture of the Aleut people indicated they had sprung from a race of mummy-makers. They had retained this custom even as they paddled and walked across a thousand miles of islands from Asia to the Great Land in the East. In the Islands of Four Mountains a rare find had been made at the time of my visit: mummies wrapped in straw matting with their artifacts and ornaments. The faces and hands felt like old leather when I touched them. They were shrunken and black with the passing of centuries, cured to bone-like hardness in volcanic caves just above the water line amid oozing fumes of burning sulphur from submarine craters. Anthropologists in the Smithsonian Institution in Washington, D.C. where the wrinkled little mummies were shipped, placed the time of their death at approximately 3,500 years ago. The only other people with as valid a claim to the discovery of America were those who might have crossed the once existing Arctic land bridge from the vicinity of East Cape, Siberia, via the Diomede Islands, to what is now Seward Peninsula; the same route traveled by vast herds of beasts like mammoths, superbisons, caribou, moose, deer, mountain sheep, goats, and bears in the general Ice Age period. Kitchen middens unearthed on the Alaska side of Bering Straits indicate the probability that Asiatic nomads landed on our Arctic beaches as long ago as 6,000 years; all of which tend to rate Columbus and Cabot as a couple of "Johnny-Come-Latelys!"

All the stranger, then, that at the time of my first visit the Aleutian stepping stones to America still bore the appearance of a foreign land. Because of the treacherous reefs and spear-pointed rocks, the *Aleutian Native* was forced to drop anchor far offshore, and the journey to land made in a power dory. The first sign of a village was an onion-topped church with the Orthodox Cross marked by an extra, slanting cross bar at the bottom. As I came nearer

I saw driftwood racks along the beach draped with what appeared to be hundreds of red, green, and white socks hung out to dry. When I landed, I discovered these "socks" to be split fish flung over the poles to harden in the wind—salmon for the red socks, codfish for white, and the fantastically green and blue fleshed cabezons and lings.

Those Aleuts who were skilled at blue-fox trapping had built themselves small, frame houses covered with tarpaper, though some of the homes were as they must have been for hundreds of years—clods of turf formed in the shape of an igloo. From the belfry of the onion-domed church came the frequent tolling of a heavy bell summoning the villagers. The most familiar sight in the community was the wind-whipped figure of a giant Russian priest, bearded to the waist, and with a long, flowing robe sweeping the grass-tops, appearing still more imposing by a high hat which made him look at least eight feet tall. Wherever he went he would be leading his flock of undersized Aleuts who seldom came up to his armpits; heading for the graveyard or coming back, to the church, or going to or returning from other mysterious pilgrimages about the village. The American schoolteacher at Nicolski, not long up from Oregon, said she didn't know how to compete for the children's attentions, and the Stars and Stripes flapping dismally in the rain-gusts looked oddly out of place in this strange land.

Before the ranching of blue foxes yielded them a cash crop, the Aleut tribes had been beachcombers. There were shellfish for the taking, and octopus to be hooked out from under the rocks at low tide. Sea birds clung to the vertical walls; trout and salmon schooled into the shallow creeks; the kelp beds swarmed with yellow and black zebra-barred Atkafish, greenlings, sculpins, and cods. Hair seals hauled out on the sands where they could be bludgeoned as they basked. The shorelines were strewn with the driftwood of two continents—spruce, cedar, teak, and sometimes bamboo, and among the tangle of wave-heaped wood could be found the hollow glass balls used by the Japanese for buoying up their nets.

Word had spread among the Aleuts that a government man had come to help them. The hopeful villagers smiled shyly at me, sometimes clutching their hats in hand, and a few even made the sign of the cross. As their confidence grew, they talked freely until it led to the happiest discovery of the trip; the sighting of a creature so rare that at first I could not believe my eyes. It began one night when the *Aleutian Native* lay anchored in Constantine Harbor of Amchitka Island, near the end of the chain. It was stygian dark and the fog was thick enough to slice with a knife when I heard a polite tap on my stateroom window. I opened the door and recognized the whispered voice of Makary Zaochney, the dwarf Aleut chief. He had something to show me. We rowed ashore in the black void of early morning, and stumbled along a footpath leading over the crest of the island, stopping only when the sound of the ocean surf seemed to rise straight up from the depths. I knew then that we were at the edge of a headland, and when daylight came I looked down with my binoculars upon a surging kelp bed and saw a creature out of the past. A light brown head and contrasting black body reared half its length up among the trailing fronds and bulbs, then fell back on the water and floated with all four feet and short tail held above the surface. The sea otter was the size of a small seal, about 80 pounds in weight, and its rich fur glistened like silk in a beam of sunshine that pierced the dawn mist for a moment. The hind feet were broadened and widened into a pair of flippers, but the stubby front paws looked in the distance like those of a land mammal. Stiff, white whiskers bristling from its face accounted for its popular name among the Aleuts of the early days—"Old Man."

Chief Makary laid a forefinger across his lips. There was a swirl among the kelp-bulbs. A small replica had appeared. It climbed onto the breast of the parent, and she hugged it in her stubby arms, licked it long and affectionately, and as the baby nursed, the mother went sculling away on her back.

"Look well," said Makary in his high-pitched stilted English as they vanished in the mist. "You may never see them again."

No one would ever know the depths of misery the little Aleut chief's forefathers had suffered because of these fabulous ocean fur-bearers. When the half-dead survivors of Vitus Bering's shipwrecked crew struggled back to their Russian base in 1742, they had almost nothing to show for their horrible adventure except a few pelts from the animals they had clubbed to death for food. But it was enough! Expedition followed expedition to the "Great Land." The Aleuts were enslaved, forced to kill the beautiful animals or be killed themselves. Because of them, Alaska was colonized and held in peonage until the sea otters were all but wiped out of existence. Then because there was no further sign of quick wealth, the Russians sold the huge, largely unexplored land mass to the United States in 1867 for $7,200,000. But even after the American flag flew over the Aleutians, the northern sea otter continued to be hunted almost without restriction until no more could be found. Many a naturalist had written them off the book of living creatures along with the passenger pigeon and the great auk when Makary shared the secret of their slender existence with me in that summer of 1931. Since that time the sea otter have continued to "come back" and spread themselves all along the Aleutian Islands and Southwestern Alaska, though the center of their population today is still among the kelp beds of Amchitka Island where I found them.

My elation at the discovery was tempered by another odd sight before I got back aboard the *Aleutian Native* that day. From a high point overlooking Constantine Harbor I spotted a dory drifting off a rocky point near the entrance to the bay. There were three men in the boat, and when my binoculars brought them close enough, I saw that one of the figures was holding a sketch-board. Another appeared to be handlining for fish over the side. The third was sighting through a camera. They were not Aleuts.

Jananee watch service," explained Makary. "Long time stay this place; take picture; write on paper." The little chief shrugged his shoulders. "All time go fishing. Sometime no use bait."

¶27 Seeds of War

We were in the summer of 1931 at peace with the Japanese nation. There was no inkling that they were sowing the seeds of war in the Aleutians; no reason to suspect that their Tokyo-San Francisco Good Will Flight by a small single-engined airplane was other than they represented it to be: a friendly gesture by an admiring people. Their *Hochi-Shimbun* newspaper and our own dailies stressed the growing amity between Japan and the United States, and there were cartoons depicting clasped hands across the North Pacific. To safeguard their heroic lone flier in case of bad weather or other mishap, it seemed natural that the Japanese would want to set up some kind of "watch-service" along the Aleutians. All this we accepted as perfectly proper procedure. But what didn't seem to make full sense to those of us who were in the area at the time was why the Japanese felt it necessary to install so many "watch-service" parties along the Aleutian Chain; why each little group of three were scurrying about like beavers on tasks which would appear to have nothing at all to do with watching for a small airplane to fly overhead.

Before leaving Constantine Harbor, Tiny Campbell, the giant red-headed mate of the *Aleutian Native*—who shared my curiosity—took me on a "fishing" trip of our own in the ship's power dory. On the rocky point where I'd seen the Japanese trio, we examined an odd sort of beacon made of bamboo, above which flew a small white flag with a red center. Beneath a waterproof covering we found a message written in Japanese characters. There was a small cache of gasoline and a box filled with rice, tea, and cookies; nothing to excite the least suspicion. Swarming hordes of brightly-barred Atkafish seemed far more interesting at the moment, and I proceeded to have the time of my life fly-casting along the edge of the kelp beds for the surfacing fish which were feeding on tiny crustaceans and which snapped wildly at a Brown Hackle floating fly. I had dismissed the "watch-service" as being of small consequence when Tiny Campbell said he'd just caught a glint of light from the top of a bluff across the harbor entrance. I laid down my fishing rod, picked up my binoculars, and from a distance of half a mile found myself staring into another pair of field glasses. The Japanese, it seemed, were watching us, too.

Before the trading schooner left Constantine Harbor on its return journey, chief Mike Hodikoff of Attu Island, farthest west of the Aleutians and much closer to Japan and Russia than to our own seat of government, came aboard to join me in my stateroom. Secretly, he confided that he was worried about the "watch-service" Japanese on his island. He said he had watched them measuring the water depths at Attu bay entrances and passes, charting the shorelines and contours. They had climbed all over the steep sides of the island planting signal flags which could be seen from the decks of ships at sea. In the little village of 27 natives, best known in the early 1930's for their exquisitely woven grass "Attu baskets," Mike Hodikoff and a woman schoolteacher constituted the only authority, and their advice had been to treat the Japanese visitors courteously. Nevertheless, Hodikoff had somehow acquired a wireless set and was taking it to the United States Coast Guard base at Dutch Harbor to have it put in working order, and to arrange some kind of a code for calling in an emergency.

The little Attu chief's near-sighted eyes blinked with suspicion behind the thick lenses of his horn-rimmed glasses. "Japenee come back some day," he predicted solemnly. "Take village."

I tried to calm his fears with an explanation of the "good will flight" and the necessity for some kind of a "watch-service," but a few days later on Atka Island I wondered if Hodikoff hadn't seen something the rest of us were missing. I had tramped far inland from the village to catch and examine some of the odd speckled trout described by the natives, and to my utter surprise came upon three Japanese squatting around a small fire of lichens and twigs, cooking a pot of rice and boiling water for tea. I walked among them, noting a plant press loaded with botanical specimens and a sack full of mineral samples. One of the party carried a small camera, and the one I took to be the leader had a pistol hanging from a black leather belt.

They recovered quickly from the surprise encounter. The leader, who said his name was Yusada, greeted me in schoolboy English. He said they were all college students attached to the "watch-service" party, and were taking advantage of the flight's delay by studying the new land. He said it reminded him of their own northern islands. He asked me what my connections were with the U.S. government and I remember that when I told him, he quickly translated the news to the other two Japs. They watched me catch enough trout to augment their lunch, and I joined them for rice and tea, fumbling with the chopsticks they offered, then dipping in with my fingers. Several times the leader suddenly addressed me in Japanese language, whether to try to catch me off guard, or by slip of the tongue, I could not be sure. It was clear, however, that they suspected me of deliberately following them from the village. And whether they liked my company or not, we were destined to become much better acquainted in the next few hours, because while we hunkered around the smudgy campfire a dank fog came rolling in off the water to blot out every landmark and wrap us in mist so dense we could see no more than twenty feet.

They let me take the lead back toward the village. There was little hope of finding the exact cove in which it lay. My chief concern was to avoid the precipitous bluffs and try to make our way safely to a level shore. Screaming sea birds were warning enough of the perpendicular walls hiding in the fog. The steady roar of the surf breaking across the sandy beaches guided us to the surging ocean. But in which direction lay the village there would be no way of telling until the opaque gray curtain lifted.

Before the darkness of night combined with the cold fog to reduce visibility to absolute zero, we gathered heaps of driftwood above the high tide line and built a roaring fire at the mouth of a natural cave. It was then that I took a lesson from these Japanese boys on how to live off the land—and the sea. They plucked a dozen kinds of shoots and roots from the edge of a creek to cook with the small sack of rice, though the real supply of emergency food came under the swirling tide waters. They showed me several varieties of shellfish and edible kelps. The choicest items of all were the spoon-sized blobs sucked from the spiny sea urchins which fairly carpeted the bottom. The orange-colored roe sacks were delicate and tasty as the finest oysters. Baiting my fly rod with limpets, I caught a half dozen green-fleshed Russian rock trout to complete one of the finest sea food cookouts of my life. The Japanese boys seemed to enjoy it, too. They relaxed and chattered most of the night, though I would have liked it better if their conversation had not all been in their own language.

The morning sun was trying its best to burn a hole through the overcast when I heard the steady chunk-a-lunk of the one-cylinder engine in the *Aleutian Native's* dory. Big Tiny Campbell had paced the deck half the night before, worrying and watching, and thought he had detected a glow in the darkness. We pitched more drift-wood on the fire and yelled at the top of our voices, and presently the dory came around a point of rocks and headed into our cove. The brawny mate eyed the Japs curiously but said nothing until after we'd let them off at the village and headed out to the trading ship for a good old fashioned American breakfast of ham and eggs and hotcakes and mugs of strong black coffee.

"You and the Japanese Boys been on some kind of party?" he asked finally.

I knew what big Tiny had in mind, but there wasn't much I could tell him. I'd seen nothing that couldn't be explained as natural curiosity on the part of the Nipponese college boys—if that's what they were. Yet, the feeling persisted that the Japanese "watch-service" could stand a little more "watching" on our part, and this was strengthened when we found more Japanese bobbing up and down in their small boats at the entrance to the main harbor on uninhabited Kiska Island, one of the finest natural anchorages and potential airfield sites in all the Aleutians.

I guess everybody aboard the trading vessel except jovial Tiny Campbell, with whom I had formed a lasting friendship, was glad to see me walk down the gangplank of the *Aleutian Native* and out of their lives at Dutch Harbor, especially owner Archer who was quite aware that I had amassed enough evidence to restore the Aleuts' rights to their co-op stores and fur farm leases. I carried my duffel bags up the beach to a boarding house operated by Mr. Pedlar, manager of the Northern Commercial Company trading post, and found myself sharing a small upstairs quarters with a surprising bedfellow. He was a man in his thirties who carried himself with military erectness. When Mr. Pedlar introduced us, the stranger's clipped speech carried the faintest trace of a hiss. The name he had signed on the register just ahead of mine was "H. Kimura, Tokyo, Japan."

Far from being secretive about his mission in the Aleutians, Kimura was sociable, very well mannered, and very inquisitive. He said that he represented the newspaper *Hochi-Shimbun* which was sponsoring the Tokyo-San Francisco Good Will Flight. He said he had been staying aboard the *Maru,* but had decided to take up short residence ashore in order to get better acquainted with the American people, and he hoped I wouldn't mind if he asked many questions.

I thought this over a minute before replying. "I'll trade with you," I said. "For every question you ask me about the United States I'll ask you one about Japan."

While the late summer rains started pouring down and I waited for a government patrol vessel to come down out of Bering Sea to let me hitch a ride to the southeastern mainland, Kimura also waited for a non-stop flier who turned out to be a *non-start* flier. We swapped small talk in the upstairs quarters of the Northern Commercial Company post for hours on end, ate our meals together, and retired to our cubby-hole bunks to sleep at night. At the end I didn't really know much more about Kimura and the "watch-service" than I had at the beginning; I was just as sure he didn't know much more about me or my suspicions, either.

There were little slips, of course, small utterances which didn't mean much by themselves, but which added to something said a few days before, or after, were like bits of chaff tossed in the wind. When sifted they revealed tiny defects in Kimura's smooth line of talk. Once, for example, when I remarked on his obvious high-born bearing, he said with some pride that he was a baron in his country, which didn't seem to tie in with his being a newspaper reporter.

Another time Kimura showed me a photograph of a scowling Russian brandishing a fist at him, and said it was a member of the secret police, the dreaded OGPU, and he smiled thinly as he told me that he had snapped the picture on the docks at Vladivostok with a hidden mini-camera. It was the first information I'd had that the Tokyo-San Francisco "watch-service" had necessitated a stop-over at one of Russia's main sea bases on the North Pacific.

Kimura also knew the location of every schoolhouse, church, and government structure all the way from the Coast Guard oil tanks of Dutch Harbor to the end of the chain, and frequently mentioned the names of native chiefs like Makary Zaochney of Atka and Mike Hodikoff of Attu. He expressed wonderment that we were utilizing the Aleutian resources so poorly that only a few hundred Aleuts occupied such a vast and rich terrain. "Five million Japanese could live well on these islands," I recall him declaring.

Kimura had expressed unfamiliarity with the *Maru's* appointments and a distaste for naval life, yet when he showed me through the vessel I couldn't help noticing that he occupied the master's quarters; that the *Maru* commander bowed to him, and that all wireless messages were delivered into his hands. It was on one of these occasions that Kimura said it looked as if they would have to call off the Good Will Flight for the season, and that the *Maru* would soon be departing westward to gather up members of the "watch-service"—who had been scattered through the Aleutians all summer long—and return them to Japan before the equinoctial storms started blasting the islands with williwaws.

Though Alaskans grumbled at the stalling tactics of the Japanese along the Aleutians in that summer of 1931, and realized they were doing considerable snooping, nobody seemed to take the matter too seriously. After all, we were one of the most powerful military forces in the world. Japan was only a small nation struggling to feed its burgeoning population, and apparently trying to improve relations with the West. The Tokyo-San Francisco flight, on its surface, appeared to be just what the newspaper *Hochi-Shimbun* proclaimed it to be: a gesture of good will to its American friends.

On my way back to Juneau aboard a Coast Guard cutter, I typed out my report on wildlife conditions in the

Aleutians, together with a recommendation on how to correct the abuses which had crept into the blue fox farming leases. In a separate statement I pin-pointed the locations of the Japanese "watch-service" parties and my observations of their numerous activities, concluding with the conversations held between me and the mysterious H. Kimura at Dutch Harbor. I did not feel sufficiently informed nor qualified to make any accusations, but expressed a willingness to supply more details if requested to do so. There were no such requests.

Six months after the attack on Pearl Harbor, on June 2, 1942, a Japanese naval force, presumed to be from Paramushuri in the Kurile Islands, was reported hiding in the mist 400 miles south of Kiska, moving silently toward the Aleutian Islands.

At dawn the next day, Japanese carrier-borne planes zeroed in out of the fog to strafe and bomb the Coast Guard Station and oil tanks at Dutch Harbor.

Attu was overrun and its natives, the schoolteacher, and little Chief Mike Hodikoff were captured.

On Kiska Island eleven U.S. weather observers were wiped out by the invaders as they landed in full force, pulled down the Stars and Stripes, and raised the flag of the Rising Sun.

As the shocking news filtered in from remote outposts and from lone native trappers, there was the alarming fact that the Japanese fleet had steamed at full speed through the islands; that they had known the precise location of every harbor, every installation, every "uncharted" reef. After ten years, the "watch-service" for the Tokyo-San Francisco Good Will Flight had paid off.

But not for long. Within a year, following thirty days of bitter fighting, we had silenced every machine gun and dragged every enemy soldier from the fox-holes on Attu. Then we moved on Kiska, the main stronghold of the enemy in the Aleutians, and there a very strange development occurred. As American and Canadian troops stormed ashore in August of 1943, there was not a Japanese to be found. Under cover of the fog they had evacuated a force believed to have numbered 10,000. They'd had enough. The futile attempt of the Emperor's war lords to seize the Aleutians had fizzled.

In the aftermath two questions stuck in my mind. Where had my boarding-house "friend" H. Kimura been on the day Dutch Harbor was bombed? What had happened to brave little Chief Hodikoff and his wireless set when the Japanese took Attu? I never found out.

28 The Swivel Chair

After weeks of suspense and strange happenings in the Aleutians, it was good to settle down to the tranquility of life in Juneau. There were many happy weekends spent at our beach cabin with Klondy and our fast growing girl and boy. We dug clams at low tide. We cast for salmon off the porch at high water. I rowed the skiff out front while the children handlined for flounders and chicken halibut. We set pot-traps for crabs. There were wonderful evenings with friends around the driftwood fires.

When the weather was right we made outboard-motored trips to outlying trout streams; all four of us stretched in our sleeping bags, sometimes alongside bear trails worn deep beside the river bank. In the fall there were big hooter grouse and blacktail deer bucks to be hunted in the mountains at timberline. Migrations of waterfowl—mallards, sprigs, teal and widgeons, snow and Canada geese—

tarried for weeks along the estuaries and tide flats before lifting off for the rice fields of California.

But the luxury of living in a comfortable home with my family, as it had before, brought with it the penalty of office routine which I abhorred. I had thoroughly convinced myself that the only really worthwhile part of wildlife management was getting out in the wild places, observing the game and becoming attuned to its ways and needs, then making recommendations on how to achieve (1) well stocked streams and forests, and (2) proper utilization by humans *of the annual surplus only*. I had come to the conclusion that you could not hoard the fish and game beyond a certain level of abundance; that when the species reached the point where the water and the land could support no more of them, the overflow—if not angled or hunted—simply spilled away and was lost through old age, predation, malnutrition, winter kills, or worst of all by diseases which might spread through their ranks and cause far more devastation than any amount of hunting, or, indeed, of all other loss factors combined. I had thought that if I could stay out in the hinterlands checking on these conditions from year to year and from place to place, that others could handle the mechanics of getting the job done.

Through the years I had worked out of the Juneau headquarters office, I had observed with some detachment the growing harassment of the Game Commission's Executive Officer as he sought without much success to apply the principles of the first Alaska Game Law to a frontier which had been for years with almost no game regulations at all. I had seen the mountainous heaps of scrawled letters from irate old timers, and the clerks pecking away at office forms and statistics. There was the never ending pursuit of violators, many of them Indians who found their old way of life threatened. There was the necessity to justify operating funds; the annual trips to Washington to be grilled by appropriation committees of the Congress. This phase of the operations filled me with dismay. I detested the thought of becoming another office worker. So it wasn't long before I started asking for more outdoor assignments, the tougher the better. The worst of them would be preferable by far to this pencil-pushing drudgery.

The four resident members of the Alaska Game Commission, in Juneau for their yearly session, had been joined by a top official from the Washington, D.C. office of the Bureau of Biological Survey. At my first opportunity I had planned to ask for an audience to suggest that I be given more field work and less office routine, but they asked me in first. I launched into my carefully prepared program of wildlife studies, and it stretched for several years ahead. The board members smoked their pipes, smiling with what appeared to be secret amusement as I put in my plea for action in far away places. I sensed they had something else in mind, and only half listened until I finally ran down. Then I found out I was not going to get away with less office work; I was going to be saddled with more of it.

They had excused the Executive Officer from the chambers, and now they proceeded to question me on many phases of the Alaska wildlife situation, meanwhile telling me something I already knew: that conditions had not been very good. After they were finished, I repeated my suggestion. When could I get away from all this red tape rat-race and get back in the wild puckerbush where I belonged?

It was then that the blow fell.

"You can't," said the man from Washington. The members had risen to their feet and were starting around the table. "You can't," repeated the man from Washington, "because you are now the Executive Officer of the Game Commission, Chief Representative of the Biological Survey in the Territory, in charge of all Alaska operations. Congratulations!" My knees wobbled as I returned their handclasps.

Though the thought of never again being able to flee from office routine into the peace of the wilderness came as a dull shock, I felt no qualms about handling the top job. I had dogteamed and snowshoed, boated, and rubber-booted the great land from one end to another. I knew it better than any other man in the Service. What is more, I knew the pioneer residents and the natives through visits at their cabins and fish-camps, and I thought I knew what they wanted and would support in the way of regulations. Of all the jobs waiting to be done in the headquarters office, none seemed so urgent to me as tackling that heap of angry letters and trying to establish some kind of rapport between these widely scattered people and the Game Commission which had been set up to give them their first measure of home rule.

It was easier than I had dared hope. Many of the letters I could answer with a "Dear Jim," "Dear Bob," "Dear Pete," because I had unrolled my sleeping bag across their cabin floors and broken sourdough bread with them, and talked wildlife far into the nights. To make it easier for them to make recommendations for new regulations, I contrived a form for distribution through the several hundred trading posts which needed only check marks for the trappers and outlying residents to express a choice on open seasons and bag limits, though with plenty of space at the end for those who still wanted to let off steam. Letters filled with scrawled profanity continued to come in from the old timers, but now they were written by friends, not enemies. It wasn't long before cross sections of opinions were available for orderly review by the Alaska Game Commission members at their annual sessions. At the same time I began to perceive that management of wild life must also include management of people; that it wasn't much use to know merely what the fish and game needed unless the people approved and supported the necessary laws. I began to realize the value of what we nowadays call "public relations."

As they made occasional trips to "Seattle and Great Outside," the Alaska residents began dropping into *their* game commission headquarters by invitation, and the big corner room in Juneau's new Federal Building became a meeting place for all manners of people. Sometimes I would look up to see an old dogmusher I'd raced down the frozen Yukon years before, and we would slap each other's backs with the pleasure of meeting again. The next visitors might be big names from Hollywood. One day the famous blackface pair, Amos and Andy, came for hunting licenses. Then John Barrymore insisted that I go down to his yacht while he displayed an exquisite collection of fairyweight fly rods and dry flies so tiny you had to use a microscope to thread a leader through the eye of the hook. Right after the great profile, came a deputy I'd served with in the early days of Nome.

I didn't want to admit it, even to myself, but I was beginning to enjoy these human contacts in the office almost as much as confronting a grizzly on a salmon stream. Stewart Edward White, outstanding naturalist and novelist from Santa Barbara, California, shook his head of white hair with deep feeling mounting almost to rage as he challenged the reasoning of the United States Forest Service and anybody else who fought against his plan to have Admiralty Island set aside as a national recreation area so that its unique bear populations and park-like scenery might be preserved for all the people of America to enjoy. I think it was then that I, myself, took up the crusade to save this wonderful island which was to culminate years later in my book *No Room For Bears.*

One of the most lovable sourdough characters I ever met, rich and famous through royalties from his books and motion pictures, "The Spoilers" and "The Silver Horde," was burly Rex Beach, retired to the life of a country squire in Sebring, Florida. Now in his middle-sixties, the gold rush pioneer had become a dedicated fisherman. He spent hours helping me "control" the swarming salmon in front of our beach cabin, reminiscing between strikes on the roaring days of the Klondike and Nome. One day he joined me for an inspection flight in our game commission sea plane and we splashed down for a pontoon landing at an isolated island where Joe Ibach, one of his partners of early adventures, was living out his allotted years in lonely contentment. As Joe waded out in his rubber boots to grasp the struts, Rex appeared in the doorway with an armful of dog-eared magazines scooped out of a rack.

"Sir," he began, "I am a young man working my way through college . . . . . ." The rest was drowned out by old Joe's obscene roars of ecstasy.

Once a year Allen Hasselborg, the irascible hermit bear man of Admiralty Island, bulled his way into the office. Every spring the fiery old curmudgeon made it a point to come to town for the chief purpose of lambasting me with vituperations he'd been composing all winter for my sole benefit. He'd spent months reading the annual regulations by candle-light, probing for soft spots. His unshorn locks and vast black beard shook with fury, and his cold eyes blazed like those of a grizzly about to charge.

"You'd think the law of averages would fix it so you couldn't be wrong all the time," he'd shout. "But no, you *Never* get anything right . . ." and so on until the typewriters in the outer office stopped clacking, and the girls held their hands to their ears waiting for us to engage in hand-to-hand combat.

After the hairy man-hater stomped out of the office, and the thumping of his bootheels faded away down the hall, the place seemed quiet as a tomb. Nonetheless, I appreciated his visits, because when I reflected on the charges he had leveled at me, I began to see a lot of truth in what he'd said. He was nobody's "yes" man. He jabbed unmercifully at every weak spot. But as long as I fronted for the game commission I came to regard his blistering criticisms as compliments, because I was the only "government parasite" he deigned to visit.

29 Full Circle

Because I had for many years set my own time for working in the wilds—which meant from before daylight to after darkness—I had a bad time trying to adjust my hours to an office clock. When there was a job to be done, I felt I had to stay with it twenty-four hours a day, seven days a week. Frequently, I'd be under a hot desk lamp far past midnight penciling on cost sheets, doodling over personnel problems, scanning law books, trying to undo mistakes which lay splattered before my tired eyes as hopeless as a lot of broken eggs waiting to be poured into their shells again. I'd be back in the morning while the town was still wrapped in sleep. The custodian of the Federal Building used to tell me they didn't need a night watchman any more.

Every time I donned my old field clothes and tried to slip out of town there would be another crisis at the office until, finally, a semblance of order began rising out of the chaos. The improvement came about not through my own "new broom" sweepings, but chiefly because the Territory's first game code needed only a fair test to prove that it was basically correct. Through its four pioneer commissioners, one from each of the judicial districts, there was representation of people right down to the humblest Eskimo. Through me as its executive officer, there was the necessary liaison between the Territory, and the Federal Government who paid the bills. My earlier travels into almost every hamlet began to pay off in another way, too. I had met outstanding woodsmen whom I now convinced to accept appointments, and see them form one of the finest groups of wildlife agents in all of America. Though there were only eight of them to patrol an area one-fifth the size of the 48 lower states, they seemed at times to cover their vast domain like a blanket. Several of them learned to fly, and soon their small planes carrying the brown bear insignia of the game commission, rigged with ski landing gear in winter and fitted with pontoons in summer, were lighting down all over the Territory. In all the country there was no other game department so advanced in the technique of aerial wildlife surveys and law enforcement.

For me there was only one sour note in this rising prestige of the Game Commission. Caught in my own trap, I could not free my mind of the truth that the wildlife agents in their green cruiser jackets, their mukluks and rubber boots, were the ones getting the job done; not me with a pencil and a green eye-shade. In the frustration of being forced to sit like a lump of tallow in a steam-heated office while the outside men daily risked their lives in their small planes and patrol boats, I grew fidgety as a setting hen. I took up pipe-smoking and blew rings like a donkey engine. I put on flabby pounds of flesh. I developed saddle sores from riding a swivel chair. I began experimenting with anti-ulcer nostrums.

It was a big day in my life—bigger than I could possibly realize—when two more visitors walked into the Juneau office which had become my prison. One of the callers was Corey Ford, a young author from New York. With his writing partner of those years, Alastair MacBain, Ford had been commissioned to do a series of conservation articles for the *Saturday Evening Post*. Alaska was next on their list. They sniffed through the office material like a pair of eager beagles, and then Ford said the words that sprung me out of my cell.

"We'd like to see a little live action," he suggested. "We'd like to get out in the forests and meet some of your bears and trout . . ." And then it came: "*We'd like you to go with us.*"

Three evenings later I wondered if they might not have changed their minds about seeing the wild side of Alaska. Hosea Sarber, the great bear man whom I had talked into accepting an appointment as wildlife agent, had led us far up a crystal-clear trout stream on Admiralty Island. Ford and MacBain had fetched along their angling paraphernalia straight out of Abercrombie and Fitch, and had experienced what they said was the greatest dry fly fishing of their lives. The upper reaches of the river were a pure wilderness of primeval evergreens and tumbling currents.

There was no sign that anybody else had ever cast a fly on its riffles. Black-speckled cutthroat to twenty inches, and red-spotted Dolly Varden trout rose at almost every cast, and the angling was made even zestier when Hosea casually called their attention to other fishers; mink, otters, *and bears.* There had been a run of salmon up from the sea, and the grizzlies had come down from the mountain berry patches to eat their fill of red flesh. In the bright daylight hours, the shaggy giants kept their distance, occasionally rising on their haunches to follow with their eyes the back and forth swishes of the fly rods, like spectators at a tennis match.

In mid-afternoon Hosea quietly reminded the New York writers that it was time we all headed back downstream in order to reach our beached speed boat before nightfall. With the coming of darkness, he said, there would be many more grizzlies moving out of the forest shadows to catch salmon; they would be bolder, even resentful of humans, and a surprise encounter at close range "could get somebody hurt."

It was a typical understatement by the great "Hozey" and at first the two writers did not catch its full significance. They continued to dally in anglers' heaven, so that when the sun went down in a last blaze of deepening red, we were still not out of the woods. In the waning light we had all seen a big grizzly swaggering against the skyline, on a bear trail we would have to follow on our way to our boat. How many others might be down in the streambed below the horizon we had no way of knowing. But we had to go through. Hosea, with rifle cradled across his arm, felt called upon to impart a few words of advice.

"If we jump one—or he jumps us—don't yell; don't run. Stand still and let me try to talk sense with him." Out of the corner of his mouth Hosea slurred a remark at me.

"Nobody knows what a grizzly's going to do. You know that . . ." He turned and started down the smoothly padded trail, his legs spread wide like a man on snowshoes as he planted his feet in the bear tracks. I knew there would be no more talking; only action if needed.

There were snorts and whoofs and splashing of water ahead as the fishing grizzlies caught our scent, and once a shadowy blob vanished in the alders within a pebble's toss. We had reached a short stretch of open meadow and then the tidal mud sloping down to saltwater when the night was suddenly shattered by horrendous roars. Our ears followed the blood-chilling outbursts as they faded into a point of timber, then seemed to turn about, hesitate, and come storming our way again.

If the grizzly was bluffing, it worked. We hustled across a windrow of clam shells to the speedboat and shoved off for the mast-head light on Hosea's patrol boat bobbing up and down in the darkness. As we climbed aboard, we looked back on the black outlines of Admiralty Island with its greatest concentration of wild grizzlies in the world; the region that Teddy Roosevelt had once tried to set aside as a national attraction. To its undisputed title of "Bear Island," Corey added another: "The Exciting Forest."

When I got back to Juneau I made a discovery of my own. I'd been gone a week. There should have been a heap of trouble on my desk. There wasn't a single letter. No telegrams. The office force had slicked up every detail, and by the grins on their faces, they'd enjoyed doing it. I learned, as other fledgling executives before me had learned, that I was not nearly as important as I'd let myself believe. It was not efficiency, but insufficiency, that had caused me to burn the midnight oil over problems better handled by others. When I ran into the custodian of the Federal Building again I told him he'd just lost himself a free night watchman.

Once the prison bars came off my office windows, I was away on a new round of field trips, though it wasn't quite like the good old days. Now, I had to do most of my travel by plane, and I had to check with the headquarters by wireless at every opportunity just in case an emergency arose. But it did give me a chance to "recharge my batteries" in the wilderness. Author Cory Ford kept coming back from New York to join me. Together, we squatted around Kenai campfires in moose and mountain sheep country while the incomparable Andy Simons puffed his curved-stem briar and spun tales for Corey's typewriter. Ford sat strapped beside me as we flew through the thermal air currents of famed Valley of Ten Thousand Smokes. In the remote watersheds of Bristol Bay we caught giant rainbow trout sometimes larger than the salmon among which they schooled. Dr. Ira N. Gabrielson, new Chief of the Biological Survey, who began to claim that he was having to climb more mountains than any other fat man in the world, fled from his own troubled desk in Washington to share in my outdoor cure for "office-itis." My role as head man in the Alaska Game Commission seemed to stretch serenely and beautifully into the years ahead.

There were little snags, of course. As their school terms rolled by, Klondy reminded me that our children Ginny and young Frank were reaching the ages when they would have to go "outside" for college. Then, there was another matter; a subtle change in what I wanted to do with the rest of my life.

As I watched Corey deftly converting his experiences into magazine articles, slyly kibitzing his skills, the writing bug which had been latent, started pumping its virus through my bloodstream again, though nothing might ever have come of all this had not Congress seen fit to throw a major roadblock across the conservation trail. In a sweeping change of federal management, it passed a new law in 1943, which combined the functions of two old line bureaus—The U.S. Bureau of Fisheries and the U.S. Bureau of Biological Survey—into one unit to be henceforth known as the United States Fish and Wildlife Service, and my hefty, brilliant field companion, Dr. Ira N. Gabrielson, was placed in charge.

"Gabe" made a special trip to Juneau to tell me what it meant to the Territory. There would be a complete fusing of the Alaska Commercial Fisheries and the Alaska Game Commission under one head man. Did I want to tackle it?

He waited a while before telling me the rest of the story. There was another job created by the amalgamation, and he was holding it open. It was my elevation to nation-wide chief of the information service for the new organization. I would be heading both staffs of expert writers, camera men, and publicity sections. All press releases, photographic files, motion pictures, and official reports would be my responsibility. I would be expected to visit wildlife refuges and fishery installations in every state of the Union—and Alaska. I would be given a free hand to devise better methods of acquainting the general public with the aims and accomplishments of the big new setup.

I pretended to mull it over, though I guess I knew all the time what I'd have to say. The revised Alaska program would call for me to attend endless meetings in smoke-filled rooms to haggle with salmon canners and other commercial fishermen, then rush by airplane to another and another. I would be dealing—or trying to deal—with people who knew far more about their business than I could ever hope to learn. What really hurt the most was that I would have to name an assistant to take over the work I liked best of all; watching over the wildlife and sport fishes; the journeys into the mountains; the visits with old timers and Indians I'd come to feel were a part of me. Finally, it was the plain truth that among the augmented field force there were several men who were as well, or better, qualified for the new job. Through the years good men had worked their way up from the bottom rungs, as I had, and this was their opportunity for promotion.

I talked it over with Klondy, and she answered my question by asking two of her own. What woman would not enjoy a spell of living in the Nation's capitol? What man would not rise to the challenge of a bigger job?

Friends and neighbors were down at the dock to see us board the steamer. As the whistle sounded our departure from Juneau, we stood on the stern deck over the rumbling wash of the propellers, watching their faces fade away, blurring into the past and fusing with the scenes of half a lifetime—Nome; sled tracks across the Arctic snowfields; boating the wild, wide Yukon; the birds of Hooper Bay; campfires on the Yukon; the mysterious Aleutians; the face-to-face encounters with bears; the friendship of Gold Rush characters and Eskimos and Indians I would treasure forever.

They were all behind me now, never to be recaptured except in our memories. The golden chain of adventure was drawing full circle, and now my way was south. But wherever the years carried us, Klondy and I both knew that our hearts would always be in the north.